SO-BBS-714

WITHDRAWN

Stafford Library
Columbia College
1001 Rogers Street
Columbia, Missouri 65216

THE SEARCH FOR ISRAELI–ARAB PEACE
LEARNING FROM THE PAST AND BUILDING TRUST

Studies in Peace Politics in the Middle East

Volumes 1, 2, and 4 are published in association with the
University of Oklahoma Press

THE SEARCH FOR ISRAELI–ARAB PEACE
LEARNING FROM THE PAST AND BUILDING TRUST

Edited by
EDWIN G. CORR, JOSEPH GINAT,
AND SHAUL M. GABBAY

Foreword by
HRH Prince El Hassan bin Talal of Jordan

Preface by
David L. Boren, President of the University of Oklahoma

sussex
ACADEMIC
PRESS

BRIGHTON • PORTLAND

Copyright © Sussex Academic Press 2007; Introduction, Afterword and editorial organization copyright © Edwin G. Corr, Joseph Ginat, and Shaul M. Gabbay 2007

The right of Edwin G. Corr, Joseph Ginat, and Shaul M. Gabbay to be identified as editors of this work has been asserted in accordance with the Copyright, Designs and Patents Act 1988.

2 4 6 8 10 9 7 5 3 1

First published 2007 in Great Britain by
SUSSEX ACADEMIC PRESS
PO Box 139
Eastbourne BN24 9BP

and in the United States of America by
SUSSEX ACADEMIC PRESS
920 NE 58th Ave   Suite 300
Portland, Oregon 97213–3786

All rights reserved. Except for the quotation of short passages for the purposes of criticism and review, no part of this publication may be reproduced, stored in a retrieval system, or transmitted, in any form or by any means, electronic, mechanical, photocopying, recording or otherwise, without the prior permission of the publisher.

British Library Cataloguing in Publication Data
A CIP catalogue record for this book is available from the British Library.

Library of Congress Cataloging-in-Publication Data
The search for Israeli–Arab peace : learning from the past and
  building trust / edited by Edwin G. Corr, Joseph Ginat, and Shaul
  Gabbay ;
  foreword by His Royal Highness Prince Hassan bin Talal ; preface
  by David L. Boren.
  p. cm.
  Includes bibliographical references and index.
  ISBN 978-1-84519-191-7 (h/c : alk. paper)
  1. Arab–Israeli conflict—Peace—1993– —Congresses. 2. Israel—
Politics and government—1993– —Congresses. 3. Arab
countries—Politics and government—20thcentury—Congresses.
4. Arab countries—Politics and government—21st century—
Congresses. 5. Middle East—Politics and government—20th
century—Congresses. 6. Middle East—Politics and government—21st
century—Congresses. I. Corr, Edwin G. II. Ginat, J. III. Gabbay,
Shaul M.

DS119.76.S43 2007
956.04—dc22

2007004560

Typeset and designed by SAP, Brighton & Eastbourne.
Printed by TJ International, Padstow, Cornwall.
This book is printed on acid-free paper.

Contents

Foreword

HRH Prince El Hassan bin Talal
President Emeritus of the World Conference on Religion and Peace
Chairman of the Arab Thought Forum

It is with great hope and humility that I recommend this thoughtful and dynamic work to anyone with an interest in building peace in the Middle East. *The Search for Israeli–Arab Peace: Learning from the Past and Building Trust* picks up the pieces of a shattered peace process and offers hope for rebuilding a framework for dialogue in our fracturing region.

It is my belief that lasting peace in the Middle East can only be achieved through a multilateral initiative that can show home-grown, regional credentials. Our worsening situation can yet be saved but only if the actors in this existential and ideological conflict agree to move away from short-term, bilateral policy-making. We must all become champions of foreign relations with equality of treatment and the promise of a more inclusive future for all.

The efforts of the contributors to this important work provide hope for the future. I share their belief that dialogue and negotiation, mutual respect and concrete investment in the lives and livelihoods of Middle Easterners can halt the threatening tide of events. Indeed, from my vantage point at the heart of a troubled region, I see that the Arab street is filled not with anger and hatred but with disillusionment and despair.

Concerned academics and politicians must press all parties in this conflict to come to the table so that a stability pact, with guarantees and responsibilities for all, may be forged through disagreement and discussion. In order to achieve this, the United States and the wider international community must show consistency in their treatment of states and their peoples and must accept the need for supra-national thinking. Similarly, all actors in the region must demonstrate a willingness to conduct themselves in compliance with the requirements of international law.

It is accepted by most observers that dealing with the particularities of the Arab–Israeli conflict is essential to rebuilding trust within and beyond the Middle East. Although the current crisis in Iraq has its own root causes and cannot be blamed on events in Israel and Palestine, it has become obvious that the United States cannot achieve its goals in the region unless it deals directly with the consequences of 1948 and 1967.

Of course, diplomatic multilateralism in the Middle East must be supported by a greater economic initiative involving oil and non oil-producing states. Indeed, the people of Palestine and the greater Middle East are in dire need of a cohesion fund to build a structural framework for hope and prosperity. I believe that the Saudi Arabian-led peace initiative of 2002 marked a positive step in this direction where a framework for negotiation might eventually lead to solid investment in the human capital of the Levant.

The recent appeal by UN aid agencies for over \$450 million in emergency economic aid reminds us that for those most immediately affected by stalled peace talks, the Palestinian issue is first and foremost an economic and existential one. In this regard, I would suggest that a vital first step to facilitating calm and considered negotiation might be taken by implementing an international protectorate for the West Bank and Gaza Strip, as proposed by the Middle East Policy Initiative Forum in May 2003. Such a temporary juridical arrangement would allow formal legal jurisdiction for the West Bank and the Gaza Strip to be taken from Israel while offering benefits to both sides as a precursor to real negotiations for a peaceful solution.

The key responsibilities of an international protectorate would be to enforce peace and to pursue a time-limited mandate of state building and restoring basic services. A final settlement based on two viable states with Jerusalem as a common capital remains the desire of a majority of Israelis and Palestinians, while the urgency of Israel's full acceptance into the wider region has never been greater.

Rebuilding trust between communities will require a brave honesty on all sides. The level of unreported violence in Palestine and Iraq has greatly hampered informed and realistic policy making. I would agree with many of this book's contributors that honesty is the first step towards healing trauma. It is imperative that Palestinians, Israelis, Iraqis and others be given a platform from which to tell their harrowing stories. The effects of trauma must be acknowledged by a truth and reconciliation process or we risk a future fractured by the impact of unvented anger.

The Middle East is not alone in its increasing dominance by what I call a 'human dignity divide', an unsustainable discrepancy between those included and excluded from decision-making and stake-holding. I believe that the key to disempowering the extremists is to create a space for civil society to flourish. Such action should mark the beginning of a process for inclusion, where democratic institutions can offer ownership to people at grassroots level and recreate a particular exceptionalism that acknowledges the diversity of the region.

It is encouraging that politicians on all sides are increasingly accepting the need for a multilateral approach to our problems. This spirit must not only cross borders but also penetrate society at the 'Track 2' level to engage with the region's free and creative political minds. The events of recent years have proved that frustrating channels of civil expression can only lead to empowerment of extremists and increased alienation of people and government.

EL HASSAN BIN TALAL
Amman, March 2007

Preface

DAVID L. BOREN
President of the University of Oklahoma

The international community and the United States must cope with, try to resolve, or contain a number of bloody and costly intra-state or regional conflicts during this early part of the twenty-first century. Principal among these is the seemingly intractable Arab–Israeli conflict. Continued failure to resolve this issue threatens to draw many of the world's major powers into a conflict across the entire Middle East. It also continues to polarize the world along sectarian lines and serves as the leading recruitment motivation of the world's most dangerous terrorist organizations.

There were those who thought that the best road to peace in the Middle East ran through Baghdad rather than Jerusalem, but, after the frustrating developments in Iraq, thoughtful leaders are counseling a re-focus on the Israeli–Arab conflict. Former Secretary of State James A. Baker, III and former House Committee on Foreign Relations Chairman Lee H. Hamilton, as Co-Chairs of the Iraq Study Group, joined by high-powered bi-partisan members wrote:

> The United States cannot achieve its goals in the Middle East unless it deals directly with the Arab–Israeli conflict and regional instability. There must be a renewed and sustained commitment by the United States to a comprehensive Arab–Israeli peace on all fronts: Lebanon, Syria and President Bush's June 2002 commitment to a two-state solution for Israel and Palestine. This commitment must include direct talks with, by, and between Israel, Lebanon, Palestinians (those who accept Israel's right to exist), and Syria.[1]

The Search for Israeli–Arab Peace: Learning from the Past and Building Trust embodies the creative thought and research of distinguished academics and practitioners on how Middle East states and outside mediating powers can get the Middle East peace process back on track. It is in large part a response to the increasingly violent and chaotic environment that began in 2001 with the second *Intifada* and the 2003 US invasion of Iraq. The situation shows few signs of abatement and threatens to expand. After the failed 1999–2000 Camp David Two Talks almost all bridges of dialogue between Arabs and Israelis have collapsed and the peace process has stagnated. The level of trust among actors trying to resolve the impasse in the Arab–Israeli conflict that had grown in the aftermath of the Camp David One Accords, 1991 Madrid Conference, 1993 Oslo Accords, and 1994 Jordan–Israel peace agreement has been greatly eroded.

This book's contributors examine what went wrong in the peace process which caused it to lose momentum and to deteriorate into an unending chain of violence and mistrust. They study how trust might be restored and sufficiently increased to allow Palestinians and Israelis to reach a peace accord that might open the way for Israeli peace agreements also with Syria and Lebanon, and the achievement of normal relations with the rest of the Arab world. The contributors to this book provide social science knowledge and review the history of Arab–Israeli relations, talks and negotiations to seek lessons to apply to the present situation.

The Center for Peace Studies (CPS) under the International Programs Center (IPC) of The University of Oklahoma (OU) has since 1996 given its greatest attention to the seemingly intractable Arab–Israeli conflict. I agree with my long-time US Senate colleague George J. Mitchel, who has had mediating roles in both the Northern Ireland and the Arab–Israeli conflicts, who said at the University of Oklahoma's second annual foreign policy conference in 1999:

> I believe there is no such thing as a conflict that cannot be solved. Conflict is created and sustained by human beings, and it can be ended by human beings. There must be a determination on the part of all concerned to bring it to an end, and that determination requires an extraordinary amount of patience and perseverance. It is important that Americans [and others] understand that these conflicts, rooted in history cannot easily or quickly be resolved. Patience is an important virtue, as is perseverance.[2]

The IPC, headed by Ambassador (ret.) Edward J. Perkins, created the Center for Peace Studies, which has been persistent and energetic in its efforts to contribute positively to the Arab–Israeli peace process. The Co-Directors of the Center, by design, have been an Israeli expert and an Arab expert, beginning with Dr. Joseph Ginat, a well-known Israeli who is also an Arab specialist in anthropology, and Dr. Jamil Ragep, a Lebanese–American and a historian of science of the Middle East. In 2006, Dr. Joshua Landis, another Arab specialist and historian, replaced Dr. Ragep. Under Dr. Ginat's leadership, the CPS has conducted and co-sponsored a half dozen major conferences focused specifically on the Middle East peace process, and several of The University's annual foreign policy conferences have had major components dealing with that peace process. Ambassador Edwin G. Corr of the IPC has been the general editor for the IPC's dozen books, of which half of them deal specifically with aspects of the Middle East peace process.

This book is a sequel to *The Middle East Peace Process: Vision Versus*

Reality, published by the University of Oklahoma Press. It, along with other books spawned by the IPC and published by the University of Oklahoma Press and other publishers, advanced solutions to different issues in negotiations for a final peace agreement on such matters as refugees, water, Jerusalem, the holy sites, borders and security. The focus of *The Search for Israeli–Arab Peace* is on achieving an overall agreement as opposed to individual components. Earlier works chiefly address acceptable compromises and solutions to major substantive obstacles to a final peace agreement.[3]

Agreements that bring peace and provide opportunity for economic and social development in the Middle East will have multiple side effects and benefits for the United States and the international community. Such agreements would enhance US relations and the image of the United States in the Middle East and the Islamic World. They would particularly help our relations with our decades-long Middle East allies such as Egypt, Jordan, the Gulf States, and Saudi Arabia that are primarily Sunni populated states. These states currently are disturbed by the failure of the United States to bring stability to Iraq and by what they see as the emergence of a menacing Shia Crescent cutting through their region from an increasingly powerful Iran through Iraq and Syria into Lebanon. Peace agreements would also better our relations with traditional European allies and Russia, who have very important economic and strategic interests in the Middle East. Settling the Israeli–Palestinian conflict is not a panacea for all US problems, but it would certainly improve the US posture in the world.

Exhortations the past year by former Secretaries of State James Baker and Warren Christopher, the Iraq Study Group report, and a recent book by former President Jimmy Carter, all urged the George W. Bush administration to return with vigor to resuscitate and achieve success in the Middle East peace talks. Former National Security Advisor Brent Scowcroft in a particularly wise opinion piece in the *New York Times* at the beginning of 2007 wrote that such negotiations "could fundamentally change both the dynamics in the region and the strategic calculus of key leaders," saying that "Arab leaders are now keen to resolve the 50-year-old dispute":

> Resuming the Arab–Israeli peace process is not a matter of forcing concessions from Israel or dragooning the Palestinians into surrender. Most of the elements of a settlement are already agreed as a result of the negotiations of 2000 and the 'road map' of 2002. What is required is to summon the will of Arab and Israeli leaders, led by a determined American president, to forge the various elements into a conclusion that all parties have already publicly accepted in principle.[4]

With this book, we contributors join these distinguished statesmen in their analysis that attention is required on the Arab–Israeli conflict. *The*

Search for Israeli–Arab Peace: Learning from the Past and Building Trust will help the public and decision makers to understand better and overcome obstacles to achieve a comprehensive peace agreement for the Middle East. The knowledge, insights and counsel of this distinguished group of Middle East experts should be heeded. The benefits could be enormous!

Notes

1   James A. Baker, III and Lee H. Hamilton, Co-chairs, *The Iraq Study Group Report: The Way Forward – A New Approach* (New York: Vintage Books, 2006), pp. xv, 54–58.

2   George J. Mitchell, "Negotiating the Settlement to Internal Wars and Terrorism: The Lessons of Northern Ireland" in David L. Boren and Edward J. Perkins (eds.) *Democracy, Morality and the Search for Peace in America's Foreign Policy* (Norman: University of Oklahoma Press, 2002), p. xvi.

3   Joseph Ginat, Edward J. Perkins and Edwin G. Corr (eds.), *The Middle East Peace Process: Vision Versus Reality* (Norman: University of Oklahoma Press, and Brighton: Sussex Academic Press, 2002); see other IPC edited and published books, e.g.: Joseph Ginat and Edward J. Perkins (eds.), *Palestinian Refugees: Old Problems – New Solutions* (Norman: University of Oklahoma Press and Brighton: Sussex Academic Press, 2001); K. David Hambright, F. Jamil Ragep and Joseph Ginat (eds.), *Water in the Middle East: Cooperation and Technical Solutions* (Norman: University of Oklahoma Press, and Brighton: Sussex Academic Press, 2006); Abdul Salam Majali, Jawad A. Anami and Munther Haddadin, *The Inside Story of the 1994 Jordanian–Israeli Treaty* (Norman: The University of Oklahoma Press and London: Garnet Publishing, Ltd., 2006): H.R.H. Prince Hassan bin Talal, *To Be A Muslim* (Brighton & Portland: Sussex Academic Press, 2004). IPC books that have major components that relate to the Israeli–Arab conflict include David L. Boren and Edward J. Perkins (eds.), *Preparing America's Foreign Policy for the 21st Century* (Norman, The University of Oklahoma Press, 1999); and, David L. Boren and Edward J. Perkins (eds.), *Democracy, Morality and the Search for Peace in America's Foreign Policy* (Norman: University of Oklahoma Press, 1999).

4   James A. Baker, III, "Talking Our Way to Peace," Op-ed, *The New York Times*, Dec. 2, 2004; Warren Christopher, "Diplomacy that Can't Be Delegated," Op-ed, *The New York Times*, Dec. 30, 2004; Brent Scowcroft, "Beyond Lebanon," Op-ed, *The Washington Post*, July 30, 2006; *The Iraq Study Report*; and Scowcroft, "Getting the Middle East Back on Our Side," Op-ed, *The New York Times*, January 4, 2007.

Acknowledgments

We the editors, Edwin G. Corr, Joseph Ginat and Shaul M. Gabbay, express our gratitude to the following individuals and institutions. The book has its origin in two conferences of experts in international relations and the Middle East that were sponsored and hosted by the Center for Peace Studies of the University of Oklahoma, the S. Daniel Abraham Center for Strategic Dialogue of Netanya Academic College, the Institute for the Study of Israel in the Middle East (ISIME) of Denver University, and the Three Cultures Foundation of Andalusia, Spain. Their support made the conference and book possible.

We thank His Royal Highness Prince El Hassan bin Talal, President of the Board of the Center for Peace Studies and one of the two International Chairmen of the S. Daniel Abraham Center for Strategic Dialogue, for writing the Foreword; and President of The University of Oklahoma David L. Boren for writing the Preface. Both have strongly supported our efforts. We also express our appreciation for President of Netanya Academic College, Professor Zvi Arad, and Senior Vice President Dr. David Altman; and, from the University of Denver, Mr. Robert E. Loup, Chairman of the ISIME Board of Directors, and the Allied Jewish Federation of Colorado.

We express our appreciation to the twenty-one contributors, whose experience, knowledge, judgment, wisdom, analyses and proposals for achieving Middle East peace are included in this volume. Their names and brief biographies are in the book. In addition we thank other expert participants in the conferences on whose words, reflections and presentations we drew. These include: Ambassador Adel Adawy, Chairman, Cairo Peace Association; Mr. Clifford Chanin, Director of the Rockefeller Foundation Legacy Project; Ambassador Shmuel Hadas, former Ambassador of Israel to Spain; Mr. Bernadino Leon, former Director, Three Cultures Foundation; Professor Gema Martin Muñoz, Professor, the Autonomous University of Madrid; Foreign Minister of Spain, Dr. Miguel Angel Moratinos; Ms. Sandra Moratinos, Three Cultures Foundation; Enrique Ojeda Vila, Director, Three Cultures Foundation; Ambassador Edward J. Perkins, Executive Director, International Programs Center, The University of Oklahoma; Dr. Shibley Telhami, Professor of the University of Maryland; and Member of Knesset Major General (ret.) Danny Yatom.

Last, but certainly not least, we wish to acknowledge and thank persons who were indispensable in proficiently helping us to organize, edit and prepare the manuscript; and who made our task enjoyable: from the University of Denver, Deborah Schlueter and Mathew Markman; from Netanya Academic College, Elie Friedman; and from the University of Oklahoma, Summer Cloud Shije and Cyrus Ali Contractor, supported by Patsy Broadway, Donna Cline and Denise Forkner.

Of great importance was the professionalism of Sussex Academic Editorial Director Anthony Grahame who guided the Editors throughout the publication process.

THE SEARCH FOR ISRAELI–ARAB PEACE

LEARNING FROM THE PAST AND BUILDING TRUST

CHAPTER 1

Introduction: Landmarks on the Road to a Peace Agreement

EDWIN G. CORR

There have been efforts – interspersed between and even during the wars and *intifadas* – to reach an accord to settle differences between the Israelis and Arabs since the United Nations (UN) founded the State of Israel in 1948. Arab nations and Palestinians resisted by war the UN's creation of Israel in Palestine, and Israelis fought back in what they call their war of independence. Palestinians remember this conflict as the beginning of their *nakba* (catastrophe). Ralph Bunche, an American, mediated on behalf of the UN to end armed hostilities. A major landmark on the road to peace was the 1979 Camp David One talks sponsored by President Jimmy Carter that resulted in President Anwar Sadat of Egypt and Prime Minister Menachem Begin of Israel signing and producing a now quarter-century "cold peace" agreement between their two countries.

Discussions based on the 1991 Madrid Conference called by the United Soviet Socialist Republics (USSR) and the United States under President George H. Bush and his Secretary of State James Baker after the first Gulf War, and the subsequent 1993 Oslo Accords, were other important milestones. Oslo led to Israelis and Palestinians entering into talks with each other, and emphasized the negotiating formula of "land for peace" and the two-state solution. The Oslo process also produced the Israel–Jordanian Peace Treaty formally signed on October 24, 1994 in Aqaba, Jordan in the presence of US President Bill Clinton by Jordan's King Hussein and Israeli Prime Minister Yitzhak Rabin.

The untimely assassination of Rabin, changes in the internal politics of Israel, and the first *Intifada* made progress difficult in the late 1990s. At the end of the millennium a new round of Camp David talks were held by President Bill Clinton with Israeli Prime Minister Ehud Barak and Palestinian Authority Leader Yasser Arafat (encouraged by an ailing King Hussein). Subsequent meetings in Sharm El Sheikh and Taba moved

Palestine and Israel very near to an agreement but not close enough. Who deserves blame for the talks' failure is much discussed. Perhaps the best explanation is that time ran out as Clinton's and Barak's governing mandates came to an end, and the process was not vigorously supported by the subsequent Israeli and US governments.

Since the Oslo Accords the private sector has been very active in the peace process by promoting dialogue and collaboration between Palestinians and Israelis. Groups from the two countries, often backed by European and US institutions, have organized meetings, conferences, cooperative activities and development projects to engage Israelis and Palestinians, frequently with the participation of representatives of other countries. Of particular note are Track II projects that have drafted unofficial comprehensive peace agreements that, according to opinion polls, have received acceptance from the majority of Israelis and Palestinians but not of their governments.

The outbreak of the Second *Intifada*, provoked in part by Ariel Sharon's September 28, 2000 visit to the Temple Mount, and escalated by Palestinians injecting into the *Intifada* armed violence and suicide bombings, coupled with the occupying Israelis' targeted assassinations with collateral killings of many civilians and the destruction of the Palestinian economic and social infrastructure, all impeded further progress toward renewed negotiations. Worsening levels of violence after 2000; in 2002 Israel's beginning construction of a separation barrier wall incorporating much Palestinian territory rather than following the 1967 boundary line; in 2004 the demise of Chairman Arafat; in 2005 the unilateral withdrawal of the Israeli Defense Forces from Gaza, the election of Mohammed Abbas (Abu Mazen) to the Palestinian presidency, the unilateral withdrawal of the Israeli Defense Forces from Gaza, and Sharon's decapitating stroke; and in 2006 the election of Hamas to a majority in the Palestinian National Assembly, and the war of Israel with Hezbollah of Lebanon and Hamas – all these events have combined to create greater mistrust and dampened hopes for a peace agreement. The atmosphere of despair was exacerbated by threats of Iranian President Mahamoud Ahmadinejad to erase Israel from the face of the map, by the continuing presence of US military forces in Iraq and civil war there, and by the growing threat of the outbreak of all-out civil wars in Lebanon and Palestine.

Notwithstanding the growing pessimism about the Middle East from 2000 to 2007, very important initiatives were launched that could eventually have positive impacts on the peace process. The Arab League's endorsement on March 28, 2002 of the Saudi Arabian initiative that commits Arab states to recognize and enter into normal diplomatic relations should Israel accept the 1967 boundaries for its borders was a tremendous breakthrough. The Quartet (the United States, European Union, Russia, and the United Nations) issued a "Roadmap" in 2003 with stipulated actions for reaching a final agreement based on a two-state solution through three stages by the end of three years. The target was not reached, but, even so, the Roadmap is not yet discarded. Perhaps the most important event was the statement of President George W. Bush in 2002 declaring the United States Government's endorsement of the two-state solution, which he has reiterated several times.

Events since 2000 greatly undermined the weak levels of trust and optimism about reaching a final comprehensive peace settlement between Israel and its Arab neighbors, even if, as mentioned, there have been some notable exceptions The principal purpose of this book is to explore how individuals, private organizations and governments can build trust. The method is to examine social science about the creation of trust and to study past experiences in the peace process to uncover indicated measures and actions that leaders of the Middle East and the mediating powers might learn and implement to get the process back on track to a successful conclusion.

The Denver and Seville Conferences on "Building Trust" and "What Went Wrong"

The content of this book derives principally from participants in these two conferences. The Center for Peace Studies (CPS), which has its secretariat in the International Programs Center (IPC) of the University of Oklahoma (OU), has been involved in the Middle East peace process since 1999, when it began to hold and co-sponsor conferences and projects aimed at contributing to the achievement of a comprehensive Middle East peace agreement. The CPS is a partnership of Bethlehem University in Palestine, Haifa University and the Strategic Dialogue Center (SDC) of Netanya Academic College in Israel, the Horizon Institute in Jordan, the Cairo Peace Association in Egypt, and OU. Because of increasing lethal violence, the lack of progress and eroding levels of trust after 2000 between Israel and Palestine, the CPS organized with strong institutional partners conferences to address how to change the situation.

The "How to Rebuild Trust between Israelis and Palestinians" conference held in Denver, September 3–4, 2004, was hosted by the Institute for the Study of Israel in the Middle East (ISIME) in the Graduate School of International Studies of the University of Denver, and co-sponsored by the IPC, SDC, and the Three Cultures Foundation of Seville, Spain. Dr. Shaul Gabbay, director of ISIME and co-editor of this book, organized the conference while Dr. Joseph Ginat, also a co-editor of this book and co-director of the IPC and director of the SDC, designed the program and recruited the presenters. Three dozen distinguished scholars and practitioners addressed the building of trust process plus Israeli–Arab countries relations. Among the presenters were Professor Shibley Telhami, Professor

Moshe Ma'oz, Director of the IPC Ambassador Edward J. Perkins, Director of the Cairo Peace Association Ambassador Adel el Adawy, and Member of Knesset Danny Yatom. The participants' presentations are the basis for many of the chapters of this book. Participants endorsed the Arab concept of *hudna* (strongly presented by Dr. Ginat) as a possible means to achieve a cease-fire between Israelis and Arabs.

The "What Went Wrong?" conference in Seville, Spain, January 21–22, 2005 was hosted by the Foundation of the Three Cultures of the Mediterranean. The Foundation was established by the Kingdom of Morocco and the Province of Andalusia, and later joined by the Peres Center for Peace and the Palestinian National Authority. It receives support from the European Union. Enrique Ojeda, director, and Sandra Moratinos of the Foundation organized the conference; and, again, Dr. Ginat planned the program and recruited the presenters. Two dozen distinguished scholars and practitioners addressed "what went wrong" in Arab–Israeli negotiations. Foreign Minister of Spain Miguel Angel Moratinos, Professor Gema Martin Munoz, General Shlomo Gazit, Director of the Horizon Institute Rateb Amro, and Palestine Parliament Member Riad Malki were a few of the presenters. As seen in the chapters of this book, the participants thoroughly examined the peace process in terms of its structural and leadership flaws, as well as the premise that more should have been accomplished.

The attendees of both conferences profited by superb interventions on the history of the negotiations, analyses, insights, descriptions of problems and opportunities, and constructive ideas for building trust and arriving at solutions to allow agreement on a final peace arrangement.

Organization and Content of the Book

The Search for Israeli–Arab Peace: Learning from the Past and Building Trust is organized into three parts: Part I: Promoting Understanding and Building Trust; Part II: Learning and Making Use of the Past; and, Part III: The Mediators. These parts are preceded by the Foreword, the Preface, and this introductory chapter. The end matter comprises Afterword, information about contributors to the book, and an index.

Joseph Ginat and David Altman in Chapter 2, "The Importance of Cross Culture Understanding in the Course of Negotiations," provide seven case studies in which unintentional breaking of trust occurred among negotiators due to one negotiating party offending the other. These intriguing cases include high-level Middle East leaders who did not adequately comprehend the opposing negotiators' behavior and cultural and religious values. Attention is given briefly to the importance of economic ties among the negotiating parties, and there is a thorough discussion of the Arab concept of *hudna*, a particular type of cease-fire that has acceptability by Arabs in the context of the current conflict situation.

Menachem Klein analyzes "The Israeli–Palestinian Wonder: Losing Trust in Official Negotiations while Maintaining It on 'Hard' Track II Talks" in Chapter 3. He asks why at the end of the twentieth century trust seemingly vanished in Track I official talks between Israelis and Arabs, especially Palestinians, and has diminished in Track III people-to-people activities and projects, but has remained strong in "hard" Track II negotiations by professionals and former government officials. Klein cites polling data to show majority support by both Israelis and Palestinians for reconciliation, peace and a Palestinian state. He describes the atmosphere, attitudes, and negotiating approaches of participants in the privately negotiated Geneva Agreement, and suggests that they be emulated by official negotiators.

The public opinion aspect is explored in Chapter 4, "Public Diplomacy in the Middle East: Big Mistake, Huge Price," by Gadi Baltiansky. He says negotiations involve the regions' leaders, the media and publics. The public role has not been sufficiently recognized nor has the public been adequately prepared to accept attainable agreements. Baltiansky faults leaders for espousing unattainable goals ("red lines"). He cites the Ayalon–Nusseibeh Agreement and Geneva Agreement that were negotiated outside officials channels as examples of how the negotiators should clearly detail the costs to each party in an achievable final agreement reached through compromises. Baltiansky urges focus on the "endgame," so that the publics will be properly informed and ready for a compromise final agreement that their leaders should negotiate.

Chapter 5, "Listening as a Value: A Narrative Approach to Building Trust," is a description by Maya Melzer-Geva of a series of workshops conducted for Arab and Jewish women in Israel in which women share and analyze personal stories that have shaped their attitudes toward "others." Leaders through guided discussion teach participants to listen, transform knowledge, and learn. Participants gain insights into themselves, understanding of others and forge bonds with one another. A shared language begins to emerge and trust builds among the women. The chapter is relevant to the interactions of Israeli and Palestinian negotiators.

Gad Gilbar and Onn Winkler point out economic benefits that ensue from successfully negotiated peace agreements. In Chapter 6, "The Economic Dividends of Egypt and Jordan from Peace Agreements with Israel," they state that neither of these two countries were required to pay an economic price within the Arab community of nations for their treaties with Israel, and the authors provide information and data to show that total economic dividends for the two countries have been substantial. They propose tourism as a possible area for rapid economic growth in the Middle

East, and argue that making peace in the Middle East and economic cooperation with Israel (within the framework of the Jordanian–Palestinian–Israeli triangle) are essential to greater economic progress and the well-being of citizens of the countries involved. Understanding this should be an incentive for seeking a comprehensive peace agreement.

One of the co-editors of this book, Shaul M. Gabbay, in "Engineering Social Capital in the Middle East: Rebuilding Trust," Chapter 7, sees trust as an outcome of social networks and proposes a structural approach for engineering social capital to build trust between Palestinians and Israelis. He describes three levels of interaction: government to government, between non-governmental organizations (NGOs), and among people-to-people groups and individuals. At the governmental level Gabbay suggests that long-run, mega projects to improve the quality of life for both peoples can contribute to building trust. NGO projects and people-to people interactions also facilitate bringing the two societies together and creating mutual trust among participants. Projects at these three levels can benefit from external support and encouragement.

The editors of this volume now move from chapters dealing with concepts and ideas about the building of trust for negotiations to examine past experiences and lessons indicated for adaptation and use in negotiations. Part II of the book is divided into four sections based on Israel's relations with its neighboring countries, the first relationship examined is that of Israel and Egypt. This is followed by descriptions of relationships of Israel with Jordan, Syria, Lebanon and Palestine.

Shlomo Gazit, who was head of Israeli Military Intelligence in 1977, begins this part of the book by describing in Chapter 8, "The Peace with Egypt: President Sadat's Visit Through 1977 Israeli Eyes." His account reveals the great suspicion and mistrust that existed between Egypt and Israel prior to the visit, and how courageous leaders (i.e., Sadat and Prime Minister Menachem Begin) risked face-to-face talks for peace. Gazit provides parts of reports and recommendations that he and Military Intelligence provided to Prime Minister Begin for the pending Sadat visit. Gazit also describes meetings with Begin prior to Sadat's arrival that give insights into Begin's and President Ezer Weizmann's thinking. This chapter supplies background for understanding better the current Israeli–Egyptian relationship.

Elie Podeh in "Normal Relations without Normalization: The Evolution of Egyptian–Israeli Relations, 1979–2006, The Politics of Cold Peace," Chapter 9, focuses on Egyptian behavior that contributes to the "cold" peace. He suggests that for Egypt warm relations with Israel are not a domestic nor regional necessity and in some ways would be a liability, and says the level of "coldness" has fluctuated through six sub-periods since 1979. Podeh describes how various issues affect Egyptian–Israeli relations: Egypt's place in the world, the nuclear imbalance, Middle-

Easternism, domestic opposition, the Palestinian problem, the economic/trade dimension, and the psycho-cultural dimension. He discusses the Egyptian education system and the media, and concludes that while the 1979 Treaty was very significant in reducing the Israeli–Arab conflict, the structural problems existing between the two countries and the psycho-cultural differences have inhibited moving to a warmer peace.

Shlomo Gazit returns in Chapter 10, "Israel–Egypt – What Went Wrong? Nothing," to argue that the basic positions of the Egyptians and Israelis during the 1979 successful negotiations prevented the development of a "warm" instead of a "cold" peace relationship. The Camp David Accords had two parts: the first dealing with bilateral peace and the second with solving Israel's conflicts with all other Arab parties. But, Israeli governments in the 1980s had no serious intent to negotiate peace with the Palestinians and Syrians. And, the Egyptians were reluctant to allow close bilateral relations to extend beyond the government sphere. That attitude will not change as long as Egyptian rulers see Israel as a rival or threat to Egypt's leader role in the Middle East. The treatment of Israel in the Egyptian media is extremely hostile and biased.

Attention turns in Chapter 11 to Jordan–Israel relations and what has caused the relationship to remain a "lukewarm" peace. In "Jordan–Israel Relations: A 'Lukewarm' Peace" Joseph Nevo writes that the Israel–Jordan peace is better than the Israel–Egypt "cold" peace, but can and should be improved. Part of the reason for the situation is that there was not sufficient preparation of the publics and initial expectations were too high. Nevo outlines the considerable benefits of the Treaty, and also its disadvantages. He analyzes the reasons for many Jordanians' opposition to the Treaty and better relations with Israel, and suggests that to improve relations the benefits from economic cooperation must be extended to and felt by the Jordanian people as well as political benefits by the two governments.

Rateb Mohammad Amro in "Rebuilding Trust and Replacing Despair and Division in the Jordan–Israel Peace Process," Chapter 12, reviews the peace process since the 1991 Madrid conference, examines present Jordanian–Israeli relations, and describes key issues to be resolved to conclude a Palestinian–Israeli peace agreement. The lack of such agreement is the greatest impediment to improving relations. He discusses how to establish trust needed for successful negotiations, arguing that people-to-people relations are essential. The commitment to build infrastructure and the promise of a better future for all peoples of the region is required. The two-state solution is key! Success will require clear, committed leadership from the United States and Europe.

In Chapter 13, "What Went Wrong in the Middle East Peace Process? The Jordan–Israel Relationship," Mohammad Al-Momani distinguishes between "cold peace" and "warm peace" and between government attitudes versus societal attitudes. He examines reasons for deterioration in the quest for peace among the following groups: international, regional, domestic Israeli, domestic Jordanian, and Jordanian elites. He argues that liberalizing the Middle East could be the best way to establish the values of peace and coexistence and thereby enhance genuine peace relationships. He supports this with the "democracies tend not to fight each other" studies, and says international players could promote democratization, especially through helping to improve the media and educational institutions.

Uzi Arad in Chapter 14, "Creative Measures Needed for a Peace Accord Between Israel and Syria," argues that in the Syrian case there is less confusion about negotiations because communication and mutual understanding have been limited. The actors and region are so changed that there may be little to learn from previous talks that has relevance in future talks. The situation must be looked at anew. The territorial issue is central to a solution, and Arad believes that land-swaps among Syrians, Jordanians, Palestinians and Israelis might open new possibilities for a regional peace solution. However, new productive talks between Israel and Syria will require substantive flexibility in negotiations (as Syria recently manifested with Turkey). The Syrian position should be probed by Israel in concert with the United States prior to a new initiative.

Moshe Ma'oz asks in Chapter 15 if "After the Lebanon War: Can Israel Rebuild Trust with Syria, Lebanon and Palestine?" He describes the deterioration in Arab–Israeli relations caused by this war, and then focuses separately on the Syrian, Lebanese and Palestinian options for returning to successful negotiations. Ma'oz notes the Arab League's March 2002 resolution to sign a peace agreement with Israel, the Quartet's June 2002 Roadmap, President Clinton's Camp David Two July 2000 "blueprint," and Sharon's disengagement from Gaza. He says overcoming the setback of the war of Israel with Hezbollah and Hamas will be difficult, but cites President George W. Bush's commitment to a two-state solution, and suggests that should Prime Minister Ehud Olmert make some meaningful, good will gestures to the Arabs, and should the United States re-assume a leading role in creating trust between Israelis and Arabs for negotiations, there still is a chance for success.

The book's editors turn now to the prospects for a peace agreement between Israel and Palestine, which many believe would remove the major obstacle to agreements with the remaining Arab neighbors and the rest of the Muslim world. They begin with Chapter 16 by Raid Malki, "The Palestinian Public and What Has Gone Wrong in Israeli–Palestine Negotiations." Malki describes his amazement at the political sophistication of the Palestinian public during its January 2005 elections. Palestinians gave highest priority to personal security, rule of law, and comprehensive institutional reform, especially judicial reform. Malki states that Palestine and Israel during the past decade have had the wrong leaders who have wasted chances to move further toward a peace agreement. Moreover, he says that draft treaties in official negotiations have not had sufficient implementation, monitoring and enforcement mechanisms. Outside powers have not pushed the Israeli and Palestinian leaders enough, and both sets of leaders have manipulated their publics for political purposes rather than to prepare them for a final agreement. Leaders must negotiate with urgency to relieve the suffering of their peoples, and must carry out their leadership obligations as rapidly as possible, such as those outlined in the Roadmap.

What would Israel require to meet its security needs to assure it existence and what are the implications of these for a sovereign independent Palestine state in the two-state solution? Reuven Pedatzur in Chapter 17, "An Israeli–Palestinian Agreement: The Security Aspects", lays out "minimum" Israeli defense requirements for a treaty with Palestine in nine areas: (1) Demilitarization of Palestine, (2) Israeli control over border crossings, (3) Required border adjustments, (4) An agreement on fighting terrorism within Palestinian territories, (5) Early attack warning stations, (6) Airspace over the West Bank and Gaza, (7) The electronic sphere, (8) The "safe passage", and (9) Jordanian inclusion in the Agreement. Pedatzur insists Israel must have concessions in all these areas. He also lays out strong demands for Israel's control of water resources. There is the question of whether Palestinians would believe the resulting Palestinian state were truly sovereign under the arrangements.

Miguel Murado, echoing other contributors to the book, in Chapter 18 questions "Did Anything Go Wrong?" He asserts that the Oslo Accords were poorly structured to achieve peace to solve the conflict because Israel was given a preferential position that allows it to manage the peace process and dictate final content of an agreement. Israeli occupation also gives it an advantage. He asserts that in the Oslo process the Palestinians were never given the status of real negotiators. Murado comments on negotiating positions of Rabin, Netanyahu and Barak, saying that at Camp David Two Barak made Arafat an offer he could not accept. Afterward, Sharon gave the Israelis what they wanted. The whole thing has not been about land but about time – delaying resolution of the conflict and achieving through military operations and settlements the land the Israelis want.

I point out in Chapter 19, "A Leaking Reservoir of Trust in Israeli–Palestinian Water Talks," that advocates for formal negotiations and a two-state solution have judged dialogue and cooperation on water – because of its symbolism of being essential to life – to be particularly important. Israelis, Palestinians, and Jordanians out of necessity have continued collaboration on water and consequently retain a certain degree of dialogue and trust in this area; cooperation on water has not become overly-politicized nor a publicly major issue. There are signs, however, that Palestinians are becoming exasperated with the inequity of water alloca-tions from sources they consider to be their aquifers and surface water. This is exacerbated by the Israeli occupation that makes it difficult and dangerous even to travel to meetings to discuss water issues. Water equity and control over water resources are issues about which Palestinians could become confrontational and organize protests and actions for redress of grievances rather than an area that has on the whole contributed to dialogue and trust.

Alon Ben Meir wraps up the treatment of the Israel–Palestine possibil-ities for peace in Chapter 20, "Rebuilding Israeli–Palestinian Trust by Unilateral Steps." Meir defines "trust," discusses mistrust, and analyzes how trust is formed. He proposes the creation of a peace track dedicated to creating continuous people–people activities that build trust. The first and most important stage of trust building is characterized by: (1) unilat-eralism, (2) unconditionality, (3) graduality, (4) realism, (5). calibration to culture, (6) simultaneity, and (7) confidentiality. Once there is response to the building trust track, action should move to Track III activities for learning each parties' history and culture and the use of confidence-building activities. Negotiators in Tracks I and II should deal with matters of substance and be independent of the steps in Track III.

Part III of the book deals with outside mediators. Cyrus Ali Contractor in Chapter 21, "The Changing Face of the Arab League," discusses the evolution of the twenty-two nation Arab League position over the past fifty years on Israel–Palestine relations and negotiations and on Arab govern-ments' relations with Israel. In doing so, he uses and describes the crucial events of the League's founding on the basis of Arabism, and Egypt's expulsion from the League, the 1991 Madrid Peace Talks, the League's involvement in the 1948 War, and Sadat's visit to Israel in 1977. He ends with the 2002 Arab peace initiative. One sees a change in the Arab official and public position of total opposition to Israel's existence to an offer of normal relations, should Israel accept the two-state solution in accord with UN resolutions.

In Chapter 22, "The Quartet and US Government Roles in Israeli–Palestinian-Arab Negotiations," I describe briefly the Quartet and then concentrate on the United States. The US during the first two decades of Israel's existence had a fairly balanced and uninvolved role, but increased greatly its involvement in negotiations thereafter. US govern-ment goals and ideals for the Middle East are discussed. I examine "lessons indicated" from various successes and failures during the past in terms of promoting a comprehensive peace, as well as lessons from US government involvement in peace mediations in other parts of the globe. The Middle East peace process has been stalled, if not worsened, since 2000, but there are some promising signs. Key external mediators, especially the United

States, should give priority to regenerating the peace process and achieving Middle East peace in the Holy Land.

Joseph Ginat and Shaul Gabbay, co-editors of this volume, close the book with an "Afterword" in Chapter 23 in which they discuss developments in 2007 and the need to begin peace talks between Israel and Palestine and Israel and Syria. They comment on the implications of Israel's withdrawal from Gaza, the Israeli–Hezbollah–Hamas War, threats to erase Israel from the map by Iranian President Ahmadinejad, and the need to remove Syria from the Iran–Syria–Hezbollah "Axis of Evil." They point to Israeli calls for renewed peace talks that increase prospects for the start of a new round of sincere and serious negotiations.

PART I

Promoting
Understanding and
Building Trust

CHAPTER 2

The Importance of Cross Cultural Understanding in the Course of Negotiations

JOSEPH GINAT AND DAVID ALTMAN

In the anthropological literature much has been written about the definition of culture. It is our belief that culture can be defined through four concepts: Beliefs, Values, Signs, and Symbols. Not including the material culture, those four terms include everything that composes a culture. In different cultures there are different beliefs, such as the belief in monotheism or polytheism. Belief includes other components; for example, in the countries of the Far East, especially in Thailand, one is not allowed to touch the nape of a child's neck for fear that the child's spirit will be irreversibly removed from the body.[1]

In western societies, any kind of killing or murder is considered a terrible crime, whereas in Muslim and other Arab societies if someone from a certain extended family (co-liable group)[2] is killed or murdered, then a member of the injured group will take revenge by killing one member of the murderer's family. Within the values of Arab culture when a woman, either married or non-married, commits illicit sexual activities, in many cases she is brutally killed by a member or members of her natal family. "Blood revenge" and the honor killing of a woman who has brought shame to her family are not considered crimes within Arab culture.[3] It is inconceivable to the western mind that the killing of a woman by her own father or brothers for her sexual behavior could be deemed honorable.

In different cultures different people express themselves by having different signs and symbols. It should be emphasized that there is no limit to the size of membership within a culture group; however, it is important to note that one individual cannot constitute a culture – it is necessary for there to be at least two or more persons.

What Went Wrong because of Not Knowing the Other's Culture?

Case History #1

In the winter of 1966, General (Res.) Meir Amit, then the head of the Israeli Mossad, was invited to visit Egypt by an Egyptian general whom he met several times in European countries.[4] In 1965–66 Egypt was in a difficult economic situation, and the Egyptians believed that the Israelis could help them receive a significant loan that would alleviate their economic problems. Despite their national differences and the fact that their countries were in a state-of-war, these two generals had established an amiable relationship that permitted President Jamal Abdul Nasser to invite General (Res.) Meir Amit to discuss such a possible solution. General (Res.) Amit felt that this situation could serve as an excellent opportunity to decrease Egyptian–Israeli tension and to perhaps cultivate the potential for the establishment of peace talks. Amit brought the idea to then Prime Minister (PM) Levi Eshkol and recommended that the PM grant him permission to go to Cairo on this secret mission. Golda Meir, a later PM of Israel, persuaded PM Eshkol that it would be wrong to let Amit go to Egypt, and convinced him that the invitation from the Egyptian general was, in reality, a trap. Golda Meir felt that Amit was being baited by the Egyptians and would be forcibly restrained from returning to Israel. The outcome was that PM Eshkol did not permit Gen. (Res.) Amit to go to Egypt.

Before continuing with this example of rejecting an invitation, the following story is pertinent. In 1959 a head of a large co-liable group of one of the Sinai Bedouin tribes visited a sheikh of a different tribe in the same region. The visiting leader was caught up in a desert storm en route to the host, and upon arrival began to clean his garments and his gear of the dust. However, when he was cleaning his pistol it discharged amongst the group present. The host sheikh's son was accidentally shot and killed. The sheikh's response to the tragedy is illuminating: he immediately ordered his son's body removed from the tent, brought the visiting leader to dine at the feast that had already been prepared, assured the visiting leader safe passage out his domain by his assigned escort, and then assured the visiting leader that "blood revenge" would be exacted.[5]

Those who are familiar with Arab culture understand that the responsibility for a guest's security lies in the hands of the host; for a host to disregard this responsibility would bring great dishonor. The fact that Golda Meir did not understand this fundamental cultural construct indicates her lack of knowledge of Arab society. This misunderstanding resulted in the loss of a singular opportunity to bridge Israeli–Egyptian differences. Although is it speculative, one can question whether the unaccepted invitation for Amit to travel to Egypt may have offered an opportunity that could have prevented the 1967 War. When President Sadat eventually came to Israel with the peace initiative, he did so because of Egyptian efforts to assuage their own national economic difficulties.[6]

Case History #2

In the fall of 1971, Egypt's war of attrition concluded; tensions remained, however, and Israelis occupied the Sinai and were installed on the East Bank of the Suez Canal. Also as a result of the 1967 War Egypt brought to a halt the navigation of the Suez Canal. Along the western bank of the Suez Canal, residents of Egyptian cities were deserted. Only Egyptian soldiers remained there within fortifications and trenches. Gen. Moshe Dayan, then Israeli Minister of Defense, came with the following proposal to PM Golda Meir: that Israel would unilaterally withdraw 10–15 miles along the Suez Canal. Dayan explained that, according to his understanding, by conducting this unilateral move the Egyptians would be able to clean and then reopen the canal for traffic, allowing commerce to recommence along the Egyptian cities that lay vacant. He felt that such a move would ease Israeli–Egyptian tensions, and perhaps change the political atmosphere. PM Golda Meir asked Dayan what Israel would get in return for such a gesture. Dayan stated that not only would Israel receive nothing in return, but Israel would not *ask* for anything in return. Meir rejected his proposal on the spot.[7]

Joseph Ginat served as the Director of the Israeli Academic Center in Cairo (October 1989–October 1992) which provided him with opportunities to conduct several research projects, one related to this particular case history. The question that bothered Ginat was this: Had PM Meir agreed to the unilateral withdraw that was suggested by Dayan, would the 1973 War have been fought? Ginat interviewed members of President Sadat's cabinet, among them: former Egyptian PM Mustafa Khalil; General Kamal Hassan Áli, who served also as PM, Foreign Minister (FM), and Minister of Defense; two other retired generals; university professors; lawyers; physicians; authors; and reporters. It is interesting to indicate that all of them said that *had Israel offered such a gesture* President Sadat would not have had a pretext for going to war. Once one sees Dayan's idea within the cultural framework of Arab society, the proposal makes great sense: the Egyptians lost the entire Sinai within several days . . . they had lost face. The reader may remember President Nasser's 'Three No's' at the Khartum Summit, following Egypt's defeat in the 1967 war: No Recognition of Israel, No Negotiation with Israel, and No Peace with Israel. Under Dayan's proposal, Israel would have given back territory, allowing the cities along the canal to be re-inhabited, traffic to recommence, and the Egyptian army to take positions on the East side of the Suez Canal.

It is possible that the Egyptians could have misunderstood the gesture as weakness on the part of Israeli foreign policy, but this would not have mattered. When we said that the Egyptians lost face in 1967, it should be indicated that all the Egyptians – without notable exception – believed that American pilots using Israeli airplanes had won the 1967 War, which began with a massive air raid eliminating the Egyptian Air Force. Psychologically it was easier for the Egyptians to face defeat by believing the effort had been undertaken by American rather than Israeli pilots. Again, Israeli withdraw from the canal would have been more than a symbol for the Egyptians in the regaining of honor and the saving of face. As indicated previously, had Meir Amit visited Egypt in 1966 it may have been that the 1967 War could have been prevented. We again emphasize that this is a source for speculation; however, there is *no doubt* in our minds after studying Dayan's proposal that had the Israeli Government adopted his strategy for returning the land, that the 1973 War would have been prevented.

Case History #3

At the end of the 1979 Camp David peace negotiations between the Egyptians and Israelis, mediated by then President Jimmy Carter, a crisis took place just hours before the signing of the Peace Treaty. The day before the official signing of the treaty, PM Begin and President Sadat shook hands having agreed upon all the articles. The following day was to be the official signing of that agreement; however for President Sadat the act of shaking hands was the most important step . . . in fact this action constituted the ratification of the treaty. That night Ariel Sharon, then a Cabinet member, called PM Begin for details of the agreement. Begin indicated that there was to be a full Israeli withdrawal from the Sinai. Sharon suggested to PM Begin that prior to the ceremony, Begin should approach Sadat to reiterate Israel's intent to give back the entire Sinai and to ask for an act of good faith in the form of allowing one of the Israeli settlements in northern Sinai to remain while the others (including the town of Yamit) would be dismantled as agreed upon in the articles. On the morning of the ceremony PM Begin, who agreed with Sharon's suggestion, conferred with President Sadat saying, "Mr. President, we are going to sign the agreement in an hour or two hours from now. I thought it would be nice if for good relations and interactions that one such small settlement of Israelis remain in northern Sinai." No sooner had PM Begin said this, than President Sadat began to perspire, become pale, and even to shiver. He stated to his assistant in a very loud voice, "Prepare the suitcases and we are leaving back home!" Moshe Dayan, who understood Arabic, fixed his eye on Sadat's face. When

Sadat looked at him, Dayan smiled and said in Arabic, "Mr. President the hasten is from the Devil," which is a famous Arabic proverb. President Sadat's face changed immediately, he regained some color and began to laugh at Dayan's reaction. PM Begin, who did not know Arabic or understand Arab culture, understood immediately from the body language of Sadat that he – Begin – created a crisis. He then said to President Sadat, "I apologize, and just forget what I said earlier."[8]

In the Western style of negotiation, one has permission to discuss, argue and bring new ideas to the table so long as it is before the signing of the accord. In the Arab culture one can discuss, argue, bring new ideas, and be very difficult in the course of the negotiations, but once one shakes hands, that is the agreement and nothing can be changed post-shaking of hands. Had Dayan not inserted the Arabic proverb and caused the change in the atmosphere, the Egyptians would have returned to Egypt without signing the agreement. This does not mean that the agreement would not have been achieved at a later stage, but we must remember that President Sadat was faced with significant internal Egyptian opposition to his steps towards signing the peace agreement with Israel. Returning without an agreement could have created more bad feelings toward the peace agreement between Egypt and Israel.

Case History #4

President Sadat received back the entire Sinai Peninsula except the one square kilometer tract of land called Taba. Egypt claimed Taba as Egyptian territory and Israel claimed it within the territory of Palestine established between the British and Ottomans in 1906. Thus the issue of Taba remained open for a later stage of negotiation. After Mubarak became president following Sadat's assassination in 1982, he re-opened the issue of Taba again, claiming it as always part of Egypt. At the end of 1987, Yitzhak Shamir became the PM of Israel, replacing Shimon Peres. It was a united government of the two largest parties with an agreement on the alternating of the posts of PM and FM after two years. It was during this time that an international arbitrary committee for Taba was established. This committee had the power to determine whether Taba belonged to Israel or to Egypt. It is important to note that significant Israeli development of a big hotel had taken place in Taba.

Joseph Ginat studied very carefully the 1906 map and it looked clear to him that Taba was in the boundaries of Egypt accordingly to the map. He had no doubt that the arbitrary committee would order the Israelis to hand over Taba. Ginat went to FM Peres, who served as the Vice Premier, suggesting Peres talk with PM Shamir with a proposal to give Taba to President Mubarak *before* the arbitrary committee's decision. Ginat explained to Peres that in Arab culture if one commits such a gesture *prior* to an arbitrated decision, the Arab leader in question cannot just say 'Thank You,' he becomes indebted to the gesture.

Had it been a case of a border dispute between two European countries with an arbitrary committee appointed to decide, and if one of the two countries had come to the conclusion that the other country was right in the dispute and would suggest to conclude the dispute prior to the arbitrated decision, then it would be expected that the country offered the property would simply say 'Thank You' and that would be the conclusion. But in Arab culture, offering such a gesture prior to the arbitrary committee's decision creates a situation of *reciprocity*. Ginat concluded the proposal by saying that President Mubarak would have two possibilities for reciprocity: (1) He could say 'The land is mine and hotel is yours,' or (2) He could say 'The land is mine and the hotel will be a joint Egyptian–Israeli venture.' FM Peres, persuaded by the proposal, approached PM Shamir with the idea; however Shamir turned it down saying, "As we have an arbitrary committee, let's wait for their verdict." Eventually the decision was unanimously in favor of Egypt's claim and Israel's withdrawal. Ginat, being in Egypt for three years as mentioned above, studied this issue and sought verification of reciprocity. All the Egyptians approached by Ginat agreed that Mubarak would have come with one of the two options above.

Case History #5: The Temple Mount/Al Haram Al-Sharif

In the Camp David peace negotiations between Israel and the Palestinians during July 2000, the issue of the Temple Mount/Al Haram Al-Sharif was one of the most difficult issues within the negotiations and probably one of the reasons for the failure of the negotiations. Although much was written about the Camp David negotiations, we would like to concentrate on the issue of the Temple Mount in the framework of "what went wrong." Both the Americans and the Israelis did not involve the Egyptians or the Jordanians in the talks, which probably would have helped in the negotiations, especially through the assistance it would have provided to Chairman Yasser Arafat in the making of decisions. Shlomo Ben-Ami, who was then the Israeli FM, wrote in his book, *A Front Without A Rearguard*, that Yasser Arafat didn't come to Camp David to negotiate on the issue of Jerusalem but he came to dictate his position and therefore remained intractable throughout the summit.[9] Ben-Ami tells us that before the Camp David summit was over, the Mufti of Jerusalem, Mr. Sabri, came with a *Fatwa* (religious edict) that there cannot be separation between the religious and the political solutions on the issue of the Temple Mount/Al Haram Al-Sharif and that such a separation does not exist in Islam. The Fatwa stated that the Muslims cannot agree to keep a religious sovereignty in such a case where Israel has political sovereignty.[10] After Camp David negotiations failed, Ben-Ami met with the Jordanian FM El-Hatib on August 22, 2000. El-Hatib indicated that to his understanding, Arafat could not compromise on both of the two issues: Jerusalem and the Palestinian refugees. Arafat could, however, compromise on one of the issues. Two days later Ben-Ami met with Egyptian President Mubarak and FM Musa. Musa wanted to be a mediator between the Israelis and the Palestinians, but indicated that he felt the Israelis did not want the Egyptians to be "in the picture."[11] Ambassador Daniel C. Kurtzer, who was at that time US Ambassador to Egypt and who later would serve as US Ambassador to Israel, said that President Mubarak was upset over the fact that he was not updated during the Camp David summit.[12] On the other hand, according to Gilead Sher, Israeli PM Barak estimated that Yasser Arafat could be more flexible if the Muslim world would support him.[13]

One can see the contradiction between the actual situation created by not involving the Egyptians and Jordanians in the talks, and the assumptions about Arafat made by PM Barak and reported by Gilead Sher. In the withdrawal from Gaza, which took place in November of 2005, PM Ariel Sharon involved the Egyptians in Israeli meetings with the Palestinians; their involvement created a better understanding between the Egyptians and the Israelis which resulted in an improved relationship. As indicated earlier, we believe that involvement of the Egyptians and the Jordanians might have helped the Palestinians (i.e. Yasser Arafat) to continue the negotiations rather than stopping them and starting the second *Intifada*. It should be indicated that in the peace treaty that exists with Jordan, it states that Israel must consult with Jordan before any negotiations or changes are made in the status of the Temple Mount/Al Haram Al-Sharif.[14]

Within the course of the negotiations related to the Temple Mount/Al Haram Al-Sharif, the spokesman for Yasser Arafat, Dr. Saeb Arekat, said that the Jewish Temple never existed and that rather, the statement that such a structure had existed in that location was a purely Jewish invention.[15] Arekat was not the only one who claimed the Jews did not have a Temple on the Temple Mount. Yasser Arafat and other Muslim scholars and politicians claimed the same. Yitzhak Reiter, in his book *From Jerusalem to Mecca and Back: The Islamic Consolidation of Jerusalem*, also studied the issue of the Temple. Reiter incorporated the works of the first Arab historians into his research: El-Maqdsai was an 11th century Jerusalemite, and Al-Mustofi, a 14th century Iranian expert on Islamic law. Both identified the El-Aqsa mosque with Solomon's Temple.[16] Sheikh Abdul Hadi Palazzi, a prominent member of the Islamic community in Italy, claims that the "Rock" on the Temple Mount/Al Haram Al-Sharif is the rock mentioned in the Jewish sources.[17] On the other hand, there are other Palestinian scholars who claim that the Jewish statement that the Temple existed on the Temple Mount is a lie. One in particular claims that the worshiping of the Hebrews was in fact a Canaanite form of worshiping and therefore a Jewish Temple could not have existed.[18] It is important to indicate that the leaders of the Muslim community in Israel – such as Sheikh Raid Selah who is the chairman of the northern branch of the Islamic Movement in Israel, Shauqi Khatib who is the chairman of the Israeli Arab Supreme Committee and Muhammad Baraka who is a member of the Knesset (Israeli Parliament) – deny any connection between Judaism and the Temple Mount/Al Haram Al-Sharif.[19]

As to the discussion related to the Temple Mount/Al Haram Al-Sharif within the entire framework of the negotiations, there were several suggestions. One was that the Palestinians would receive "custodial sovereignty" of the Temple Mount/Al Haram Al-Sharif.[20] The concept of custodianship was proposed by US President Clinton to Yasser Arafat; however, the one-on-one meeting between them failed, as Arafat rejected the proposal outright.[21] Another proposal to solve the issue of the Temple/Mount-Al Haram Al-Sharif was established by President Clinton and PM Barak, and was then reported to President Chirac of France by FM Ben-Ami. The proposal was for there to be two "jurisdictional sovereignties": the first, that of the Temple Mount's surface, would go to the Palestinians; the second, underneath the surface, would belong to Israel.[22] According to Gilead Sher, the Americans proposed another solution in which Israel would give the sovereignty to the United Nations Security Council. The Security Council would delegate the sovereignty to the Muslim Council, which in turn would delegate the "control" of the Temple Mount/Al Haram Al-Sharif to the Palestinians.[23]

We consider that all the proposals suggested in the Camp David Summit related to the Temple Mount/Al Haram Al-Sharif were wrong-headed. Using the term "sovereignty" is a mistake, as neither the Palestinians nor the Israelis would agree that the other party would have any kind of sovereignty over the Temple Mount/Al Haram Al-Sharif.

The issue of the Temple Mount has occupied the mind of Joseph Ginat since the early 1990s. Ginat and Professor Ephraim Ya'ar conducted research to create a solution for the Temple Mount/Al Haram Al-Sharif issue.

> We wrote a draft of a concrete proposal and submitted it to a number of the region's leaders, including the late PM Yitzhak Rabin, and FM Shimon Peres. It was also submitted to Danny Naveh, who served as Benjamin Netanyahu's Cabinet Secretary. When Ehud Barak was elected PM we sent him the proposal as well. We received no negative comments on our proposal; however, Danny Naveh did not comment at all. While Rabin, Peres, and Barak reacted positively to the content of the proposal, due to the charged political nature of the issue they were unable to embrace it publicly.
>
> We considered discussing the subject in an academic framework, and we therefore applied to the Rockefeller Foundation for funds to convene a

conference on the issue of Jerusalem. The representative of the Rockefeller Foundation, Mr. Clifford Chanin, was at first reluctant, but once we convinced him that representatives of the Palestinians and other Arab countries would agree to participate in such a conference, he agreed to support it.[24]

Three meetings were organized to discuss a framework for discussing Jerusalem. At the July 1998 conference in Bellagio, Italy, Arab participants were hesitant to deal with the Temple Mount issue, and preferred instead to focus on the political issues such as Jerusalem's sovereignty. The first meeting resulted in a draft thinking-points paper. At the December 1999 second meeting in Amman, Jordan, no clear consensus on a solution was reached. During the third meeting, which took place in Jerusalem in January 2000, a proposal was reached by participants entitled, "Negotiating Jerusalem: Guiding Principles."

> Except for one Israeli scholar who abstained, all the participants voted in favor of the proposal. We presented the proposal to the Israeli PM through the minister in charge of Jerusalem, Haim Ramon, only two hours prior to the press conference. It was forwarded to the Palestinian Chairman Arafat through Abu Ala, President of the Palestinian Parliament. The guiding principles of negotiating Jerusalem were presented to King Abdullah of Jordan and President Mubarak of Egypt at the same time by the Jordanian and the Egyptian participants of the conference. At the January 23rd press conference there were many Arab journalists representing not only the Palestinian Authority but the regional Arab media as well. We were subsequently notified that Chairman Arafat accepted the proposal. This proposal, which is comprehensive of the entire negotiating process, has relevance to the Temple Mount problem . . . [25]

The full text of "Negotiating Jerusalem: Guiding Principles" is provided in Appendix A.

Ginat's entire focus in the conducting of the conferences on Jerusalem was to concentrate on the Temple Mount/Al Haram Al-Sharif and to see how the Arab partners would discuss the issue. However, all of the Arab participants suggested that instead the issue of Jerusalem – excluding the holy places (i.e. the Old City and mainly the Temple Mount/Al Haram Al-Sharif) – be addressed. In private talks with some of the participants as well as other Palestinians, it was explained that the Temple Mount issue was very sensitive and therefore it was suggested that all other aspects of Jerusalem be considered, but not the Old City. In the paper "Negotiating Jerusalem," the issues were "*Governance* of the city must be respectful of Jerusalem's important pluralistic and multicultural character. The protection and preservation of the unique religious interests of Christians, Jews, and Muslims must be guaranteed, and freedom of worship and access to holy places must be granted. *The status quo* in the administration of holy places should be maintained, and a coordination mechanism among the various religious authorities should be introduced."[26]

Ginat spoke with many people during the conference, and subsequently in preparation for this essay both authors (Ginat and Altman) interviewed several Palestinians regarding the issue of Jerusalem and the Temple Mount/Al Haram Al-Sharif. At the time of the conference, and again in 2005, Palestinians emphasized their belief that success could be achieved in negotiating Jerusalem only by doing it in two stages. The first stage had to be exactly what was achieved in the Guiding Principles of the conferences (refer to Appendix A). The interviewees emphasized that only after several years during which these Guiding Principles were implemented and both peoples were living in peace, should the second stage take place, that of negotiating the future of the Temple Mount/Al Haram Al-Sharif.

Ginat and Ya'ar, in their proposal for a solution regarding the Temple Mount, distinguished between the religious and the political aspects. The Muslim world, immediately after the 1967 War, established a committee for Jerusalem that focused on Al-Haram Al-Sharif. The chairman of the committee, which was elected by all entire delegates of the Muslim world, was King Hassan II of Morocco. Yasser Arafat was elected as a deputy chairman. Thus the Muslim world representatives distinguished between the religious and political aspects of Jerusalem and the holy places.[27] It was inappropriate from the very beginning of the Camp David Summit to deal with the issue of the Temple Mount/Al Haram Al-Sharif. Israel had to discuss this issue with representatives of the Muslim committee of Jerusalem, and not mesh it together with the political issue of a Palestinian state. In the Ginat and Ya'ar proposal the term 'sovereignty' was completely eliminated. It was the late King Hussein's conception of the holy places that was, and remains, the most realistic.

> My religious faith demands that sovereignty over the holy places in Jerusalem resides with God and God alone. Dialogue between the faiths should be strengthened; religious sovereignty should be accorded to all believers of the three Abrahamic faiths, in accordance with their religions.[28]

The Ginat and Ya'ar proposal was that there would not be any sovereignty appointed, but instead the management of the Temple Mount/Al Haram Al-Sharif would be given to representatives of the Muslim world. The idea was that the management would include the Palestinians along with four other Muslim nations, such as Jordan, Egypt, Morocco, and Saudi Arabia. Ginat and Ya'ar met with Shlomo Ben-Ami and later with PM Ehud Barak; these meetings took place before the Camp David Summit. The meeting with Barak lasted for almost two hours, although unfortunately the proposal was not discussed at the Camp David Summit. Sher explains that Barak used to consult with many people, but when he finally made a decision he did so with a tight group of advisors.[29]

We believe that had the proposal been discussed, in which the term "sovereignty" was not used at all (as this was the biggest 'landmine' in the whole issue), then the management of the Temple Mount/Al Haram Al-Sharif would perhaps have been handed to representatives of the Islamic Committee for Jerusalem. When negotiating, it is imperative to understand the culture of the other. If the Muslim world has established a committee that has been dealing with the Muslim holy places in Jerusalem by separating the religious and political issues, then why should Israel avoid dealing with this committee when discussing a solution for the Temple Mount/Al Haram Al-Sharif?

Case History #6: The War in Iraq

The focus of this essay is 'knowing' the culture of the other, and the things that go wrong because of not knowing the other's culture. It is not our purpose to criticize the reasons or validity of the war in Iraq; rather, we would like to point out that by knowing the culture of the Iraqis the Americans could have saved the lives of US and other Coalition Forces soldiers.

In March 2003, when the first stage of the war took place and the Coalition Forces were advancing towards Baghdad, Ginat met with one of the assistants to Ambassador L. Paul Bremer, III, US Presidential Envoy to Iraq and the Administrator of the Coalition Provisional Authority. At that meeting, Ginat predicted that the Coalition Forces would have more casualties after securing Baghdad. Ginat felt that the Americans were not prepared for the day after the first stage of the war. He explained to the assistant that Iraq is built not only of Sunni, Shiite, and Kurds, but also of tribes and federations of tribes.[30] Under the tribal customs there is a tradition of "blood revenge,"[31] the rules of which are to kill a person from the other group that caused the killing of the extended family (co-liable group) member. However, there is another solution in which the injured group accepts "blood money" or *diyya*. Usually when there is the killing by accident or by premeditated murder, the elders of the aggressor's collective responsibility unit will seek the services of a mediator(s). The mediator will approach the elders of the injured group to try to establish a cease-fire for a certain period of time, and then offer "blood money" to the injured group as a compensation for the loss of the dead family member's future contributions to the collective responsibility unit. There are cases where the injured group will not accept "blood money," and persists in seeking the death of a member of the aggressor's collective responsibility unit. On the other hand, there have been many recorded cases in which the group has accepted the "blood money." Once they have done so, and have shaken hands, there should be no threat of reprisal.

In the course of any war there are casualties; soldiers and civilians. All Iraqis killed in the course of the war belong to particular tribes. The suggestion of Ginat was that the American intelligence or any other appropriate unit should be tasked with establishing delegations of officers to tribal elders according to a map of Iraq that denotes tribal boundaries. On visits to the tribal Sheikh the officers should express their regret for the tribes' casualties and ask for the Sheikh's help in approaching the injured families with a view to asking them to accept the traditional *diyya* (blood money). Based on earlier experiences of similar situations, it would be reasonable to expect that at least 50 percent of the injured families would have accepted *diyya*. These families would not, then, have exercised their obligatory threat of "revenge" on Coalition Forces. In general the Iraqis are more rigid than Arabs in neighboring countries on the issue of negotiating blood disputes. However, even though negotiations would take longer and the percentage refusing *diyya* and taking "blood revenge" would be higher than the regional norm, there would have been a possibility of reaching a 50 percent acceptance. Other factors also affect revenge or settlement: the economic basis of the tribe may directly influence their decision to accept *diyya* or not. For example:

> A group whose economy is based on wage labor will be anxious to resolve a blood quarrel quickly because their daily and regular trips to their places of work will make them vulnerable to the revenging group. If the economy of the group is based on the raising of herds the movements of group members are not regular. Consequently, in contrast to the wage labor situation, a revenge is less likely to be perpetrated.[32]

Sedentarization increases both the dependency of family members on the earnings of wage labor and significantly increases the repetitive daily patterns of individuals, as they must go to work at a certain time and adhere to workplace schedules, which in turn increases their vulnerability to reprisals. They in turn would be more likely to choose *diyya* as it eliminates the likelihood of danger. Urbanization also affects the "blood revenge" patterns, as groups that under traditional situations might have had limited interaction are faced with increased "daily interaction between the groups that is unavoidable and thus the chance of a continuation of the conflict is higher."[33] Tribal leadership is also critical; if the leader seeks to increase group identity or cohesiveness, then he will encourage revenge.

> By deliberately increasing tension a leader can make his group aware of their collective responsibility, in this way promoting group cohesiveness. Even if the leader does not advocate a revenge he can achieve cohesion by not permitting a cease-fire agreement.[34]

An obstacle to negotiating the blood quarrel may be found when in an urban setting the tribal leadership remains obstinate or refuses *diyya*. The revenging family leadership may fear the dilution of collective identity and seek to increase tension. The increased daily interaction of family members from the injured and revenging collective responsibility units directly increases the likelihood of a "blood revenge." But as mentioned above, the membership may seek resolution because the likelihood of interaction has become so much higher. This allows opportunities to negotiate "blood money." One has to know and see the economic situation of Iraq as a result of the war: increased unemployment, decreased security, industry at a stale-mate, and reassertion of traditional affiliations. All these factors lead to an increased use of *diyya* as opposed to "blood revenge."

To the best of our knowledge the Americans have not used this approach of addressing "blood revenge" directly. We must assume that those who look for revenge and ambush American soldiers also provide shelter for insurgents.

There is controversy between military experts, not necessarily only American experts but those from other countries in the world, regarding the question of the appropriateness on the part of the American forces in the killing of the two sons of Saddam Hussein, Udai and Qusai. Experts question – was it the right thing to do? Or, because these two men were surrounded in a certain building, although though they fired upon American forces, would it not have been better to have more patience, and try to catch them alive, instead of killing them? The idea behind this approach is had they been caught alive, the intelligence (CIA) could have extracted important information which could have been essential for the American effort. However, this issue as we have mentioned, is for military analysts and experts, and not a subject for analysis here.

What is within the scope of this study – knowing the culture of the other – is what happened after two sons were killed. In Muslim societies, autopsy (post mortem) is not permitted. It has the connotation of defiling the body of the individual. It is obvious that Americans had to do it for various reasons. However, it should have been done internally, and not in a public fashion. For several days, all the television networks throughout the Arab world showed the bodies with the stitches of the autopsy. Most of the Iraqi people hated the sons of Sadam Hussein. They were brutal, and especially Udai acted in immoral ways. Several Iraqi informants told the authors that at the events of wedding ceremonies in Baghdad, Udai would send his bodyguards to kidnap very beautiful brides from the very ceremony, and would rape them, causing tremendous humiliation. There were cases in which brides then committed suicide. This type of behavior was known among the Iraqi people, and as indicated, there was great hatred toward them as individuals and as the sons of Sadam Hussein. However, once the autopsies of the bodies were done, all those who hated Udai and Qusai looked at the issue as a Muslim body having been defiled. Instead of having the Iraqi people expressing happiness over the killing of Udai and Qusai, they instead were upset because of the defilement of the bodies of two Muslim people. Udai and Qusai were no longer seen as two cruel individuals, and instead became two Muslims whose bodies were on display. The Americans thus achieved the opposite of what they had intended. The authors believe that this was done in the framework of not knowing "the other." It would have been acceptable to show the bodies of the two killed brothers prior to the autopsies, and explain later that the DNA proved that they were the sons of Saddam Hussein, without putting the autopsied bodies on display.

One week after taking Baghdad, in April 2003, someone told representatives of the CIA that a head of a tribal federation located on the Jordanian–Iraqi border gave shelter to Saddam Hussein's brother. According to several Iraqi informants, the Bedouin leader was for several years a CIA agent and was known for having good relations with Saddam Hussein. Being a friend of Hussein would make it easier to be an agent. Several hours after the rumors reached the agency, several jets leveled the entire compound of the Sheikh (tribal leader); 28 people were killed, among them the Sheikh himself. But Saddam Hussein's brother was not present. The rumor had succeeded in misinforming the CIA. It is not in the scope of this essay to analyze the difference between gossip, rumor, and information versus intelligence. However, in a nutshell, intelligence is the analysis of information; it doesn't appear that in the short time between the collecting of the information and the air raid of the compound that adequate time was allowed for vetting the information as actual intelligence. The consequences of the air raid and the killing of the Sheikh was that there was immediate ambushing and killing of Americans and other Coalition Forces. It is important to understand that the killing of such a prominent figure of a tribal federation meant that reprisals were taken not only by his particular tribe but by the entire federation of tribes. In late July and early August of 2004, the brother of the late Sheikh went to Jordan. The authors are aware that he was seeking reconciliation with the Americans. Had the Americans seized the opportunity, and given him a position in the provisional government, this could have led to immediate reconciliation and stopped the tribal federation's 'blood revenge' associated with the Sheikh's death (see Appendix B).[35]

Bombing the Sheikh's compound was a mistake – not in the framework of knowing the culture of the other but a purely tactical mistake on the part of US forces. But not seeking a way of reconciliation and not using the opportunity offered by his brother is within the framework of not *wanting* to know the culture of the other.

Case History #7: Encounters Between Israelis and Palestinians

It is not only Americans who often do not understand the culture of the other; but as mentioned above, Israelis often do not, or do not wish to, understand Arab culture. The authors would like to conclude this section with an example that is similar to Case History #6.

From the very beginning of the second *Intifada* (September 2000) there were several brothers and cousins from one of the co-liable groups of the El-Támra tribe, located in the Judean Desert east of Bethlehem, who belonged to Fatah and attacked Israeli targets. Israeli forces killed one of these men, which in turn resulted in their increased attacks. The cyclical nature of the conflict caused not only increased Israeli casualties but also casualties among the co-liable group. On one hand, it was a war between the Palestinian Liberation Organization (PLO) and Israel, but on the other hand, the leaders of the local Palestinian organization were Bedouin of a certain co-liable group and famous tribe. The Israeli authorities knew that they were of the El-Támra tribe and should have viewed the situation according to Bedouin customs: seeking Bedouin assistance to mediate the conflict. The authors discussed this issue with several Bedouin leaders who verified that a delegation of Bedouin dignitaries sent to the leaders of the co-liable group, whose members were attacked and killed by the Israelis, could have quietly reached a long-term *hudna* (cease-fire; see below).[36]

It is possible that Israeli expert analysis may have concluded that, as the members of the El-Támra Tribe were incorporated within the PLO, attempting to solve the problem under the structure of tribal law would not have been a feasible. The authors would like to base their argument, however, by reminding the readers about the first encounter between the PLO and Hamas in Gaza. Several weeks after Israel turned Gaza and Jericho over to the Palestinians, as the first stage of the Oslo agreement, and after Yasser Arafat came to Gaza, there were encounters between Hamas and the PLO in the streets of Gaza. These encounters were shown live on television, with Palestinians in uniform shooting at Hamas members, and vice versa. On television, one could see bodies, both dead and wounded people. Suddenly, some of the people in uniforms belonging to the Palestinian police forces lifted their weapons in the air above their heads, turned around, threw their guns on the ground, and ran away from the scene. Other policemen, in the same uniform, continued fighting. What is the explanation for these different modes of behavior? What is the peculiar situation? The police forces of the PLO were comprised of members of two groups – one of local Gaza people, who were members of various Gaza families. The second group represented people that were brought, according to the agreement between the Israelis and the Palestinians, from training camps of the PLO that were located in Tunisia, in Sudan and in

Iraq (Israel agreed on a certain number of people to be brought in as a police force to the Territories).

Those who were of the import group did not have relatives in Gaza, and they could continue to fight. Those who were from Gaza understood that the members of families of the injured from Hamas, upon seeing the footage on television, would take revenge. In other words, even if you are serving the authorities, you are still part of the collective responsibility unit. This example demonstrates that had the Israelis used Bedouin as mediators in Case History #7 described above, they could have potentially reached an agreement with the terrorists who belonged to the PLO but were members of one of the co-liable groups of the El-Támra Tribe.

None of the above-mentioned cases have dealt with the Arab side of not knowing the other's culture. There is no question that the Arabs, especially the Palestinians, have made many mistakes by not having an understanding of Israeli culture. The authors have sought to concentrate in this chapter on the Westerners' lack of understanding of the other's culture. However, we cannot avoid one extremely important issue, and this is the issue of the Jewish Temple on the Temple Mount. As has been aforementioned, the authors believe that this is an occurrence of a group "not wanting to know the other's culture." Yasser Arafat, on many occasions, stated that the Jewish Temple did not truly exist on the Temple Mount. He actually did not tolerate the mentioning of the Jewish Temple's location on the Mount by anyone in his presence. In a meeting with the US Secretary of State Madeline Albright, she used the term "Temple Mount." Arafat became angry, emphasized the name of the place as only 'Al Haram Al-Sharif', and then stormed out of the room.[37] In discussions between the authors and various Palestinians, the latter in a polite way said that they were not sure of the existence of a Jewish Temple on the Temple Mount/Al Haram Al-Sharif. The same was true with Arabs from other Arab countries, such as Jordan and Egypt. It appears that in the socialization, and perhaps even in the indoctrination, of Muslims that the issue of the Jewish Temple is dealt with as "if it existed, it must have existed elsewhere." Yasser Arafat indicated on several occasions that it was true that the Jewish Temple existed, but near Nablus. It is true that there was a Temple on Mount Gerizm, but it was a Samaritan Temple.[38]

There is no other alternative, to avoid misunderstandings and mistakes in any kind of relationship and especially in negotiations for peace in conflicts, but to learn in depth the culture of the other party.

How to Rebuild Trust?

Building trust is a process, it is not done overnight. One of the most important components is to build economic ties between the parties. If the

Israelis and the Palestinians establish joint-economic ventures, to be located on the border, then both sides will share a *mutual* interest in the keeping of peace. But in order to reach this stage, a prerequisite required is a cease-fire. It is difficult, and perhaps impossible, to sit and talk when there is bloodshed that leads to ever increased hatred. The key is to discover the formula for the reaching of a long-term cease-fire that would enable the parties to sit around the peace table and build the foundation of a peace agreement.

Hudna[39]

Over the course of the second *Intifada* no efforts on the part of the Bush Administration have broken the Israeli–Palestinian deadlock. The Mitchell Report did little to address the root causes of the violence and only provided political guidelines for returning to the negotiating table. The Tenet Cease-fire document attempted to formalize the *de facto* cessation in violence while providing a timetable to move toward implementing the Mitchell recommendation. Neither side thought the Tenet Cease-fire capable of implementation. President Bush then sent Assistant Secretary of State for Near Eastern Affairs William J. Burns and Special Envoy Marine Corps General (ret.) Anthony C. Zinni to push the Israelis and Palestinians toward the Mitchell and Tenet reports. To date all US efforts to break the Israeli–Palestinian stalemate have failed. President Bush proposed the "Roadmap," none of the articles found within having been implemented up to the present, January 2007.

The Bedouin terms *hudna* and *átwa* mean "cease-fire" or "armistice." Ginat's research indicates that in cases of Bedouin blood quarrels the term *átwa* is used. *Hudna* is used to describe the cease-fire agreement between Bedouin or Arab troops and non-Bedouins or non-Muslims.[40] This is not to say that *hudna* is mentioned in the Qur'an, which it is not, but that it is a variation of cease-fire denoted in the Muslim tradition. Peacemaking is given significant prominence as a practice of the Prophet Mohammed; for example, he is recorded to have "made peace (*salaha*) with the polytheists on the day of *Hudaybiyyah*." Several other terms beside *hudna* are used throughout the text: *muhadana* (cease-fire), *ahl al-muhadana* (people with whom a cease-fire was established), *muwadeená* (separation of fighting forces), *sulh* (agreement, peace), *musuleha* (peace-making), *áhd* (pact, peace treaty). Among Israeli Arabs, Palestinians, and Jordanians the peace-making process that they understand as *hudna* has become something of a sacred concept. It is not religious *per se*, but its violation invokes the fear of Heaven's retribution; for example, a member of the *hudna* violator's family may become deathly ill or may die. Because of this sacred element, when a person has signed or shaken hands to rat-ify a *hudna* agreement he will not violate it. The time limit for the *hudna* has then been established and will be honored; this does not however suggest that the person will not act against the *hudna* after its expiration. The annulment of other peace agreements or treaties does not carry the severity of the annulling of a *hudna*. Sheikh Ahmad Yassin, the Hamas leader assassinated by Israel on March 22, 2004, on many occasions stated that "*hudna má al-Yahud wala sulh*" (It is alright to have a *hudna* with the Jews, but not to sign a peace treaty).

European incursions into the Middle East, from the Crusades to the nineteenth century, consistently demonstrated their inadequate knowledge of the Muslim religion and culture. Despite this, the Crusaders and Salah al-Din reached eight *hudna* agreements: four initiated by Salah al-Din and four by the Crusaders. The Crusaders had observed that when the Arabs bound themselves to an oath, they honored it. For the Bedouin, they are similarly honor-bound when an oath is taken by placing his hand on the Qur'an or by even raising his right hand to evoke the same sentiment; he may not make it falsely. During many of the various nineteenth-century conflicts between Muslims and Europeans, negotiations were conducted and *hudna* agreements ratified: for example, between the French forces and those of Ábd Al-Qadir in Algeria, and between the Moroccans and the Spaniards in Tatouan, in northern Morocco. The first Ábd Al-Qadir–French *hudna* was signed on February 28, 1834, and was essentially a conventional European cease-fire agreement other than the fact that references to Western type cease-fires were replaced by both the term *hudna* and the French agreement to introduce Islamic codes in the document's wording (i.e. the agreement is between General Desmichels and the "Prince of the Believers Ábd Al-Qadir"). The second *hudna* (May 30, 1837) is formally known as the "Treaty (*hudna*) of the Tafna," and again features prominently Islamic components such as: freedom of religion, building of mosques, and the jurisdiction of the *qadi* (religious judge) over Muslims to judge according to Islamic law. During the nineteenth-century war in Tatouan between the Moroccans and Spaniards, several attempts were made and failed before a *hudna* was finally ratified. This led the way for a *sulha* pact.

Throughout the relationship between Arab countries and Israel, all cease-fire (*waqf al-nar*) agreements with Israel have been treated as *hudna* agreements by the Arab states post-signing. After the 1948 War, a convening in Rhodes by the representatives of Israel, Jordan, Syria, and Egypt resulted in cease-fire agreements. The "Green Line" was formalized and the area referred to as the "Triangle" (the Arab villages from Umm al-Fahm to Wadi Ára and Kafr Qassem) was transferred to Israel. The agreement was referred to as a *hudna* by all Arab press.

A Proposal to Stop the Second Intifada by Introducing the Hudna Concept

A meeting between Eyal Erlich, Ábd al-Wahab Darawshe (a Muslim former member of the Knesset and an experienced mediator in blood quarrels), and Joseph Ginat under Eyal's initiative took place to discuss the possibility of proposing a Palestinian–Israeli cease-fire under the *hudna* system. The conclusion of the discussion was that reaching a *hudna* would stop the bloodshed for an assigned period. The three met with Yasser Arafat who was in favor of using the *hudna* concept; he suggested a period of one year with the option to renew for another year if talks had not yet been conclusive. Arafat emphasized that the Palestinian Authority (PA) legislature had to approve the proposal, which was subsequently done. On March 25, 2001, the trio sent a letter to PM Ariel Sharon suggesting the *hudna* concept as a possibility for stopping the bloodshed (see Appendix C). The May 21, 2001 answer of the letter was as follows: "Thank you for forwarding the material to the Prime Minister's Chief-of-Staff, Uri Shani. Your proposal and that of the other gentlemen is very interesting, and we will take it under advisement at a latter date . . . Danny Ayalon."

On June 6, 2001, Ginat traveled to Cairo to meet with Dr. Osama Al-Baz, senior political advisor to President Mubarak, who showed interest in the *hudna* idea. It should be noted that in the summer of 2001 the Egyptian government signed a *hudna* with two terrorist organizations active in Egypt, the Islamic Jihad and al Gamaá al Islamiyya. This *hudna* remains effective to date. The three then met with President Moshe Katsav, in a meeting on November 14, 2001, and Katsav responded favorably: "I find your initiative very interesting. I know a little about Arab culture. Only a few weeks ago, I was invited to a large *sulha* ceremony in an Arab village. There had been a blood feud between two clans. They agreed to a *hudna*, and then to a *sulha*. I think it's a fine idea."

President Katsav agreed to address the Palestinian legislature in Ramallah; however preparations came to an abrupt halt after the Israeli capture of the *Karin A* weapons ship (February 2002). It should be noted that PM Sharon had already decided against the *hudna* concept prior to the incident. The trio's idea was that the *hudna* would be signed between Israel and the Palestinian Authority; Hamas and Islamic Jihad would sign the *hudna* agreement as a prerequisite, binding the Palestinian Authority as the responsible agent for the two groups' adherence.

Since the Israeli Declaration Decision No. 3281 of February 20, 2005, which furthered the previous Decision No. 1996, to withdraw from the Gaza Strip from June 6, 2004 onwards, the Egyptians have become increasingly interested in reaching a *hudna* between the Israelis and the Palestinians. Omar Suliman, the head of the Egyptian Intelligence and also a member of the Egyptian Cabinet, has been making regular visits to the

Gaza Strip. He has been meeting high-ranking Israeli officials in order to find a way for the withdrawal to be bilateral with the cooperation of the Palestinians, and to make sure that in the period following disengagement, there would not be any attacks by Qassam missiles and mortars on Israeli settlements. In order to achieve this, the Egyptians realize that the best solution will be to reach a comprehensive *hudna*. Omar Suliman has invited representatives from the Hamas and Islamic Jihad to Cairo in order to discuss the possibility of a *hudna*. However, although the Hamas and Islamic Jihad had agreed to a cease-fire between them and the PA, it was a *waqf al-nar* agreement, with no mention of the word *hudna*.

Hamas, the Islamic Jihad, and the El-Aqsa Brigades agreed to have a *tahadiyya*, but *hudna* was not mentioned. *Tahadiyya* loosely translates as a cessation of fire. The Islamic Jihad and El-Aqsa Brigade did not keep the *tahadiyya* where the Hamas honored their word. However, the Hamas did state that the *tahadiyya* was effective only until January 1, 2006.

Concluding Remarks

It is not a crime to swallow one's pride. Israel and Israelis will lose nothing by adopting a Muslim term or concept. One can fight terrorism but cannot fight suicide bombers – there is no return and no regret for a person embarking on a mission with an explosive belt. A *hudna* might just be the way to stop this senseless cycle of violence.

What has been presented in this chapter is an approach to overcome a psychological barrier in order to stop bloodshed. Negotiations according to the "Road Map" can start only when there is no violence. Before the second *Intifada*, tens of thousands of Palestinians worked daily in Israel, but at this point in time (January 2007) there are approximately one quarter of a million "guest workers" from different countries around the world such as China, Thailand, Philippines, Romania, Hungary, etc. working in Israel. If a comprehensive cease-fire were to be implemented, then Palestinians could replace a percentage of these "guest workers." Alleviating the heavy unemployment in the Palestinian Authority would gradually change the attitude towards Israel of many Palestinians. When stomachs are full and survival is not the daily imperative, then a peaceful socialization may begin. With a long-term cease-fire in place, tourism would increase, international companies would begin once again to invest in Israel and the Palestinian Authority territories, and the economies of both parties would begin to improve.

There is no question that there will be difficulties and obstacles on the way to a comprehensive peace; however, when both parties learn to know the culture of the other, establish a long-term cease-fire, sit at the negotiating table and discuss how to work towards peace, then both sides will prevent misunderstanding and a repetition of what went wrong, and they will gradually build trust.

Appendix A: Negotiating Jerusalem: Guiding Principles

Negotiating Jerusalem:
Guiding Principles

January 23, 2000

> *First released to the Office of the PM of the State of Israel at 0900 hours, January 23, 2000 in Jerusalem.*
>
> *Released to the Office of the Chairman of the Palestinian National Authority at 1000 hours, January 23, 2000 in Abu-Dis.*
>
> *Subsequently presented to: His Majesty King Abdullah bin Al Hussein of the Hashemite Kingdom of Jordan and to President Mohamad Hosny Mubarak of the Arab Republic of Egypt.*

Recognizing the historic opportunity that Arabs and Israelis have at the beginning of the new millennium to secure comprehensive peace between them,

being cognizant of the looming deadline for a final settlement of the Palestinian–Israeli conflict,

believing that neither party can resolve the conflict unilaterally,

understanding the central importance of Jerusalem to Palestinians and Israelis, religiously, culturally, and politically,

considering the significance of Jerusalem to Muslims, Jews, Christians, and other communities and to many states, including Jordan, which has played a significant role in East Jerusalem for several decades,

accepting the principles of equity, fairness, and reciprocity among the parties in searching for a lasting settlement,

having examined and debated the issue of Jerusalem in several sessions over the last two years, and having overcome serious disagreements in the process,

we, a group of international academics and practitioners, including Israelis, Palestinians, Jordanians, Egyptians, Americans, and others, acting as individuals,

resolved to put forth the following **Guiding Principles** for a final settlement of the Jerusalem issue:

Neither the imposition of annexation nor the partition of Jerusalem could serve as a basis for the final status of the city. Jerusalem is to be the capital of both Israel and Palestine in Jewish West and Arab East of the city, respectively and on equal footing.

Palestinians and Israelis shall be sovereign over their respective capitals as stipulated in the first principle above.

The unique religious, cultural, and historical importance of the walled part of Jerusalem to both sides requires special arrangements for this part to be negotiated by the parties.

The wholeness of Jerusalem should be upheld, with open access to Israelis and Palestinians alike.

Governance of the city must be respectful of Jerusalem's important pluralistic and multicultural character. The protection and preservation of the unique religious interests of Christians, Jews, and Muslims, must be guaranteed and freedom of worship, and access to holy placed must be assured.

The status quo in the administration of holy places should be maintained, and a coordination mechanism among the various religious authorities should be introduced.

Principles of self-governance of all communities and at all levels must be equitable and democratic.

It is necessary to resolve the issue of Jewish neighborhoods/settlements in and around Jerusalem, beyond the 1967 "green line," and to reconcile existing realities with the existing agreements between the parties and with relevant international resolutions.

Residents of Jerusalem, including non-citizens, shall be subject to equitable rules and regulations to be agreed upon by Israel and the Palestine Liberation Organization.

Municipal arrangements in Jerusalem must be consistent with above principles. Among the possible arrangements consistent with these principles is the establishment of two municipal councils in the two respective capitals and a coordination commission for the entire city with equal representation.

No unilateral steps that would affect the final status and boundaries of Jerusalem, beyond the 1967 green line, should be take prior to a final agreement.

Participants

Dr. Mohammed Ali, Jordanian
Mr. Rateb M. Amro, Jordanian
Dr. Taisir Amre, Palestinian
(Amb.) Tahseen Basheer, Egyptian
Prof. Dale Eickelman, American
Dr. Khalil Elian, Jordanian
Dr, Bahieldin Elibarchy, Egyptian
Prof. Abraham Friedman, Israeli
(Gen.) Shlomo Gazit, Israeli
Prof. Joseph Ginat, Israeli
Dr. Motti Golani, Israeli
Dr. Mohammad Jadallah, Palestinian
Prof. Mohanna Haddad, Jordanian

Prof. Manuel Hassassian, Palestinian
Prof. Saad Eddin Ibrahim, Egyptian
Mr. Abdullah T. Kanaan, Jordanian
Dr. Menachem Klein, Israeli
Prof. Moshe Ma'oz, Israeli
Mr. Rami Nasrallah, Palestinian
(Amb.) Edward Perkins, American
Dr. Hussein Ramzoun, Jordanian
Dr. Yitzhak Reiter, Israeli
Prof. Shimon Shamir, Israeli
Prof. Shibley Telhami, American
Mr. Khalil Tufakji, Palestinian
Prof. Ephraim Yaar, Israeli

This project was funded by the Rockefeller Foundation and sponsored by the

Center for Peace Studies of the International Programs Center at the University of Oklahoma.

Appendix B: Letter to President Bush (unabridged)

PRESIDENT OF THE UNITED STATES   AUGUST 1, 2004
GEORGE W. BUSH

Re: Reduction of Insurgent Actions Against U.S. in Iraq

Dear President Bush,

One of the largest Federation of Tribes in Iraq is the Dulaim Federation. The tribe includes a very large area of Iraq, including the cities of Fallujah and Ramadi. The head of this federation was Sheik Malik Harbit. He was known as someone who worked with the CIA for many years. During the first phases of the present war in Iraq, American intelligence received faulty information that Saddam Hussein's brother was hiding in the home of Sheik Malik. On April 14th 2003, six days after the fall of Baghdad, American forces attacked Sheik Malik's house in Ramadi. 26 people including Sheik Malik were killed. Saddam Hussein's brother was not at the house.

Among the Bedouin and other Middle Eastern societies the families have a collective responsibility for "Blood Revenge," against someone who injures a member of their family or tribe. In some cases the problem can be resolved by paying "Blood Money" to the injured party. Since April 14, 2003, there have been many attacks against American soldiers and civilians by members of this Federation of Tribes. There exists an opportunity to reconcile this Federation of Tribes with American interests in Iraq. The late Malik Harbit's brother, Munther, is in Jordan now. He would like to negotiate with the U.S. He would like for the Federation to have representation in the new Iraqi government. In return the entire Federation of Tribes he represents will cease hostility against American troops and the new Iraqi government.
. . . I believe it can be a turning point in U.S. and Iraqi relationships.

On May 10th 2001, I sent you a letter predicting a possible Al Qaeda attack in the United States. I also sent a documentary that I conducted concerning "Suicide Bombers." You should have also received my book about "Blood Revenge." I am currently a Visiting Professor at the University of Oklahoma in the Center for Peace Studies . . .

Sincerely,

Professor Joseph Ginat, PhD.
Professor of Anthropology and Middle Eastern Studies
Vice-President and Director of Strategic Dialogue Center, Netanya Academic College
Co-Director Center for Peace Studies, University of Oklahoma

Appendix C: Letter to Prime Minister Ariel Sharon (unabridged)

(The letter was written in Hebrew. The following is a translation.)

25 March 2001

To: Prime Minister Ariel Sharon
From: 'Abd al-Wahab Darawshe, Prof. Joseph Ginat, Eyal Erlich

A Suggested Political Move that May Rapidly Achieve a Cease-Fire with the Palestinians and a Renewal of the Peace Process

Sir,

We respectfully suggest this idea of ours out of a profound understanding of the heavy responsibility placed on you, and a sincere wish to assist in putting an end to the bloodshed in our region. Should you decide to adopt this suggestion, it would require you, or your representative, to travel to Egypt and meet privately with President Mubarak, in order to inform him of this suggestion. If President Mubarak agrees to join this effort, we estimate that in all likelihood a cease-fire may be achieved within a relatively short time, without any concessions on Israel's part. If our suggestion is indeed accepted, we recommend a meeting with President Mubarak at the earliest possible time, prior to the Amman conference.

Our suggestion would require a short introduction. To explain its origins: The blood-feud has been a part of Arab custom and Islam for many centuries. Arab culture also evolved an important traditional mechanism for resolving conflicts peacefully, a device intended to break the vicious circle of blood-feuds. This mechanism is especially effective in cases of conflicts between families.

Our suggestion is based on a simple idea: the implementation of this traditional mechanism to promote the political ends you have stated: a cease-fire as a condition for negotiations, without any concessions on Israel's behalf. Approaching the Palestinians with a conflict-resolution mechanism rooted in their own culture, well known to them and respected by them, enhances its chances of success.

The mechanism is as follows: when a family finds itself under threat of a blood-feud (regardless of who caused the conflict, whose fault it is, who started it, etc.) it appoints a delegation of dignitaries (Shaykhs), who approach the potential avengers in the other family and suggest a cease-fire *("Hudna"* in Arabic).
Normally, in "ordinary" conflicts among Palestinian families, the family approached by the delegation of Shaykhs agrees to declare "Hudna" (a cease-fire) for a period of several months, sometimes longer. During this period the threat of vengeance and violent acts is removed, and the families conduct dignified talks, mediated by the Shaykhs, in an attempt to reach a resolution. These resolutions normally conclude with financial remuneration, at which point a *sulha,* or peace

ceremony, between the families takes place, and the bloodshed is ended once and for all.

Haifa University Prof. Joseph Ginat, who has studied Arab societies for years, has dealt with blood-feuds and mediation of conflicts in several studies. As an authority in this field, he is of the opinion that this suggestion may work, if brought before the Palestinians. Prof. Ilai Alon, of Tel Aviv University, who specializes in the study of negotiations in ancient times, also supports this suggestion.

One should remember that Salah a-Din, one of the greatest Arab military leaders, reached several *hudna* agreements with the Crusaders. In some cases the Crusaders were the ones seeking *hudna,* in other cases the initiative came from Salah al-Din. Most significantly, these *hudna* agreements were made between a Muslim hero and Christians, thus the procedure is not valid for Muslims only.

We suggest that you approach President Mubarak (perhaps King 'Abdullah as well), and ask him to be your partner in an attempt to reach *hudna,* a move mediated by him and carried out under his aegis. If President Mubarak accepts this appeal, it would require maximal commitment on his part to ensure the success of this measure. As we have already said, this move (if agreed to by Mubarak, and later by the Palestinians) should initially achieve a cease-fire in the occupied territories. It is our estimation that such a cease-fire, rooted in Palestinian culture and regarded as sacred, would be honored by most Palestinians.

Assuming the cease-fire *(hudna)* would be declared for six months, peace talks with [Palestinian leader Yasir] 'Arafat may start within a brief period of several months, with the view of finalizing an agreement. Extending the *hudna* for a period of years may very well be one of the central provisions of such an agreement.

We believe that if 'Arafat follows the example set by Salah al-Din and agrees to some sort of *hudna* (or formally declares his agreement to the eminent mediator, President Mubarak), it would be possible to proceed to the next stage, a "delegation of dignitaries representing Israel". Such a delegation, consisting of men alone, would appear before the Palestinian parliament and request a *hudna.* We are of the opinion that the high point of the ceremony should be the attendance of the Israeli Prime Minister, speaking from the heart and into the hearts, in a spirit compatible with the Arab honor issue. President Mubarak and other Arab leaders (such as King 'Abdullah) would play a pivotal role in convincing most Palestinian organizations to agree to such an armistice. If 'Arafat and his parliament agree to declare *hudna,* a cease-fire will become effective immediately and all violence will cease.

Incidentally, Shaykh Yassin himself spoke several times in favor of a *hudna* with the Jews and Israel, although his terms were unacceptable. The most important aspect of these statements was the recognition that *hudna* with Israel is possible. We think that the suggested move may work. In any case, such a course of action will show the Arab world that you understand its mentality and respect its customs. You are willing to talk and would like to achieve peace and put an end to the bloodshed. We see no harm coming from the suggested course of action.

We are convinced that you will give this suggestion all due consideration. We are at your disposal at any time, so as to help promote a cessation of violence and bloodshed. An exploratory visit where we can meet with Dr. Osama al-Baz, President Mubarak's senior advisor, should be considered (before sending your representative or meeting yourself with President Mubarak).

Sincerely,

'Abd al Wahab Darawshe, Prof. Joseph Ginat, Eyal Erlich

Notes

1 Personal communications from the Geologist, Jacob Kolton. He worked in Thailand and was invited to the dinner of a local family. Not knowing the culture he hugged the seven year old child of the host and patted the back of the child's head; the parents screamed and cried saying he killed their child and that it was irreversible.

2 Emanuel Marx presented the term 'Co-Liable Group' in his referring to the five-generation collective responsibility unit known in Bedouin culture as *Khams*. See Emanuel Marx, *Bedouin of the Negev* (Manchester: Manchester University Press, 1967).

3 See Joseph Ginat, *Blood Revenge: Family Honor, Mediation, and Outcasting* (Brighton & Portland: Sussex Academic Press, 1997).

4 Personal communications from Meir Amit. Before heading the Israeli Mossad he headed the Intelligence of the Israeli Defense Force. Also see Meir Amir, *Head to Head: A Personal View of Great Events and Secret Affairs* (Tel Aviv: Or Yehuda, Hed Arzi Publishing House, 1999) [in Hebrew].

5 Personal communication from Muhammad El-Aasam, a famous Bedouin Judge and Mediator.

6 When President Sadat came to Israel it was kept as a secret almost to the last moment even from the Chief of Staff and the Head of Intelligence. However, when the secret became known to the Chief of Staff, Gen. Mordachai Gur, he immediately reacted to PM Menachem Begin, claiming the coming of Sadat to Israel was a trap. Joseph Ginat interviewed Gen. Gur about his statement and he admitted that he did not know why he had that spontaneous reaction. He was suspicious of Sadat's intentions, so Gen. Gur's first instinct was 'trap.' Gen. Gur has since voiced his regret for his reaction, and stated that it was a mistake.

7 In the last two years of Moshe Dayan's life, Ginat had the privilege of serving as his personal advisor on Arab affairs. This took place after Dayan had resigned from Begin's cabinet as FM. He then spent much of his time talking to Palestinian and Arab leaders. Ginat had the privilege to participate in and arrange some of those meetings. Ginat asked Dayan for details about his proposal and about Golda Meir's reaction: he said that she was very impatient and rude and even told him he should perhaps be committed to a hospital (mental institution).

8 Personal communication from Egyptian Gen. Kamal Hassan Ali and Minister Ezer Weizman, the then Israeli Minister of Defense and Camp David partici-pant. In the years 1985–1988 Joseph Ginat served as advisor to PM Shimon Peres on Arab Affairs as well as to Minister Ezer Weizman, who served as a Minister without a portfolio on Arab Affairs on the Israeli Cabinet (later, Weizman became President of Israel).

9 Shlomo Ben-Ami, *A Front Without A Rearguard: A Voyage to the Boundaries of the Peace Process* (Tel Aviv: Miskal-Yedioth Ahronoth Books and Chemed Books, 2004), p. 223 [in Hebrew].

10   Ibid., p. 224.

11   Ibid., pp. 253, 255.

12   Gilead Sher, *Just Beyond Reach: The Israeli–Palestinian Peace Negotiations 1999–2000* (Tel Aviv: Miskal-Yedioth Ahronoth Books and Chemed books, 2001), pp. 253–5 [in Hebrew].

13   Ibid., p. 163.

14   *The Jordanian–Israeli Peace Treaty 1994, Article 9B.*

15   Ben-Ami, *A Front Without A Rearguard*, p. 219.

16   Yitzhak Reiter, *From Jerusalem to Mecca and Back: The Islamic Consolidation of Jerusalem* (Jerusalem: The Jerusalem Institute for Israel Studies, 2005), p. 35. Both the first and second temples could have only existed on the northern part of the Temple Mount/Al Haram Al-Sharif, as the southern part was only developed in 20 BCE by Herod the Great and it is in this section of the Temple Mount/Al Haram Al-Sharif where El-Aqsa is situated. One of the possibilities is that both temples' ruins are under the Dome of the Rock. The British archeologist Kathleen Kenyon, who excavated south of the Temple Mount/Al Haram Al-Sharif wall, wrote "The site of the Temple is not in doubt . . . the retaining walls of the platform of Herod's Temple are still visible today, now crowned by that supreme example of Moslem architecture, the Dome of the Rock." See Kathleen Mary Kenyon, *Jerusalem Excavating 3000 Years of History* (Thames and Hudson, 1967), p. 158.

17   Adbul Hadi Palazzi, *"The Jewish–Moslem Dialogue and the Question of Jerusalem"* (Jerusalem: Institute of the World Jewish Congress, Policy Study No. 7), 1997, pp. 8–11.

18   Reiter, *From Jerusalem to Mecca and Back*, pp 36–37.

19   Ibid., p. 35.

20   Ben-Ami, *A Front Without a Rearguard*, p. 220.

21   Ibid., p. 184.

22   Ibid., pp. 281 and 286.

23   Sher, *Just Beyond Reach*, p. 247.

24   Joseph Ginat, "Temple Mount-al-Haram al-Sharif: A Proposal for Solution" in *The Middle East Peace Process: Vision Versus Reality*, Joseph Ginat, Edward J. Perkins, and Edwin G. Corr (eds.) (Norman: University of Oklahoma Press, 2002; Brighton: Sussex Academic Press), pp. 371–82.

25   Ibid., p. 372.

26   Ibid., p. 373.

27   In the talks between the Egyptians and the Israelis following the late President Sadat's visit to Israel (November 24, 1977) Israeli PM Menachem Begin was willing to agree to self-rule for each denomination regarding the holy places in Jerusalem. He also suggested that countries which do not border Israel – such as Saudi Arabia, Morocco, and Iran – could participate in the management of the holy places. See Menachem Klein, "Temple Mount: A Challenge, Threatening, and Promising on the Path to an Agreement," in Yitzak Reiter (ed.), Sovereignty of God and Men: Sanctity and Political Centrality on the Temple Mount (Jerusalem: The Jerusalem Institute for Israel Studies, 2001), p. 273 [in Hebrew].

28   Quoted from Menachem Klein, *Jerusalem: The Contested City* (London: Hurst & Company, 2001), p. 163. Adnan Abu-Odeh – who was a minister in

the Jordanian government and was very close to the late King Hussein – introduced in 1992 the idea of separating political sovereignty and religious sovereignty. See Adnan Abu-Odeh, "Two Capitals in an Undivided Jerusalem," *Foreign Affairs*, 17 (1992), pp. 183–88. After the failure of Camp David, Shlomo Ben-Ami suggested functional sovereignty that would be handed to an alliance of the three kings: King of Jordan, King of Morocco, and King of Saudi Arabia. In a meeting with the US Ambassador to Israel, Martin Indyk, Ben-Ami brought up the idea of the sovereignty being handed to the three kings so that it would not happen and that the Palestinians wouldn't have the sovereignty either. The idea being the solution would be sovereignty for God, Ben-Ami, ibid., pp. 243–45.

29 Sher, *Just Beyond Reach*, p. 131.
30 See, Charles Tripp, *A History of Iraq* (Cambridge University Press, second edition, 2002), pp. 265–66. This book references the use of the tribal entities by Saddam Husain. He allowed various tribes to have judicial rights and other self-determination. Chapter deals with the resilience of Saddam Husain's regime, page 37 mentions the regime's policy concerning Tribal Civil and Criminal Disputes. See also, Amatzia Baram. "The Missing Link: "Badu" and "Tribal" Honor as Components in the Iraqi Decision to Invade Kuwait" in Joseph Ginat and Anatoly M. Khazanov (eds.), *Changing Nomads in a Changing World* (Brighton: Sussex Academic Press, 1998), pp. 155–70. See also some clues in Amatzia Baram, *Between Impediment and Advantage Saddam's Iraq* (Washington, D.C.: U.S. Institute of Peace, 1998); and Amatzia Baram, *Culture, History, and Ideology in the Formation of Ba'thist Iraq, 1968–89* (New York: St. Martin's Press, 1991).
31 See, Joseph Ginat, *Blood Revenge*.
32 Ibid., p. 25.
33 Ibid., p. 26.
34 Ibid., p. 26.
35 Appendix B is a letter written by Ginat to US President Bush after he discussed the issue with Dr. David Altman, who recommended that Ginat write the letter. It should be noted that this was in fact the second letter written to President Bush; the first letter was sent on May 10, 2001 explaining the phenomenon of suicide bombing. In the first letter Ginat wrote also, "I will not be surprised if in the near future Bin Laden will attack targets inside the United States and not only American targets outside the United States." The first letter was delivered via diplomatic pouch whereas the second letter was delivered by a mutual friend. Both letters were never acknowledged.
36 The discussion of the issue was with Sheikh Áqel. It is interesting to note that one of the leaders of the PLO is Salah El-Ta'amra, who is a member of the El-Ta'amra Tribe. He is married to Princess Dina, who was King Hussein's first wife. Salah, in 1982, was one of the commanders of the PLO in Lebanon, and fell into the captivity of the Israelis in the encounters in Lebanon (1982). Amalia and Aharon Barnea, she a print journalist and he a television correspondent who is a specialist on the Middle East, became friends with Dina; when Salah was in captivity they arranged with the Minister of Defense, at that time, Ariel Sharon, to bring Salah from the camp of captivities to a hotel in Tel Aviv together with Dina for several days. Salah was also, in 2003–2004, a

member of the PA Cabinet. See Amalia (Argaman) and Aaron Barnea, *Gone into Captivity* (Tel Aviv : Edanim Publishing Ltd., 1986) [in Hebrew].

37   Ben-Ami, *A Front Without a Rearguard*, pp. 568–69.

38   In the time of the Second Temple (516 BCE–70 CE) there was a Jewish Priest who fell in love with a Samaritan woman, married her, and he became a Samaritan. The Samaritans do not marry outside their ethnicity, but Jews will accept their religion. This Priest was the one who built the Samaritan Temple on Mount Gerizm.

39   Discussion of the *hudna* is based on a paper that was published: Joseph Ginat, "*Hudna*: Origins of the Concept and its Relevance to the Arab–Israeli Conflict" in Arab–*Jewish Relations: From Conflict to Resolution? Essays in Honour of Professor Moshe Ma'oz* (Brighton & Portland: Sussex Academic Press, 2005), p. 252.

40   Ginat, *Blood Revenge*, p. 253.

CHAPTER 3

The Israeli–Palestinian Wonder: Losing Trust in Official Negotiations while Maintaining it on "Hard" Track II Talks

MENACHEM KLEIN

Trust is an illusive concept. Its aspects are as many as the sides involved in building and maintaining it. This subjective concept can be measured and quantified, yet it will remain mostly a mental–psychological attitude determined by the eyes of the beholder as he perceives the "other." In addition, trust in the Israeli–Palestinian peace process is a generic title under which one can find a mix of wishful thinking, vision, hope, a keen wish to give peace a chance, and a will to test the other sides' intentions. Finally, trust changes as the circumstances change. Trust between a couple that just married is different from trust of a divorcing couple. In both cases trust is needed, although in different forms. Therefore, there is a need to make a clear distinction between changing circumstances and engaging in the wrong type of trust. The Israeli–Palestinian interaction from the 1993 Oslo agreement until the election of the Hamas Government in 2006 leaves the impression that the sides were engaged in a partnership-building project rather than in a divorce and disengagement process. This can partly answer the question that is the subject of this chapter: Why was trust destroyed in the official talks in Track I and in people-to-people meetings, while it was maintained in "hard" Track II negotiations?

Losing Trust

Three following inter-related reasons sharply reduced Israeli trust in peaceful coexistence with the Palestinians to almost zero. First and foremost, it was due to waves of Palestinian terrorist attacks that turned main Israeli cities into a frontier and took the lives of more then 1,000 people.[1] These attacks caused traumatic and post-traumatic effects on the Israeli mind. The Israeli people concluded that the Palestinians are not their partners in a peace process but rather a hostile nation, if not an ill society that highly values suicide bombers. Palestinian suicide attacks began in 1994, but until 2000 the Israeli people hoped they could be stopped by a political agreement. Then came the second reason for the Israeli's loss of trust – the collapse of the final status talks in 2000. The psychological effect of Palestinian terror, together with the end of the political process, shattered the Israeli hope of having a better future. Finally, the Israeli mind was shaped by the spin and propaganda campaign on Barak's "generous offer" at Camp David that Arafat answered with a pre-planned *intifada*. It provided the Israelis with "arguments" and a mythological narrative in which the Israelis are colored in white and the Palestinians in black. The Israelis' perception of Arafat changed from an ill old man who moved from armed struggle to compromise to a demon – to that of a master of terror. The Israeli mind re-created the old perception of the Palestinian leader and Palestinian society.[2]

It is worth noting that this is not the most pessimistic analysis of the changing Israeli mind. Baruch Kimmerling goes much further when he includes the Israeli occupation and colonization in the process mentioned above:

> The fact of occupation and rule over a territory and its population was absorbed into the Israeli consciousness and became part of its identity. Today most Israelis have grown up under the present reality or immigrated into it (more than 1 million from the former Soviet lands, Ethiopia and even from the United States) and cannot imagine life within the narrow pre-1967 war borders. Moreover, "peace" is an abstract and incomprehensible notion, while land is a tangible asset. If Israeli casualties caused by wars and Palestinian terror, or resistance movements (depending on one's values), were regarded in the past as a painful national calamity, they were slowly routinized and perceived as an inevitable cost of Israel's existence. In the past, governments that failed to prevent war or protect the personal safety of their citizens were voted out. Today, casualties only empower governments – a situation that reflects a high level of national cohesion on this issue. It's true, as pointed out above, that many Israelis say they are prepared to give back land for peace, but their words remain untested.[3]

On the other side, in the Palestinian territories, a mirror image emerged. During the Oslo years, Israel expanded its settlements and built more roads for the exclusive use of settlers and the Israeli army, forcing native Palestinians to use by-pass roads and make their trips longer. To the collapse of final status talks the disappointment from Israel's offers during the Oslo talks and its operations in the occupied territories, one must add the popular criticism on the poor performance of the Palestinian Authority. Led exclusively by Fatah the Palestinian Authority failed to achieve its political goals of liberating 1967 territories, founding a Palestinian state with Arab Jerusalem as its capital, and assuring the return of at least some of 1948 refugees. These together with the corruption of some of the Palestinian Authority senior officials caused Fatah's electoral defeat in 2006.[4]

Furthermore, Israel's anti-terror measures since the outbreak of the second *Intifada* include methods of heavy collective punishment, the exercise of massive force during waves of army raids, and short-term re-occupation of cities and populated zones. According to the Palestinian Centre for Human Rights from the outbreak of the second *Intifada* up to mid-December 2006, 4,059 Palestinians civilians were killed, 24,000 were wounded by Israeli Forces, and 49,979 houses were totally or partly demolished. According to B'eTselem, the Israeli Information Center for Human Rights in the Occupied Territories, at the end of 2006 Israel kept in detention about 10,000 Palestinians. The United Nations Office for the Coordination of Humanitarian Affairs found that in late September 2006 the West Bank system had 528 checkpoints and barriers established by Israeli forces to prevent fully or partly Palestinian free traffic and movement. Additionally, the anti-Israeli campaign in the Palestinian media and mosques further reduces the Palestinian trust in peaceful co-existence with Israel and renews negative perceptions.

Public opinion polls by the Truman Institute at the Hebrew University and the Palestinian Center for Policy and Survey Research in Ramallah showed in December 2001 that there was consistent and overwhelming support for reconciliation but a split in confidence regarding its feasibility.[5] Almost three-quarters (73%) of the Palestinians and 76% of the Israelis supported reconciliation between the two peoples under conditions of peace and the existence of a Palestinian state, but only 46% of the Palestinians believed that reconciliation was possible compared to 65% of the Israelis. Forty-one percent of the Palestinians and 31% of the Israelis believed that it "is not possible ever." Similarly, a majority of Palestinians (69%) did *not* believe that lasting peace was possible between Israelis and Palestinians compared to a majority of Israelis (52%) who thought that lasting peace was possible.

Results also showed that the overwhelming Palestinian support for reconciliation was based on cold calculations of interests and needs rather than friendship, forgiveness, or tolerance. Thus, an overwhelming majority of the Palestinians (85%) supported open borders to free movement of people and goods in the context of a peace agreement. Similarly, two-thirds of the Palestinians supported the creation of joint economic institutions and ventures. However, even in the context of a peace agreement, a majority of Palestinians opposed other forms of cooperation, stopping incitement against the other side, and teaching in schools against irredentist aspirations. Israelis, on the other hand, were less supportive of open borders (49%), were supportive of joint economic ventures (65%), but much more supportive of a ban on incitement (60%) and the teaching against irredentist aspirations (46%).

In November 2002 there was a surprisingly small impact of the two-year-long *intifada* on Palestinian and Israeli sentiments towards reconciliation in a state of peace and the establishment of a Palestinian state. Under such conditions, 73% of the Palestinians and 75% of the Israelis would have supported a process of reconciliation, despite the ongoing hostilities. While Palestinians would have mainly supported open borders and economic cooperation, Israelis more so than Palestinians, favored changes in the school curriculum and cessation of incitement in public discourse and social interaction.

In December 2003, 29% of the Israeli public supported immediate resumption of the negotiations with the Palestinians. An additional 29% supported it if the Palestinian government made a serious effort to stop violence. Forty-two percent of the Israeli public believed and 52% did not believe that there are serious partners for peace talks among the Palestinian leadership. In June 2004 support for mutual cessation of violence remained very high (90% among Israelis and 79% among Palestinians). If such cessation were obtained, 55% of the Palestinians would support taking measures by the Palestinian Authority to prevent further armed attacks on Israeli targets. Support for long-range reconciliation between the two peoples also remained very high (73% of Palestinians and 80% of Israelis) even though 42% of the Palestinians and 28% of the Israelis believed such reconciliation is not possible ever. In June 2005, 53% of the Israeli public supported Ariel Sharon's disengagement plan. Among Palestinians, 72% viewed Sharon's plan to evacuate settlements in Gaza as a victory for Palestinian armed struggle (45% among Israelis). Sixty-two percent of the Israeli public supported dismantling most of the settlements as part of a peace agreement with the Palestinians.

Interestingly, December 2006 polls show strong preference in both publics for the comprehensive settlement option with 58% of the Israelis and 81% of the Palestinians supporting this track compared to only 30% of the Israelis and 16% of the Palestinians supporting an interim track. When asked on the parameters of a comprehensive settlement along the lines of President Clinton's proposal and the Geneva Initiative, 52% of the Israelis and 48% of the Palestinians supported the package. A majority of 58% among Palestinians and 63% of the Israelis agree with the proposal that after reaching a permanent agreement to all issues of the conflict, there would be mutual recognition of Israel as the state for the Jewish people and Palestine as the state for the Palestinian people. 52% of the Palestinians and 55% of the Israelis believe that a majority of their public supports such a proposal. However, both publics are only partly aware of the majority support for such a step on the other side. Only 44% of the Palestinians and 42% of the Israelis think the other side public supports this step.[8]

Therefore, when international mediators considered how to rebuild trust and by what means can they help put the peace process back on track, their offers included the following components: a stable cease-fire, stopping all forms of terrorist attacks and Israeli army operations against non-combat civilians, implementing an Israeli withdrawal from posts and areas its army occupied since the eruption of the second *Intifada*, freezing settlement expansion, and dissolving illegal outposts. These were the main principles of the 2000–2001 reports made by CIA head George Tenet, Senator George Mitchell, the vision of President George W. Bush, and the Quartet Road Map of 2002. These American presidential representatives hoped to manage the conflict through interim plans rather than to solve it as President Clinton tried in 2000 and failed. Their joint wrong assumption was that both the Palestinians and Israelis are ready for an interim plan only. Therefore, Tenet and Mitchell ignored the permanent status, whereas Bush and the Quartet Road Map left it very vague. But the Oslo stage process had shown that this strategy is doomed to fail. The Oslo agreements were not implemented successfully; they intensified the sides' competition and their race to collect negotiation chips before the final status talks opened instead of increasing compromise and building trust.

The Israeli mainstream concluded that in the absence of a partner, unilateral withdrawal from parts of the occupied territories must take place. Unilateralism in the Israeli strategy had two goals. First, in the short run, it aimed to protect Israel from Palestinian terror by building around the Gaza Strip and inside the West Bank security walls and barriers. Second, in the longer run it aimed to keep Israel from becoming a bi-national state by excluding most of the Palestinian population from its immediate control. Therefore in summer 2005 Israel pulled out its civilian and military personnel from the Gaza Strip.

In March 2006, Ehud Olmert, leader of the Kadima party (established by Ariel Sharon) was elected Israel's Prime Minister based upon his plan to continue unilateral withdrawal from more parts of the occupied West Bank. But shortly it became clear that the unilateral experiment failed to bring more security to Israel. The Hamas government refused to recognize Israel and different Palestinian armed groups fired Qassam rocket on Israeli cities. The Israeli war against Hezbollah in Lebanon in summer 2006 – during which Hizballah launched rockets on all Israeli north and north center areas – forcing one-third of the population to seek safety in safe rooms or shelters – showed the failure of the Israeli unilateral withdrawal from South Lebanon in 2000. Thus, in late 2006 Israel remained with no political strategy. It neither enjoyed stability nor was it successfully managing its conflict with the Palestinians.

Developing Trust in Track II

Interestingly, although Oslo trust was destroyed on official and popular levels, it survived in many "hard" Track II meetings that continued while the conflict escalated. The distinction between "hard" and "soft" Track II was introduced by Hussein Agha, Shai Feldman, Ahmad Khalidi and Zeev Schiff.[9] "Soft" Track II is aimed at an exchange of views, perceptions and information between the sides involved to improve their mutual understanding. "Hard" Track II, on the other hand, is more politically oriented. It is not only about achieving better knowledge of the other side but also about helping negotiate, and, if possible, even achieving breakthroughs that will help reach a political settlement between the sides.

Surprisingly, the atmosphere in those meetings was totally different than in the popular and official interactions. Trust remained in force and helped the participants reach positive results. However Track II participants failed to transfer their achievements to the official level and influence directly their leaders. I will show this in the following cases.

In December 2000 a small group of Israelis and Palestinians met in Amsterdam under the auspices of the Dutch foreign minister in an attempt to contain the *intifada* and find a compromise to issues that the sides have debated since Camp David 2000. A few meetings in Jerusalem followed in which the participants drafted a joint statement for a cease-fire. They gave the document to their respective leaderships, but could not instill in the leaders the trust that had guided them.

A month later in January 2000, in another Track II event sponsored by the University of Oklahoma, the participants concluded a document on the principles of a final status agreement on Jerusalem.[10] The paper was submitted to the relevant leaders and, unlike most of Track II products, was also made public. The publication of the document somehow affected the Israeli public and consequently its leadership's mind, as was seen in the Israeli proposals in Camp David 2000 to divide Jerusalem. (Several participants in that exercise are contributors to this book.)

In another Track II meeting led by the Israel Palestine Center of Research and Information, IPCRI, the participants agreed on a road map for Jerusalem; i.e., a plan to integrate east Jerusalem into the Quartet Road Map phases. A similar document on an economic road map was prepared by IPCRI. Once again the way from Track II to Track I was blocked.

The best and most impacting Track II event is the Geneva Agreement. In my view (and I do not pretend to remain objective on this), it is the model from which we can learn most in terms of creating mutual trust and joint interests.[11]

Herein lays the question: How did Track II participants succeed in maintaining trust and cooperation in a worsening context?

At the negotiation of the Geneva agreement, trusting each other did not eliminate deep disagreements, moments of anger, and complaints on re-opening discussions of issues that were unofficially concluded. Throughout the negotiation, each side had doubts about the other side's determination to reach an agreement and questioned the other side's motivations. The sides could not avoid the division into "us" and "them," but this division did not overpower the talks. A coalition was built over the bloody ethnic line that bridged the imbalance between the occupier and the oppressed. It is easier to build such a coalition as long as one side has come to a better understanding of the other side's concerns, fears, and interests.

Open communication also includes acknowledging the domestic debates within each delegation and the respective political problems in marketing the issue at stake. In an intensive negotiation it is almost impos-sible to hide domestic debates within each delegation. Therefore, instead of denying them or trying to exploit the other side's domestic division in order to further your original position, it is better to exchange information on difficulties and find a joint way to overcome them.

For that purpose the sides involved in negotiating the Geneva Agreement maintained open channels. In order to find pragmatic solutions to negotiation debates, the sides used a tactic that in South Africa was called "walking in the woods." A representative from each side who enjoyed his leader's full confidence met on a daily basis in order to find a practical solution to negotiation problems. In addition, similar dialogue was held among other delegation members. The purpose of these commu-nication channels was not to collect intelligence on the other side's positions in order to exploit weaknesses or impose a solution. Rather, the purpose was to study the issue at hand from both sides' perspectives in order to finalize a win–win agreement, instead of playing a zero-sum game. The Geneva Initiative succeeded to become the term of reference regarding the final status agreement (alongside President Clinton's parameters) because it was massively distributed and promoted inside the region and internationally. However, the Geneva Initiative did not enjoy the critical mass to force the relevant leaderships to endorse it and adopt it as their policy guideline.

Research on the Israeli–Palestinian final status talks lead me to conclude that the above-mentioned elements characterizing the Geneva Agreement talks have been missing from the Israeli–Palestinian official negotiation.[12] Israeli interests overpowered the Palestinian ones when Israel tabled its positions. The Palestinian needs and views were shaped along Israeli criteria, not as the Palestinians saw them. Thus the Israeli "red line" determined what the Palestinians would get or how much Israel was ready to give-up. A red-line strategy fuels disagreements and mistrust. It is based on a unilateral, ultimatum-style statement of the limits of one's concessions. The approach is a hierarchical one in which the relations are always between superior and inferior rather than an egalitarian approach in which each side embraces a win–win strategy.[13]

Conclusion

Any discussion on trust faces a dilemma: must trust exist before the sides can negotiate or is trust an outcome of a signed and implemented peace treaty and a result of peace building? Which comes first – trust or peace agreement? The Geneva Agreement and similar Track II activities show that some trust can be achieved prior to the conclusion of a peace agreement. After all, are not all peace treaties signed by bitter enemies that acquired the needed trust to conclude an agreement? Thus, the argument that the lack of trust prevents final status negotiations should be accepted as no more than an excuse not to negotiate. However, we should bear in mind that the type of trust needed to manage a successful negotiation is different from the trust that will emerge later when the peace is well based. The first is limited, characterizing the negotiators and their interaction with each other. The latter defines wider circles and defines mutual popular relationships of parties involved in peace building outside the negotiation room. The second type can come only if the first type exists. The way to achieve mutual trust between two enemies is through trustworthy negotiators, and trustful negotiation methods.

Notes

1   See the report on losses on the three-year anniversary of the al-Aqsa *Intifada, Journal of Palestine Studies,* Summer 2004, pp. 162–64.

2   Klein Menachem, "Arafat as a Palestinian Icon," *Palestine–Israel Journal,* Vol. 11 (2004/5), pp. 30–38.

3   In his review of *How Israel Lost,* by Richard Ben Cramer, Salon.com, July 19, 2004.

4   For further analysis see my article "By Conviction, Not by Infliction: The Debate over Reforming the Palestinian Authority," *Middle East Journal,* Vol. 57 No. 2 (April 2003), pp. 194–212; Nigel Parsons, *The Politics of the Palestinian Authority From Oslo to al-Aqsa* (New York and London: Routledge, 2005).

5   <http://www.pchrgaza.ps/intifada.htm>; see also the report of the Palestinian Human Rights monitoring report in <http://www.phrmg.org/initifiada%20statistics.htm>. See also *Journal of Palestine Studies,* ibid. On child casualties in the *Intifada* see Menachem Klein, "The *Intifada* – the Young Generation in the Front" in Charles W. Greenbaum, Philip Veerman and Naomi Bacon-Shnoor (eds.), *Protection of Children During Armed Political Conflict: A Multidisciplinary Perspective* (Antwerpen and Oxford: Intersentia, 2006), pp. 45–56.

6   <http://www.btselem.org/english/statistics/Index.asp>.

7   <http://www.ochaopt.org/documents/Closure_count_analysis_sept06.pdf>.

8   The following data are from <http://truman.huji.ac.il/>.

9   *Track II Diplomacy Lessons from the Middle East* (Cambridge, MA: MIT Press, 2003), p. 3.

10 The papers presented in this track can be found in Joseph Ginat, Edward J. Perkins, and Edwin Corr (eds.), *The Middle East Peace Process – Vision Versus Reality* (Brighton: Sussex Academic Press, 2002); another Track II paper by the same organizers was published in Joseph Ginat and Edward J. Perkins (eds.), *The Palestinian Refugees: Old Problems – New Solutions* (Brighton: Sussex Academic Press, 2000).

11 The Geneva Agreement is in <http://www.heskem.org.il/Files.asp>; on the agreement itself see my article "The Logic of the Geneva Accord," *Logos*, Vol. 3 [2004] No. 1 in <http://www.logosjournal.com/ issue_3.1.pdf>. My book on the Geneva Initiative is forthcoming by Columbia University Press.

12 Menachem Klein, *The Jerusalem Problem – The Struggle for Permanent Status* (Gainsesville: University of Florida Press, 2003); Jeremy Pressman, "Visions in Collision – What Happened at Camp David and Taba," *International Security*, Vol. 28, No. 2, Fall 2003, pp. 5–43; Shimon Shamir (ed.), *The Camp David Summit – What Went Wrong?* (Brighton & Portland: Sussex Academic Press, 2005).

13 On the "red lines" strategy, see my *The Jerusalem Problem*, pp. 164–79.

CHAPTER 4

Public Diplomacy in the Middle East: Big Mistake, Huge Prices

GADI BALTIANSKY

While formal negotiations usually take place behind closed doors, public diplomacy can be found everywhere by everyone. This kind of diplomacy is not only influenced and guided by the traditional one, but has often tremendous impact on the content of the negotiations. This two-way street has characterized the peace process in the Middle East in the last decades. Perceptions, public images and conventional misleading were part of the process and part of its failure. In this chapter I will mention a few examples of what has been done and, moreover, what should have been and still can be done.

First of all, both sides need to agree on a common goal, and to publicly announce that goal. The goal should be clear, realistic, and obtainable. Until now, the presented goal was wrong and misleading. Public statements from both sides, formal declarations and international official and public voices called for an impossible aim.

The most famous examples are UN Security Council Resolutions 242 and 338. The first described the goal as being "a just and lasting peace" while the second described it as "a just and durable peace." Clearly, both resolutions mention the word "just", and emphasize the need for a lasting solution of this nature.

This is a goal that can never be fulfilled, and anyone who calls for a "just peace" is in a sense acknowledging that peace cannot be obtained. One's justice will be the other's injustice. Any future agreement between Israelis and Palestinians will never fulfill the condition of being completely "just for all," and therefore what we witnessed over the years was an ongoing phenomenon that created illusions between the two peoples and the international community.

In the framework of any endgame status agreement, Jews will probably not be able to live in Hebron or Nablus, and will definitely not enjoy sovereignty over those cities and the areas around them. Many Israelis and Jews around the world will connote this as a great injustice. Judea and Samaria (known also as the West Bank) compose the region where the Jewish nation was created. Hebron is known as the "City of the Forefathers," and Nablus is mentioned many times in the Bible as an important place for the development of the Jewish people, its culture and legacy. Hence, it is impossible, in any form or fashion, to label the negation of the right of Israeli Jews to live in Hebron as a just solution.

Similarly, the endgame status agreement will not allow a mass return of Palestinians exiled after the 1948 War. Some of the villages and townships where they resided no longer exist, and other parts that remain have been settled by Jewish Israelis. No Israeli government will recognize the so-called "right of return" and its subsequent implementation in the form of massive immigration of Palestinians to the State of Israel. Those Palestinians who are attached personally and nationally to places where they and their ancestors were born will not interpret an agreement that denies their "right to return" as constituting a "just peace."

The ongoing talk about a "just peace" as the ultimate goal is not only misleading, but potentially very harmful. It is obvious that when both sides are close to reaching an agreement (as in Camp David or in Taba), both peoples will look for the "just peace" that has repeatedly been promised to them. They will not find it, and therefore they will make it more difficult for leaders to reach an agreement, and subsequently may oppose such an agreement once it has been reached.

This is why the peace treaty goal that I propose should be an "obtainable peace" and a "practical solution." The historical narratives should stay in the books of historians and the endgame status agreement should be based on today's reality, with eyes set to the future. Anyone who seeks unachievable goals will undoubtedly fail, and hence, negotiations should channel efforts and energy to finding practical solutions and compromises to the differences between Israelis and Palestinians.

Another goal that should be publicly clarified is the explanation of which conflict is to be solved. Many Israelis are nourished by the popular narrative that in 1967 a war was thrust upon Israel. As a result, territories that were occupied by Palestinians were added to the State of Israel. For Israelis, this is why the 1967 conflict should be solved by a territorial compromise. In contrast, most Palestinians believe that the conflict that needs resolution is that of 1948, as it was this war that resulted in the "*Nakba*" (the Palestinian Disaster) – the establishment of the Israeli state and the subsequent displacement of the Palestinian people. Though the public debate in Israel revolves around a discussion of the territories, the Palestinians reach for a solution that deals with a much broader problem. I offer the following: Instead of attempting to rectify problems of 1948 or 1967, the conflict at hand is that of 2006. As such, it is important to face the current reality and not the old narratives. The publics of both sides should also know the real interests and concrete "red lines" of each side. Past negotiations, from the Peace Talks with Egypt (1977–1979), through the talks at Wye Plantation (1998), and until the preparation of Prime Minster Ariel Sharon's Unilateral Disengagement Plan (2003), have all demarcated false "red lines", and as a result have damaged the public's faith and trust in its leaders. In the early 1970s Moshe Dayan, former Israeli Defense and Foreign Minister, said that it is better to have Sharm el-Sheikh without peace rather than have peace without Sharm el-Sheikh. Prime Minister Begin publicly emphasized the importance of having the oil resources, airports, and settlements in the Sinai. Eventually, the decision to return every last grain of sand of the Sinai Peninsula to Egyptian hands made it difficult for the Israeli public to comprehend what was and was not truly important.

Similar phenomena were witnessed when Prime Minister Binyamin Netanyahu argued that every additional percent beyond 9% withdrawal from the Judea and Samaria territories is equivalent to a withdrawal from Tel Aviv. Additionally, his then Foreign Minister Sharon declared that every withdrawal beyond 9% poses a real threat to the security of Israel. The two of them went on to sign the Wye Memorandum (1998) in which Israel committed itself to withdraw from 13% of the West Bank. A more recent example is the 2003 declaration of Prime Minister Sharon that the fate of *one* Gaza strip settlement, Netzarim, is the same as the fate of Tel Aviv. Similarly, Sharon argued that Israel should never evacuate the Kfar Darom Settlement because of its vital strategic value. Despite these strong declarations, Sharon offered a disengagement plan several months later that included Netzarim, Kfar Darom and all the settlements in the Gaza Strip.

The Palestinian side also needs to decide on its true and indelible "red lines," especially in matters concerning the refugee problem. If the fulfillment of the "right of return" is considered a red line, the Palestinian side will have to acknowledge that an agreement will never be reached if they publicly claim as much, since no Israeli leader will be able to accept such a claim. But if, as I believe, the Palestinian leadership understands that the practical solution to the refugee problem cannot involve mass return to Israel, they should publicly say as much. They will thus prevent false aspirations of their people, which will only serve to bring about an agreement in the future.

False red lines create false public myths that are very hard to deal with when reality must overcome empty slogans. The real interests of both sides call actually for the opposite: To identify the vital red lines, which if crossed would only result in discord. By doing so, everything else should be left to negotiations. In this case, both Israeli and Palestinian public opinions will be much more receptive to the end result.

Another mistake that has repeated itself over the years is the stressing of the dividends of peace rather than reiterating the price of peace. I recall how in the early stages of negotiations with Syria we promised the Israelis that they would be able to eat *hummus* in the markets of Damascus, and that they would be able to travel to Europe by car via Lebanon and Syria. In Oslo we told the Israeli public that we would have peace, quiet, and security.

On the Syrian issues, we did not speak enough about yielding Mount Hermon to Syrian sovereignty, and about the Syrian demands for a strip along the northeastern shore of the Lake of Galilee. On the Palestinian issues, we were cautious to speak about dividing Jerusalem or on the scope of the expected withdrawal. The Syrians spoke mainly about the territorial dimension, and tried to not elaborate at all on the upcoming signs of normalization. The Palestinians expected after Oslo an immediate economic renaissance ("Gaza will become Singapore") and a gradual dismantling of settlements. Needless to say, all sides witnessed exactly the opposite of the expected.

The "lets emphasize the fruits of peace" policy is, of course, logical in three respects:

1   Human nature instinctively tells us that if we want to "sell" a product (whatever it may be), we should immediately emphasize the pros and limit the discussion on the cons. Obviously, one would want to seed optimism and talk about the fruits of peace rather than spell out the prices and cost.
2   The opposing side limits the discussion on the negative aspects, so why should we be the first to do otherwise? We suspect that if we talk about the price, without the other side also doing so, we will end up with the bad end of the bargain.
3   Neither of the sides can be sure about the eventual real costs of a peace agreement, and each side is therefore careful about elaborating specifically on what the costs will be.

Despite the above three points, I think the preferable way to handle the situation is by simultaneously describing the bonuses of reaching an agreement, and presenting the prices and sacrifices each side will be forced to make in the most realistic and detailed way. At the end of the day, a message of this type would be realistic, practical, and effective, and could prevent future crises. One of the greatest risks involved in reaching peace agreements is the negative reaction to those who have approved the agreement. The most effective way to avoid, or at least to reduce, this risk is to share the possible prices and potential concessions.

An illustration of this can be seen in the Camp David talks of July 2000 when Israeli Prime Minister Barak for the first time spoke of a withdrawal that would be larger than 90% of the West Bank. The Israeli public initially found it very difficult to digest, but slowly began to accommodate to these new developments. By December 2003, when the Geneva Accord was published, 47% of the Israeli public supported the territorial solution in the Accord, which specified a complete withdrawal from the West Bank and Gaza "with the exception of some settlement areas in less than 3% of the West Bank that would be swapped with an equal amount of territory from Israel." A year later, support for the same solution, as described in the same question, increased to 55% of the Israelis. Both polls were conducted jointly by the Palestinian Center for Policy and Survey Research and the Harry S. Truman Research Institute for the Advancement of Peace at the Hebrew University of Jerusalem, and were published in the Israeli daily *Ha'aretz*.

A similar phenomenon occurred with Israeli discussion about the Jerusalem issue, and the slow transition from the myth of "United Jerusalem Forever" to the acknowledgment that Israeli interests will require them to cede some Arab neighborhoods inside Jerusalem to the Palestinians. This discussion was considered taboo due to three decades of being told by their leaders that the city shall never be divided. However, once Prime Minister Barak stated that it would be in Israeli interests to allow the more than 200,000 Palestinians living in East Jerusalem and the area in which they reside to become a part of Palestine rather than a part of Israel, that would add to the Arab-Israeli population, Israelis accomodated to the idea. This will undoubtedly be part of any future agreement.

A similar phenomenon happened with the Palestinian public regarding the refugee problem. For many years Palestinians heard only the slogans about the right of return, until they were exposed to painful but necessary compromises on the issue in the context of the Ayalon–Nusseibeh agreement and the Geneva Accord. Then, and only then, a real debate within Palestinian society began regarding the refugees and a possible solution to this problem. The above-mentioned poll found that in December 2003 only 25% of the Palestinians supported the Geneva Initiative solution for the refugee problem. Only a year (and many open discussions) later in December 2004, support had increased to 46%. Once again, one can witness an agreement unfold, as a transition from empty slogans to a practical understanding of the compromises takes place. Additionally, this materializes only after a detailed account is given to the public regarding the price each side would be forced to pay.

To conclude, I will mention two more points which leaders need to emphasize in the public debate:

1   A transition from a zero-sum game to a win–win situation. It is not coincidental that both Hebrew and Arabic have translations for the term "zero-sum game," and lack translation for the term "win–win situation." We in the region are used to a life with battles and wars that

necessarily create a winner and a loser. It is the obligation of leaders on both sides to tell their publics that winning is possible only if the other side feels they have won too.

2   A transition from a gradual process to an endgame. Without spelling out and clarifying the endgame, neither of the sides will have incentives to act in the first stages – this was both Oslo's and the Roadmap's mistakes. Both sides argue, and rightly so, that it is hard to convince the public to agree on certain concessions if the end result is not clear. In order to bridge between two peaks the solution does not necessarily lie in many small strides. Rather, what are needed to bridge between the two peaks (or sides) are large and courageous steps. By avoiding a gradual and long process, one can avoid also the negative influence of extremists who are eager to sabotage any future agreement.

The Geneva Initiative model, which simulates all these lessons, proposes a practical and doable solution to all problems without entering to historical narratives. The suggested model clearly details the price each side has to pay, and emphasizes the endgame, the end of the conflict, and the end to all claims. In contrast to conventional wisdom, according to which leaders need to prepare the Israeli and Palestinian publics for an agreement, it appears to me that both publics are now in need of preparing their leaderships. The same poll conducted jointly by the Palestinian Center for Policy and Survey Research and the Harry S. Truman Research Institute for the Advancement of Peace at the Hebrew University of Jerusalem, indicates that support for the general content of the Geneva Accord is 54% on the Palestinian side, and 64% on the Israeli side (December 2004).

The patient who is wounded and bleeding understands that he needs to undergo an operation to save himself, even if it may be a painful one. Strangely enough, the doctors (our leaders) are hesitant if not afraid to perform this operation. A loud and clear voice should be heard first and foremost from Palestinian and Israeli civil societies, but also from the international community, calling for both sides to reach a permanent status agreement that will put and end to the conflict. If we all act in the required fashion, we will not have to discuss the question of "What Went Wrong?" but rather can talk about "What Did We Do Right?"

CHAPTER 5

Listening as a Value: A Narrative Approach to Building Trust

MAYA MELZER-GEVA

A Moslem woman from Nazareth recounts the following story:

> When I first began my studies at the Hebrew University in Jerusalem, in the course I was taking, psychology, I was the only Arab among seventy Jewish women and a few men. I started wearing this pendant of an olive tree, which for me was a symbol of being connected to my land and my identity, and to Palestine and all the other things I'm connected to. That's how I went to the university, wearing this pendant every day. Then one Thursday evening I was returning to Nazareth by bus, as I always did. As usual, there were many female soldiers standing in the central bus station, and they were checking IDs and so on. One of the soldiers saw the pendant, pointed at it, and asked, "Aha? Do you have a boyfriend in *Golani*?" (an Israeli army brigade whose emblem is an oak tree). I got home and decided to take it off. Some time later I found another pendant and started wearing it – this one, which says *Allah* in Arabic. It's not that I'm all that religious or even traditional; in fact I'm quite secular, but still, I was pretty much alone there in Jerusalem, so I continued wearing it.
>
> A few years ago I went to the U.S. on my own for a few weeks, and I visited all sorts of places, including New York. When I went into Sbarro's in the middle of Manhattan, the guy serving me noticed the *Allah* pendant, and asked, "What is that?" "It is a sign of my god," I told him. He asked, *"Anti arabiya?"* ("Are you Arab?") And I replied, *"Anta?"* ("And you?") He said, "I'm from Morocco." When I said, *"Ana falestiniyya"* ("I'm Palestinian"), he started piling food onto my tray. I sat down and ate alone, and when I left the restaurant I stood in the middle of the street in Manhattan and started crying. That's it . . .

This story was told during a narrative discourse workshop that brings together Arabs and Jews from neighboring communities in the Galilee, and in which they take part in a constructivist process that evolves with them.

The workshop was developed and is implemented by MA'ARAG, the Association for the Advancement of Education in a Multicultural Society. The data gathered is the product of workshop observations, participation in meetings with workshop facilitators, interviews with them, and participant feedback employing open-ended questions. A Moslem–Arab evaluator and I evaluated the pilot workshop to enhance our understanding and apply cultural knowledge toward improving it.

The primary objective of the narrative workshop is to rebuild trust through gaining insights into the complexity of the Arab–Jewish conflict and finding effective methods for dealing with it. A listening dialogue is the means employed to achieve this objective, through learning to understand other worldviews, identities and ways of life, and developing awareness of inter-subjective learning.

The workshop consists of 8–10 meetings, each lasting approximately four hours, with a maximum of 14 participants. The meetings are led by two facilitators, one Jewish and one Arab, and are conducted in Hebrew. The meetings are held according to a preplanned program. In the first meeting each of the participants relates a personal story that has shaped his or her attitude towards the "other." The facilitators create a setting of listening, and the participants do not react during the telling of the stories. A box with cards and pencils is placed in the center of the circle to facilitate an immediate channel for reactions without interrupting the narrator. The stories are told in succession, with a brief break after each one. They are recorded and transcribed in time for the next meeting. Once all the participants have told their stories, they express their opinions on and feelings toward them, and discuss the experience of listening.

At the next meeting, each participant receives the text of his or her story, and a moderated intrapersonal process takes place. The participants experience the rereading of their own narrative, while clarifying their own place in the story. The facilitators ask questions such as: Why did you choose the story you related? What does your choice teach you about yourself? How did the story you related shape your attitude toward the "other"? Are there any motifs or parts of the story you related of which you were unaware? What do you think of your story now? The participants then extract core motifs and significant expressions – such as "exile," "homeland," "minority," "lack of knowledge," "naiveté" – as part of the reflective process and toward conducting an interpersonal dialogue.

An interpersonal process, in which the participants identify the points at which each story converges with the others, follows the intrapersonal process: In which parts of the story is it possible to identify with the narrator? What are the symbols appearing in the story? What typifies the characters and environment that have been described? Are there other ways of viewing the story? The last question creates a multilayered kind of *Rashomon* which reveals shared, complementary elements, as well as dissimilar and conflictive ones. Thus, connections are formed between the stories and within them, with overlapping or opposing links. Conflicting motifs paradoxically serve as a basis for dialogue by reexamining the listener's boundaries of tolerance.

The facilitators employ additional methods to trigger stories and broaden the participants' perspectives. One is to bring to the participants objects that are meaningful and which evoke levels of memory, symbolism, emotion, or thought. Some examples are a memorial candle, a dowry chest, a charm, or a reed tray. Another method is to bring formative and constructive texts, such as religious and national texts, literature, poetry, and songs. This shared learning of cultural assets reveals connections between the personal story, text or object and its cultural layers. A selected cultural asset can have a variety of connections to the normative cultural ethos: it can be congruent with it or contradict it; support or criticize it; relate and identify with it, or reject it.

The workshop also provides a theoretical framework for subjects such as multiculturalism, phenomenology, and interpretation. It also addresses the anatomy of intercultural encounters by employing the iceberg metaphor, on which I will elaborate later. This framework facilitates conceptualization of the processes that take place in the workshop. The final meetings are devoted to discussing the options of applying the insights learned to real life situations – Jewish and Arab citizens from neighboring communities, school environments, university students, etc. Thus, an alternative educational process is created, which is based on shared learning, creating new knowledge, and deepening understanding.

I shall now focus on three core issues from the workshop that constitute cornerstones for rebuilding trust: (a) listening; (b) transformation from a position of a lack of knowledge (or possessing pseudo-knowledge) to a state of learning; and (c) employing autobiographical stories. The three issues are interlinked and constitute a holistic narrative concept.

The first issue is listening, which is the desire and ability of the listener to hear the storyteller and understand his or her point of view. Listening is facilitated by adopting a position that is free of judgment toward the participant's ideas and emotions. It can be acquired and inculcated through awareness of the barriers to listening, such as disagreement and judgmental stances, a desire to give advice or correct the speaker, excessive interpretive or analytical preoccupation, and thinking of a response. Listening is not only a cultural characteristic according to which good manners dictate that one should not interrupt an interlocutor, but rather a state of awareness, a state of mind, a value that has behavioral manifestations. The discussion that follows the listening focuses on the thoughts and feelings of the participants in their experiences both as listeners and storytellers: What did they notice? What disturbed them? And, in particular, what are the barriers to listening? (What is difficult or impossible for me to hear?) It is immensely difficult to exercise restraint when faced with a painful or infuriating story. Educating toward complexity, toward loosening the constraints of listening and containing other voices, can enhance this skill.

The second issue is shifting from a position of lacking knowledge (or possessing pseudo-knowledge) to a state of learning. The intercultural encounter can be likened to an encounter with an iceberg, or one between two icebergs. In encounters with the "other" we experience what is visible "above sea level": behavior, speech, and appearance. Below the surface are expectations, norms, and beliefs, and deeper still are gender and time perceptions, attitudes toward authority, codes of communication, fears, values, myths, collective memory, symbols, stereotypes, and so on. Ignoring the larger, unseen part of the iceberg is liable to lead to collision or in other words, to misunderstanding and conflict.

This disregard can also stem from pseudo-knowledge, a dangerous state of mind in which people claim knowledge but their firm knowledge is superficial, stereotypical, and closed to dialogue. In the workshop, learning through stories lowers the sea level to expose more and more of one's own and the other's 'iceberg' or culture.

The intrapersonal process that occurs is just as profound in clarifying and constructing identity. This learning fleshes out the identity of the storytelling individuals who listen to themselves within the complex dialogue that takes place in the workshop. Schur writes about identity being influenced by the accumulated experience of people in interactive processes.[1] Listening facilitates interactive processes that create a change from a position of lacking knowledge, or of unequivocal and superficial pseudo-knowledge, to a position of learning, investigating, and inquiring. Participants in the workshop report that they undergo an inner change of becoming aware of the complexity of their own identity as well as those of the other participants. The intrapersonal change creates a dynamic in the complex fabric of the interplay between collective narratives and personal ones.[2]

The third issue is employing autobiographical stories. The stories are intended to allow each participant in the workshop to express his or her own life experience, which is meaningful and relevant to intercultural relationships. The autobiographical stories facilitate a retrospective and reflective view of the experience that influenced and shaped each of the participants' worldview. The story facilitates an encounter with a subjective process that continuously rewrites the attitude of the storyteller toward the past, the present, and the future. The biography relates to the "self" in time- and context-dependent perspectives that do not presume to be permanent, consistent, or objective. The "other" is also not absent from the biographical story and representations of the "self" and the "other" play an important role in changing long-term personal and collective consciousness. Participants report that the process of selecting the story to be related in the workshop is a meaningful, complex, and occasionally difficult and painful process. The selection process incorporates the original context in which the story occurred in the past with the present context of the narrative situation.

What are the advantages of the personal narrative approach to building trust?

1   Jackson asserts that a narrative contains the perception that an individual has no reality other than in relationships with others, and all narratives allegorize abstract subjects as "intersubjective dramas."[3] The stories told in the workshop are intersubjective dramas that cross-reference intra-cultural elements, such as the personal story and the collective story or two stories from the same culture, with intercultural elements, as well as stories from different cultures. The act of connecting the stories creates a complexity between local and global places, between individual experiences and the human condition as a whole, and between the life experience of individuals and the collective tradition and history of their culture.

2   Narrative discourse evokes emotions such as empathy, irritation, fear, identification, and shame, and creates emotional involvement. It is human, and has a dominant element of sharing. Emotions are a human foundation for communication and discourse.

3   The personal story contains collective elements, which are easier to listen to in an autobiographical context. A narrative discourse enables participants to see the pain, joy, and fear, and enables learning and knowledge by peeling off the "layers of demonization." The autobiographical story is less threatening. It evokes messages of "I" rather than "We." It says: "The tree that symbolizes my roots in this country is important to me as a symbol of my identity." It does not say: "I have a right to this land, I was here first."

4   A story is a holistic unit. The subject always appears in context. It facilitates learning of the connections between the components of the storyteller's consciousness. The full significance of human actions, states MacIntyre, can only be studied by means of narrative, which positions the action in the continuum of a personal life story and in the context of the culture and tradition in which the action takes place.[4]

5   The stories contain powerful experiences for the storyteller that mediate between shared external "reality" and internal, personal, creative imagination. The connection between the inner world of the individual and his or her sociocultural world is expressed in symbolic phrases and metaphors whose meanings embrace these dimensions.

6   Narrative discourse is a proclaimed and subjective process that constantly rewrites attitudes toward the past, the present, and the

future.[5] This dynamic enables change, flexibility, and complexity, from which new trust can emerge.

7   A story is a transformative tool. The very act of telling the story aloud and conducting a dialogue about it creates an awareness of the story's being one possible version of viewing reality. Identity relates to a process of construction and reproduction through time, directly or in opposition to others.[6] In its complexity, the story facilitates a space for change.

In the feedback from the workshop, the participants reported that they underwent a meaningful experience, and many spoke of a new experience, different from their experiences in other workshops. They gained numerous insights and discussed the processes of inner contemplation they had experienced and also responded to one another's stories. A discourse based on understanding the pain of the "other" began to emerge. The participants expressed commitment to the group and a desire to continue meeting. Some began talking about the end product and purpose of the workshop, while others suggested focusing on the process and giving it time. Some spoke of "lacking knowledge," the extent to which each story reveals something new, and how much we do not know.

The various workshops yielded a database of stories that constitutes considerable learning material. Connections were made between the stories: awareness of dilemmas, rifts, pain, fears, and frustrations through which people can connect with themselves and with similar or different "others." The workshop created an empathic, supportive, attentive, and inquiring dynamic that motivated the participants to continue searching and studying. They forged bonds with one another through their stories, and a shared language began to emerge.

The Middle East conflict is replete with attempts at establishing discourse aimed at finding a solution. In many cases, conventional discourse contains declarative, monolithic attitudes and arguments with a linear logic. The dialogue is "flat," one-dimensional and limited. In a discourse of rights, such as this one, the participants reconstruct what they know and say what they know how to say. In contrast, narrative discourse is a complex discourse of identity; it is substantial and multidimensional, and expands the prism through which a person observes the reality of his or her life. The monolithic "I" transforms into a polyphonic "I," and the monolithic collective transforms into a polyphonic one.

I would like to close with a story about a couple that decided to obtain couple counseling to try to rebuild their relationship. The woman declared that she did not trust her partner. The counselor responded, "Trust is like an egg; once it breaks, whichever way we put it back together, it will never again be a perfect egg." The couple divorced some time later.

Israel and its neighbors cannot get a divorce. I once heard someone say,

"If we cannot hang onto one another, we will hang alongside one another." Perhaps the broken egg we glue back together will not be perfect, but metaphorically speaking, a path towards renewed trust will be hatched from it. The components of the narrative approach – namely, inculcating listening to the "self" and the "other" as a value to guide our interactions, constantly being in a position of learning, and adopting a multidimensional attitude toward reality – are conditions for rebuilding trust between us. Together they create a space that can serve as fertile soil for producing complex solutions.

An understanding of the value of listening, and how to communicate your positions and ideas, are essential to the building of trust and meaningful negotiations. Helping both Israeli and Palestinian negotiators to comprehend and value listening might enhance the prospects for successful negotiation of a peace agreement between Israel and Palestine.

Notes

1   E. Schur, *The Awareness Trap* (New York: Quadrangle, 1976).

2   D. Bar-On, *The 'Others' Within Us: A Socio-psychological Perspective on Changes in Israeli Identity* (Beer-Sheva: Ben-Gurion University of the Negev Press, 1999); E. Witztum and Y. Goodman "Disorder, narrative, therapy: Narrativized and culturally-sensitive strategic intervention in a Haredi population" in E. Leshem and D. Roer-Sterier (eds.) *Cultural Diversity as a Challenge to Human Services* (Jerusalem: Magnes, 2003), pp. 275–309.

3   M. Jackson, *Minima Ethnographica: Intersubjectivity and the Anthropological Project* (Chicago: Chicago University Press, 1998).

4   A. MacIntyre, *After Virtue* (Notre Dame: University of Notre Dame Press, 1981).

5   E. Ochs, "Stories that step into the future" in D. Biber and E. Finegan (eds.), *Sociolinguistic Perspectives on Register* (New York: Oxford University Press, 2001), pp. 106–35.

6   O. Lofgren, "The Nationalization of Culture," *Ethnologia Europaea*, Vol. 19, 1989, pp. 5–23.

CHAPTER 6

The Economic Dividends of Egypt and Jordan from Peace Agreements with Israel

GAD G. GILBAR AND ONN WINCKLER

"The need for *trust* arises from our interdependence with others."[1] This is a bit of wisdom that has relevance not only for individuals but for states as well. As such, *trust* has been identified as a key element in conflict resolution, based on the formula of the "win–win situation." In the most long-standing international conflicts, such as the two major world wars, the winning side dictated an overall regime change to the losing side, including a peace treaty in line with the winning side's interests. In the case of the Arab–Israeli conflict, however, the situation is totally different insofar as there is no "winning side" or "losing side" in terms of dictating a peace treaty according to the interests of one at the expense of the other. Thus, the only option of "peace building" is through the "win–win" formula. The basic thesis of this chapter is that the peace treaties between Israel and Egypt (March 1979), and later between Israel and Jordan (October 1994), have provided tremendous economic gains for both Egypt and Jordan, in line with the "win–win" formula.

Past Economic Dividends

Prior to examination of the past peace economic dividends, it should be emphasized that neither Egypt nor Jordan was forced to pay any economic "price" in the Arab arena for their peace agreements with Israel, but that the economic dividends of those agreements, both direct and indirect, were substantial.

Egypt

Egypt's direct economic dividends of peace consisted mainly of the following five factors. First, the reopening of the Suez Canal in June 1975 has since contributed more than $30 billion to the Egyptian public revenues. By the fiscal year of 2002/2003, Egypt's revenues from the Suez Canal amounted to $2.3 billion annually. Second, as part of the peace treaty itself, Egypt enjoys an annual grant of $2.3 billion from the US (for both military and civilian purposes). Third, Egypt gained back the oil fields in Sinai and was also able to develop the oil fields on the east bank of the Suez Canal following stabilization of the political–security situation in that area. Fourth, following the first Sinai agreement in 1974, Egypt was allowed to reconstruct the cities along the Suez Canal that had been almost totally destroyed in the War of Attrition and the October 1973 War. Fifth, the signing of the Camp David Accords in August 1978 marked the beginning of a surge in foreign investments and tourism revenues. In 2004, Egypt's tourism receipts amounted to more than $6 billion. All in all, Egypt's direct economic dividends from the peace treaty with Israel have amounted to more than $12 billion annually on average since 1979 until the present.

An examination of Egypt's economic structure over the past three decades, as well as its sources for alternative hard currency earners, other than those related to peace with Israel, both directly and indirectly, reveals that there are very few other options available. By the year 2002, Egypt's total merchandise exports amounted to $6.6 billion, including oil. Manufacturing and agricultural exports amounted to only $3.1 billion, of which approximately $2 billion was earmarked for Iraq. Following the abolishment of Saddam Hussain's regime in April 2003, the hard currency earnings derived from the peace agreement with Israel assume even greater significance.

To the aforementioned direct economic dividends from the peace with Israel, one should also add the two main indirect dividends. First was the creation of a large number of new work opportunities in various economic fields as a result of the surge in foreign investments. Second was the growth of huge foreign communities in Cairo, comprised of diplomats and representatives of the foreign companies operating in Egypt. Following the signing of the Egyptian–Israeli peace treaty, most of the Western countries located their largest embassy in the Middle East in Cairo. Thus, there has been a substantial increase during the past two decades in the number of diplomats in Cairo, each of whom requires the services of Egyptian workers that are paid in foreign currency. Moreover, these foreigners are consuming a wide variety of goods and services while in Egypt. Although these indirect economic dividends cannot be measured accurately, their contribution to Egypt's, particularly Cairo's, employment and hard currency earnings is beyond any doubt.

Jordan

Overall, Jordan had several economic aims in the peace treaty with Israel (October 1994). The first was to negotiate a substantial reduction in the size of the external debt, especially the short-term debt. The second aim was to find a stable source of financial aid following termination of the aid previously received from the Arabian Gulf oil states. The third aim was to achieve a rapid increase of revenues from tourism. The fourth aim was to increase foreign investments in order to create a vast number of new work opportunities and a new source of hard currency, given the chronic balance of trade and payments deficit. The fifth aim was to alleviate the severe water shortage. Overall, it seems that after just one decade, most of these aims have been at least partially achieved.

First, as a part of the peace treaty with Israel, many Western governments cancelled the Jordanian debt. By early 1995, only a few months following the signing of the peace treaty with Israel, Jordan's total external debt was $5 billion, down from more than $9 billion four years earlier, in 1991.

Second, as a result of the peace treaty with Israel, Jordan regained a massive amount of foreign aid. As part of the treaty itself, Jordan receives an annual $250 million in cash from the US. In 2001, the official development assistance to Jordan amounted to $432 million, representing 5% of the Kingdom's total GDP. In May 2003, Jordan received an extraordinary cash grant of $500 million from the US as compensation for the losses incurred from the War in Iraq, bringing the total amount of US aid to Jordan in 2003 to $750 million. This huge grant enabled the Jordanian government to keep its expenditures at a normal level without increasing the budgetary deficit. In addition, Jordan was scheduled to receive another $200 million in early 2004, making the total US aid package to the Kingdom $450 million in 2004.

Third, one of the most important economic benefits to Jordan of the peace treaty with Israel was its development of the tourism industry. The 1990–91 Gulf Crisis caused a great deal of harm to Jordan's tourism industry, which started to recover only in 1992. Three years later, by 1995, the tourism industry was already contributing more than 10% of the total Jordanian GDP. By 1997, the tourism receipts had increased to $774 million, representing 11.1% of the total GDP, and by 1998 had further increased to 12%. In 1999, the number of tourists in Jordan reached 1.35 million. However, the onset of the *Intifada* al-Aqsa in late September 2000 and the terrorist attacks of September 11, 2001 led to a sharp deterioration in tourism activity in Jordan, as in the other Middle Eastern countries. This deterioration, it should be emphasized, was not the result of making peace with Israel.

The fourth economic dividend of peace was the sharp increase in foreign investments in Jordan, as well as in Jordan's exports to the US from the Qualifying Industrial Zones (QIZs), which are granted privileged access to the US market. As part of the peace treaty with Israel, these zones were established in order to promote Jordanian–Israeli economic cooperation. In order to qualify for QIZ status, products must have at least 35% of their appraised value added within the zone, with a minimum of 11.7% coming from Jordan, 8% from Israel, and the remainder from a Jordanian QIZ, Israel, the US, or the Palestinian National Authority (PNA). Alternatively, Jordanian and Israeli companies can contribute 20% of the value added. By mid-2002, ten QIZs were operating in Jordan, attracting foreign investments of $540 million during the years 2000–2003. By the year 2002, the total Jordanian exports to the US amounted to JD (Jordanian Dinar) 304.4 million ($430 million), increasing from only JD 5.6 million ($8 million) in 1998. By 2003, Jordan's exports to the US climbed to $660 million, representing 28% of the total Jordanian exports. Thus, the US replaced Iraq as Jordan's most important trade partner. Jordan's exports to Israel (including the PNA) have also substantially increased during the past few years, rising from only JD 4.3 million in 1996 to JD 87.1 million in 2002.

Tourism as an Alternative Option for Rapid Growth in the Middle East

For the Arab non-oil-based economies, particularly Jordan, Egypt, and the Palestinians, the tourism industry has many advantages, of which the following are the most prominent. First, governmental revenues can be expanded through taxation. Second, the tourism industry serves as a major catalyst for the development of other economic sectors, mainly construction, transportation, textiles, agriculture, and fisheries, insofar as they supply the goods and services used in the tourism industry. Third, the tourism industry promotes foreign investments, especially in the construction of new hotels and tourism sites. Fourth, the tourism industry seems to be more effective than other industries in generating a considerable number of new jobs at a wide variety of skill levels.

Conclusions

In light of the current economic situation in Jordan and Egypt, as well as among the Palestinians in the occupied territories, rapid economic growth is crucial in order to maintain political stability in these areas. The World Bank report on the Jordanian economy from early 2003 claims that, "with a labor force growing at 4%–5% per annum, Jordan needs at least 6% GDP growth to stabilize unemployment." According to the prevailing estimates,

Egypt and Jordan need an annual GDP growth of 7% in order to absorb the new entrants to their labor forces. These high growth rates can be achieved only through the implementation of two changes. First, there must be a rapid decline achieved in fertility rates. Although both Jordan and Egypt have managed to reduce their fertility rates, the current rates remain very high, at an average level of more than three children per woman. As Michael Todaro accurately stated regarding the crucial issue of fertility decline: "every year that passed without a reduction in fertility means a larger multiple of the present total population size before it can eventually level off." Thus, the introduction of comprehensive family planning programs is crucial in these countries. The second, and by no means less important, change critical to promoting "peace economic dividends" is the enhancement of stability in the regional political–security situation.

In conclusion, it appears that peace in the Middle East and economic cooperation between the Arab countries and Israel, particularly within the framework of the Jordanian–Palestinian–Israeli triangle, is no longer a matter of choice, but simply a matter of their basic economic survival.

Notes

This chapter is based on the article: Gad G. Gilbar and Onn Winckler, "The Economic Factor of the Arab–Israeli Peace Process: The Cases of Egypt, Jordan and Syria" in Elie Podeh and Asher Kaufman (eds.), *Arab–Jewish Relations: From Conflict to Reconciliation?* (Brighton & Portland: Sussex Academic Press, 2005), pp. 190–209.

1   Edward C. Tomlinson and Roy J. Lewicki, "Trust and Trust Building." [<http://www.beyondintractability.org/m/trust_building.jsp>].

CHAPTER 7

Engineering Social Capital in the Middle East: Rebuilding Trust

SHAUL M. GABBAY

Trust is the absence of fear. Mistrusting the other is based on the fear of the other's potentially hurtful actions. Mistrust occurs in the present based on the possible actions of the other in the future. Trust is the foundation of any healthy relationship, whether it be between individual human beings, organizations, or governments. The existence of trust allows for the buildup of productive ties, while its absence results in the allocation of scarce resources to preempt or deter potentially hurtful actions.[1] The perception of what the other might do is as important as the actual action. Mistrust of the other is usually based on past interactions where trust has been broken. Perceptions constrain and affect realities, particularly in the case of trust. The higher the level of perceived mistrust at present, the more likely that it will have real consequences in the future. "If people define a situation as real, it will be real in its consequences."[2] One actor's actions, which are based on the mistrust of the other, affect the actual trustworthiness. Perceptions about trust create reality.[3]

Trust is a human motivation, the foundation of human relationships. Though we can analytically aggregate trust to abstract entities (such as organizations – states included), trust lies at the individual level – among human beings. If we can change perceptions to be more trusting, we will be able to move in the direction of answering the question of "how to rebuild trust."[4] In this chapter I follow the calls for employing network theory and analysis to the Arab–Israeli Conflict.[5] In line with the theme of the conference on "How to Rebuild Trust between Israelis and Palestinians" (September 2004 in Denver, Colorado), I ask the following: What are the social structural/network characteristics that could engineer social capital between Israelis and Palestinians to restore and begin building some basic (and fundamental) level of trust?[6] The following is an analysis of how to build a network with sustainable incentives for actors to participate in order to change the perception of trusting the other, first by trusting the stability of the network itself.[7] In the following sections I begin by delineating the relevant theories and associated findings of social structure and social capital and their specific effects on the level of trust. I then apply these theories and findings to the Israeli–Palestinian conflict.

Relevant Patterns of Social Interactions

Social Networks and Social Capital

Social structure is a network of actors who are in some way connected through a set of relationships. Social capital is defined as "the set of resources, tangible or virtual, that accrue to a player through the player's social relationships, facilitating the attainment of goals."[8] In the interest of building and/or increasing the level of trust, we ask, "What characteristics of ties and forms of social structures are associated with increased levels of trust?" Once we identify these social structures, we can move to restructure – "engineer" – ties to achieve our goal.[9] There are two structural/network analytical levels which are correlated with increased level of trust: (1) the dyadic, actor-to-actor strength of tie, and (2) the structural, overarching arrangement of actors in a network.[10]

The Dyadic Level

Theoretical arguments and supporting empirical findings suggest that relative to weak ties, strong ties are associated with higher levels of trust.[11] Consider Figure 7.1:

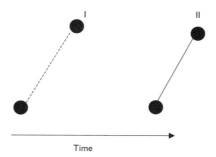

Figure 7.1   Strengthening a weak tie

Actors A and B are weakly connected in the first illustration but strongly connected in the second. The level of trust is higher in the second illustration, where the tie is stronger. There are three commonly used measures of strength of ties: frequency of interaction, duration, and emotional closeness.[12] People who know each other longer, feel closer emotionally, and interact more frequently are defined as having a stronger tie, which is characterized by a higher level of trust. The simplest of these three to manipulate is frequency of interaction – the principal tool for social engineering.[13] Once the frequency of interaction has been increased by (for example) exogenous incentives for intensified (positive) interaction, the tie has been engineered to be stronger and will therefore be associated with a higher level of trust.

If reality was the first illustration in Figure 7.1 and we are interested in building (or rebuilding) the level of trust between actors A and B over time,[14] we could use power, resources, and incentives to motivate the two actors to interact (positively) more frequently – thus creating a stronger tie, in which a higher level of trust is inherent.[15]

Multiplexity of Ties

Ties are rich in content; each two actors could have multiple sets of content in their relationship. At the individual level, for example, a relationship containing business transactions could also be based on personal friendship, a friendship relationship but not a family tie, or a family tie. Each (joint) project between two actors could be seen as one kind of content tie.[16] The more projects – the more multiplex the tie – the more interdependence – the stronger the tie is. The greater the multiplexity (more content – more projects) of a tie, the greater the dependency level between actors.

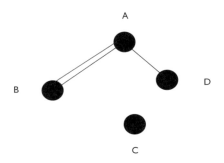

Figure 7.2   Multiplexity of ties

Figure 7.2 is a graphical illustration for the multiplexity of ties. Actors A, B, and C share two kinds of ties. These could be business transactions that include more than one project. The strength of ties between these two actors will increase as their interdependency on each of these issues of business increases. The existence and continued interaction at one level will most likely depend also on the positive interaction at the second level and vice versa.

Levels of Interaction

For analytical purposes I suggest three levels of societal interactions, which are illustrated in Figure 7.3.

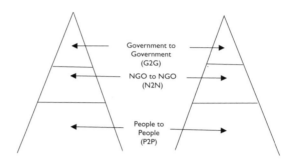

Figure 7.3 Levels of interaction

First (considered the most important in its effect on the other two) is the government-to-government (G2G) level. One example of this level is the Oslo agreement of 1993 between the Israeli government led by the late Prime Minister Rabin and the Palestinian Liberation Organization (PLO). At present (winter 2007) the level of interaction between Israelis and Palestinians is very fragile. The replacement of Chairman Arafat by Mahmud Abbas temporarily created a more hopeful atmosphere for renewed formal negotiations, but the subsequent election of Hamas brought interactions almost to a standstill, although some discussions between Palestinian Prime Minister Abbas and Israeli leaders continue. Another example of the government-to-government level is the professional water committee, which was established as a result of the Oslo agreement and which is an ongoing outcome of this level of interaction. This level continues to operate despite the challenges of the al-Aqsa *Intifada*. This level of ties is long term in character and is important mostly because it serves as the judiciary framework enabling all other levels to exist according to the law. Prior to the Oslo agreements, Israeli law prohibited Israelis from contact with PLO officials. This level is mostly contractual in nature. When discussing long-term infrastructure projects, this level of interaction may be the only relevant one.

The second level of interaction is between Non Governmental Organizations (NGOs) from both the societies (N2N). At this level cooperation is not restricted and/or derived from the G2G level. Non Governmental Organizations act according to their inherent interests and could facilitate the fostering of ties between the two societies. Moreover, since the goals of NGOs are in the nature of the "public good," their work exemplifies the joint interest of people from both societies. Examples are the joint projects of the Red Crescent and Magen David Adom – Palestinian and Israeli paramedic organizations that operate in Israel and the West Bank and the Gaza Strip. The overarching norms that each of these organizations adheres to and which are, for the most part, similar act as glue and promote mutual interest and cooperation.[17]

The People to People level (P2P) is the most common tie that has been used over the years. This level can, and usually does, operate despite the absence of the Government-to-Government interaction, though it cannot operate if the law in one society prohibits interactions with members of the other. The best and most widely known illustration of this level is the informal agreement known as the Geneva Accords that was signed by representatives of the Israeli and Palestinian societies.[18] In the P2P level the tie is not necessarily economic, nor is it necessarily based on formal agreements. Rather the tie is based on people's genuine interest in maintaining interaction, sometimes with the explicit goal of ending the conflict. Other examples at this level are business ties, which are based on economic cooperation between peoples in the two societies.

The three levels are, of course, analytical. Empirically, there are crosses between them, as for example in the role of particular NGOs, such as the Peres Institute for Peace, that are aimed at facilitating the interaction at the P2P level.

Given that the level of trust is correlated with the strength of the tie, it follows that the more (positive) ties that exist between the two societies at each of these three levels – individuals, NGOs, and formal, diplomatic, state-to-state levels – the stronger the resulting trust levels over all will be. Therefore, an investment should be designed with this focus at the core. Meaningful incentives should be made available at the level of the international community to encourage joint, mutual, and multi-tiered levels of interaction.

The question remains: How can the dyadic tie be strengthened in order to overcome its fragility? How can projects be designed to sustain the increased level of interaction needed to provide a stronger and more trustworthy tie? More precisely, in terms of Figure 7.1, how can A and B be motivated to intensify positive and cooperative interaction over time while confronting destructive challenges?

I argue here that this motivation should come from the outside as an exogenous pressure – creating incentives (financial are the most visible and effective) for increased positive interaction. The multi-actor "structural approach" addresses this challenge and is discussed next.

Trust at the Multi Actors Level – International Network of Actors

Theoretical arguments and supporting empirical findings suggest that, compared with open social structures, closed networks are associated with higher levels of trust.[19] Consider Figure 7.4.

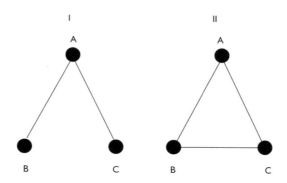

Figure 7.4   Closed and open networks

For the three actors[20] A, B, and C, in illustration one, A has a tie to B and C, yet there is no tie between B and C.[21] In the second illustration, B and C are connected, just as A is connected to B and to C – the social structure/network is closed.

Since in the second illustration all actors are connected – if one actor deviates from the norm of the social network, the other pair can sanction against that deviating action, while in the first illustration, actor A enjoys a structural advantage.[22] In the second illustration all know of the structure of ties in the network (namely, A knows that B and C are connected and share information, B knows that A and C are connected, and C knows that A and B are connected). Since each is aware of the risk of sanctions for any deviations, each is careful to avoid deviations. The sanctioning power against deviation sustains the existence of the norm over time. All actors contribute to the higher level of trust which is higher in the second illustration compared to the first. Moreover, if the triadic structure is reinforced by additional actors (e.g., Figure 7.5), the trust level is increased further as there are others to whom the normative structure of the network is relevant and of interest.[23]

Dyad Level Interaction with Social Structural Level: Stronger Closed Networks

Strength of ties is also a function of frequency of interaction. The more frequent the interaction in each dyad and the greater the multi-actor interaction in a network, the greater the level of trust that is expected. Sanctioning against defection is more effective. Actors will be more cooperative. The greater the level of interaction in the network, the more stable it is over time. The perception about the long-lived and the ongoing function of the network becomes more and more established and the perception itself affects the trust level as each actor considers his/her actions in the long run – multiple transactions with others in the network, as opposed to unilateral, opportunistic, one-time transactions.[24] Over time – and across interactions – an actor in the network considers each decision in terms of the benefit of continuing his/her participation in the network.

Engineering Social Capital in the Middle East: Applying the Theory to the Israeli/Palestinian Tie – Rebuilding Trust

I have delineated two levels for building social capital: the dyadic level and the structural level. I have also discussed the multiplexity of ties as a function of various layers of interaction and have argued that we know the structural requirements for creating social capital by engineering the social structure to build trust. I will now apply these contentions to the Middle East conflict – specifically the Israeli–Palestinian conflict. Social capital is a positive outcome derived from the network of actors. In our case, we are interested in trust for its own sake, specifically the trust level between Israelis and Palestinians.

The Palestinian–Israeli conflict, which has been at the heart of the Arab–Israeli conflict, is considered one of the most complex, intractable conflicts of modern times.[25] Since the year 2000, the Israeli–Palestinian conflict has been characterized by an unprecedented decrease in the level of trust. At present, the Israeli–Palestinian formal peace efforts have, for the most part, stagnated.[26] At the informal level, perceptions of trust between Israelis and Palestinians are at their lowest level historically.[27] The Israeli–Palestinian relationship at present is consumed by mistrust. Moreover, the level of mistrust has reached the very basic level of human need – the need for personal safety.[28] Israelis are concerned first and foremost with their daily personal security, and are engulfed with the anxiety of awaiting the next unstoppable suicide attack. Palestinians do not trust Israeli intentions and face daily hardships derived from Israeli security efforts, including what Palestinians perceive as random attacks on their homes and children.

The Israeli–Palestinian Tie – The Dyad Level

Earlier I discussed the dyadic, actor-to actor level. The suggestion here is that positive, frequent interactions between Israelis and Palestinians will increase the trust level. At the core of the trust between Israelis and Palestinians are the individuals, both Israelis and Palestinians.

Since the beginning of the second *Intifada* (Palestinian uprising) that began in October 2000, the frequency of interaction between Palestinian and Israeli individuals has plummeted. The election of Hamas and its refusal to recognize Israel put the situation at a new low. The interactions that do occur are often marked by violence. Much fewer business and social transactions have decreased the level of interactions. Clearly, the third factor, emotional closeness, has been transformed at best into emotional distance and at worst open hostility.

With the recent changes in Palestinian leadership, unless Hamas changes its position toward Israel, the level of mistrust between Israelis and Palestinians is so high that it is doubtful if they would engage either in joint projects or in the dyadic-level tie. Even if they would attempt such projects, it is most improbable that actors on either side would stay involved in them for more than a short while. The memory of past events, which shattered the hope of trust between Israelis and Palestinians, is likely too painful for independent, direct, serious, and long-term commitments to be negotiated.[29] It is therefore prudent to move to the next level of structure – the multi-actor level (structural approach).

Finally, even with the recent change in Palestinian leadership there is still a critical need to create an overarching structure, which will be independent of particular individuals. Thus we must look to the next level of social engineering.

The Israel–Palestinian Ties embedded in a Multi-actor Network

Given the multi-actor proposition I put forward earlier in the chapter, the tie between Israelis and Palestinians is, at present, characterized mostly by non-relationship. One of the most obvious strategies to bring about a more positive tie between Israelis and Palestinians is to embrace this contentious tie in a closed network structure. This could be done by adding interest-driven dimensions for the Israeli–Palestinian tie (the core) – as a part of a global network of actors on the periphery. Consider Figure 7.5, opposite.

Embedded at the core of the network is the Israeli–Palestinian tie characterized at present by a very low level of interaction (very weak tie). Surrounding the core some of the (possible) peripheral actors of the international community are depicted.

On the dyadic level both Israelis and Palestinians have strong ties with other actors in the international arena. The Israeli–US tie has been the focus of numerous comments and study.[30] The tie between Europeans and Palestinians has also been important. The tie between Israel and Jordan is yet another dyadic, independent tie to build upon.[31] The latter relationship, which has been the focus of several studies, continues to be a relatively strong one, particularly when compared with the Palestinian–Israeli tie. Moreover, peripheral actors such as Saudi Arabia, Russia, and China have independent trustworthy ties.[32]

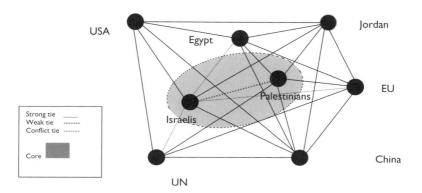

Figure 7.5   Embedding core conflict dyad in peripheral social structure

Peripheral actors today are interested in containing the Israeli–Palestinian conflict (particularly in the context of globally fighting radical Islam and terrorism). This goal increases the motivation (benefit) for actors at the periphery to participate and invest resources in embracing the core Palestinian–Israeli tie.

The more multi-actor joint projects that facilitate interactions between Israelis and Palestinians, the greater the possibility for increasing trust and security among the participants. This is true not only for the Israelis and Palestinians directly involved with the projects, but also for others, including family and friends of those directly involved and the general public involved in far-reaching networks around the world.

Overarching Strategy: Embedding Core Dyadic, Mistrustful Ties

Within Trusting, Closed Social Networks

Given these observations, I will briefly suggest several strategies for the rebuilding of trust between Israelis and Palestinians; these are long-term mechanisms for the buildup of closed systems embedding the Israeli–Palestinian relationship as a core within them. I follow the three levels suggested earlier in this chapter: Government-to-Government level where mega-infrastructural projects are involved; the Government to

Government (G2G), Non Governmental Organizations to NGOs (N2N), and People to People (P2P) levels. I will provide examples of strategies for all three. It should be noted that these three levels are structural levels whose relationships and outcomes always overlap in reality. The overlap itself contributes a cohesive bond that can strengthen and provide ongoing support for the three analytically separate levels.

The present problematic, dyadic tie between Israelis and Palestinians should be embedded in a larger network of interested peripheral constituencies such as Egypt, Jordan, Turkey, Europe, the United States, Russia, China, and others (see Figure 7.5).

The stronger the perception at each juncture that the Israeli–Palestinian conflict is just one part of a long-term, committed network which includes other actors on the periphery, (1) the greater the level of trust will be throughout the network, and (2) the lower the relative weight of the daily developments (such as violent acts) will be. In this case, dyadic relationships characterized by a higher level of trust (such as Egypt–US, Jordan–US, Egypt–Jordan) at the periphery act as a reinforcing mechanism for the core Israeli–Palestinian tie.

Strategy I: Long-term Dependency Projects

Long-term projects that build on regional interests create the perception that the general network is worthwhile and encourage cooperative efforts. These projects are, of course, dependant on active participation and/or approval at the Government-to-Government level. Important examples include (1) water projects such as conservation, desalination, protection of aquifers, and sewage treatment; (2) projects to produce and manage energy; (3) waste management projects; and (4) environmental protection megaprojects. As I suggested earlier, even in the midst of the current conflict, ongoing cooperation at this level already exists between some Israelis and Palestinians; for example, professionals interacting in the areas of energy, water, and environmental studies.[33]

Water, energy, waste management, and environmental health are issues that both Israelis and Palestinians must deal with; because they are regional in nature, they can be handled more cost effectively when considered on a regional, cooperative level.[34] The benefits of joint, regional investments (as opposed to unilateral ones) are straightforward from economic and practical standpoints. This is particularly the case with relatively large (mega) infrastructure projects that require substantial initial investments. In fact, polls show that a majority of Israelis and Palestinians agree on the need for such cooperation. More than two-thirds of Palestinians and Israelis support the creation of joint economic institutions and ventures. Projects at this level also present investment opportunities for outside constituencies at the international level.

It is beyond the scope of this chapter to delineate in detail the importance of these projects economically and physically. These arguments have
been extensively discussed in writings and conferences devoted to these
issues. The focus of this chapter is on the social dimensions of these
projects, specifically the buildup of trust. The buildup of trust between
participants is straight forward as they face joint challenges in the implementation of projects, an exercise that in itself leads to the buildup of trust
over time.

I contend that, in addition to the trust-building process that results from
working together, these long-term, joint projects will increase the perception within both societies that the interdependence of Israelis and
Palestinians will continue for years – indeed, for generations. As a result,
the daily attempts of extremists from both societies to disrupt the relationship will receive less weight and the hopelessness of resolving the conflict
will diminish. This perception was well described at a conference in Aspen,
Colorado in 2003, which was organized by Professor Marshal Kaplan of
the University of Colorado School of Public Policy. Israeli, Palestinian,
and American professionals discussed issues related to infrastructural
projects, specifically in the areas of housing, transportation, and the environment. The following citation from the report supports and illustrates
my argument about the magnitude of daily challenges (e.g., the numbers of
suicide bombings and acts of Israeli retaliation) and the commitment of
participants to continue with their efforts despite these challenges.

> Relatively soon after the conclusion of the Aspen Forum, there were several
> suicide bombings in Israel and a series of military responses by Israel. While
> dismayed at the tragic turn of events, the Israeli, Palestinian, and U.S. partic-
> ipants in Aspen indicated through e-mails, faxes, and phone calls their
> commitment to sustain the Forums and agreed-upon work program
> concerning next steps. *'We began something very important in Aspen. We hope
> the violence that has begun again will soon end and progress towards peace will
> continue.'* The success of the forums and the work programs associated with
> the Forums will encourage citizens and political leaders to support returning
> to the peace table.[35]

A similar example emerged from a professional forum titled "The Water
Working Groups," sponsored by the University of Oklahoma's
International Programs Center, Center for Peace Studies (CPS), a consor-
tium of Bethlehem University (Palestine), Haifa University (Israel), the
Horizon Center for Studies and Research (Jordan), and the University of
Oklahoma (U.S.). The proceedings of the forum and its professional
conclusions are available in the forum's final report. The following part of
the final report was self reported by the participants in the conference; it
describes the interaction and the buildup of trust I claim is a long-term
buildup of regional social capital. The participants are discussing the

relationships that developed over two succeeding forums – the first held in Cyprus, and the second, near the Dead Sea.

> As reported of the first Southern Tier meeting participants in Cyprus, the second group engaged in open and frank discussions. The inclusion of first-meeting participants enabled the second meeting to quickly re-establish trust and build upon the interpersonal relationships developed among some individuals in Cyprus. Several second-time Southern Tier participants commented on their developing friendships as a result of the repeated opportunity for dialogue and exchange. Strengthened group ties were not limited to attendees from Cyprus: a first-time participant stated he felt like he had been at the first meeting, such was the inclusive atmosphere generated by previous participants. The second meeting also included more female participants than the first meeting, and female members were particularly supportive of each other's participation and suggestions.

This passage clearly illustrates the argument of this chapter. First, the ties that formed at the first meeting strengthened over time. The relationships exist between individuals, the participants of the forum. Second, the trust and relationships which developed among participants in the first forum assisted in the creation of trust among other members of the second forum who did not participate in the first forum.

Strategy II: NGOs to NGOs

Non-Governmental Organizations (NGOs) enjoy a unique position in all societies, but they play a particularly critical role in the development of a civil society or a nation "in the making," such as Israel in the 1950s and the Palestinian society today. The NGO role takes on a heightened importance in a time and in a region of conflict such as the one in which Palestinians and Israelis now find themselves. Whatever the NGO agenda is in a given society, it is, by its nature, interested in the public good or public cause. The impact of the public cause usually crosses borders. In the Israeli–Palestinian societies, several important NGOs have an important role in issues related to the conflict. The advantages of involving NGOs are many. NGOs have local expertise and links with local actors. They are often able to gain access to areas of conflict where official representatives should not or cannot go. Since warring factions generally regard NGOs as impartial, humanitarian do-gooders, NGOs are effective as operating partners in peace initiatives. Furthermore, non-governmental groups often have the best access to people in need, and they have networks that can be mobilized quickly. Many of the larger NGOs have a long experience of working with government agencies and are knowledgeable about government requirements, specifications, and budget procedures, but maintain their ability to operate in a very flexible manner. Decisions can be decentralized, and operations can be jump-started. NGOs can deploy considerable resources, often within hours. NGOs are often able to track down key personnel about whose existence the government may not even be aware. NGOs frequently display impressive creativity in solving practical problems, and play an important role in paving the way for the implementation of conflict-resolution measures.

The positive effect of NGOs in the Israeli–Palestinian conflict is illustrated by the critical role of think tanks such as The Economic Cooperation Foundation (ECF), pioneered by former Israel Justice Minister Yossi Beilin (which was established after the Oslo agreements), as well as the Israel Palestinian Center for Research and Information (IPCRI).

It is not the focus of this chapter to describe the important work that these two organizations do, but rather to highlight the effective role they play as NGOs which, most critically, do not abide by political and state interests. These organizations have created an extensive web of ties based on mutual trust in both Israeli and Palestinian societies. The extensive relationships that ECF (located in Tel Aviv, Israel) has with Israeli and Palestinian political and security figures has enabled it to develop professional reports to be used by both sides to tackle issues related to solving the conflict. Moreover, because of its non-governmental position, ECF was able to act as an informal channel for interaction between the Israeli and Palestinian leadership, particularly in tense times when the formal channels are not available because of political constraints.

IPCRI, an NGO established by Gershon Baskin and situated at the border of Jerusalem and Beit Lechem, serves as a bridge between the two societies. At the time of its creation, Terje Larsen, Director of the Norwegian Labour Union's applied social research institute FAFO, was working on a survey of living conditions in the Gaza Strip and the West Bank. This work put him in contact with actors on both sides. In a meeting with Yossi Beilin of the Israeli Labor Party, and his associate Yair Hirschfeld, a social scientist with the Israeli NGO Economic Cooperation Foundation, Larsen and the Norwegian Deputy Foreign Minister Jan Egeland offered to facilitate a secret back channel in Norway between Israel and the PLO that eventually led to the Oslo Agreements.

Since NGOs have the ongoing interest and resources to support joint interactions between Israelis and Palestinians, NGOs play an important role in facilitating the interaction at the People-to-People level. Examples are the Peres Institute for Peace, which oversees and supports numerous People-to-People projects, as well as IPCRI.

Strategy III: Professional People-to-People Efforts

Two good examples and empirical manifestations of People-to-People efforts are the conference on "How to Rebuild Trust Between Israelis and

Palestinians," held in Denver, Colorado, in September 2004, and the conference organized by the Three Cultures Foundation in Seville, Spain, in January 2005. At these two conferences, Israeli, Palestinian, Jordanian, Egyptian, European, and American scholars, in a positive, friendly, and respectful atmosphere, tackled the issue of building trust between Palestinians and Israelis. The close camaraderie of Israelis and Palestinians at the end of the conferences, in an environment where participants from the US, Europe, Jordan, Egypt and others were also actively involved, were real-life examples embedding the two non-trusting parties within a network of interested, supportive participants. In effect, it was a real-life representation of the strategy depicted in Figure 7.5. Although the setting was not a long-term project such as those recommended above, it did provide an opportunity for participants to engage in a short-term project during which expected outcomes of trust-building did occur.

The strategy depicted in Figure 7.5 is based on the premises of networks of identities.[36] In the above real-life examples of the conferences in Denver and Seville, participants built relationships based on their professional affiliation within academia. All were willing to listen, share, and discuss a crucial question (project) – in this case, trust-building.

Discussion

The perception of the long-term stability of the overall network (enhanced by financial incentives for cooperation and accountability measures for progress) can significantly reduce the mistrust between Israelis and Palestinians. Moreover, it can create an environment for positive, personal interaction that will increase trust levels at the core dyad.

The main challenge in applying this model to the Middle East conflict concerns the creation of incentives for those on the periphery to join and invest in the proposed network. The primary question that arises is "How can incentives be created that will benefit not only the overall network but also the individual players?" This is a particularly complex question when the individual constituencies' needs/benefits contradict the interest(s) of the overall network, and therefore the questions must be addressed in the initial design phase of cooperative projects.

The role of the international community in embedding the Israeli–Palestinian tie cannot be emphasized enough. This is true for all three levels presented in this chapter. Numerous writings have focused on the critical involvements of various members of the international community, such as the role of the Quartet (US, Russia, European Union, and the UN) in trying to foster the Road Map since its initiation. Writings have also documented the role of Norway's government and NGOs (FFO) in the Oslo agreements. While no significant progress was made in

Washington during the bilateral talks agreed upon at the Madrid Conference in 1991, under the auspices of Norway a secret unofficial channel began operating between Israelis and the PLO. The unofficial talks continued throughout early 1993 and culminated in the initialing of a joint Declaration of Principles (DoP) on August 19, 1993.[37] In the Israeli–Palestinian cooperative efforts, the role of the international community is critical. For example, the funds and monitoring process provided by USAID is critical. As a Palestinian professor of engineering working on joint projects with Israeli Technion professors as well as Egyptian and Jordanian professors put it:

> It is very simple – if there were no German, Belgium, and American organizations which are specifically interested in our cooperative projects – we would not have these projects. If we did not have the opportunity to apply for funds from USAID and have their direct involvement with our cooperative development project, we wouldn't be able to work together. . . [But] because of that we have established at our university a department specializing in the funding process. They work closely with Israelis, Jordanians, and Egyptians to find these opportunities and take full advantage of them.[38]

Another Israeli professor, an expert on water, says,

> These foundations are interested in projects such as sewage and water, but they are also interested in mere cooperation. We apply to these foundations because we know that our cooperative efforts give us an advantage in actually receiving the funds . . . Without these funds it would have been very hard to still go ahead together.[39]

This critical role of third parties goes beyond providing funds. Other functions are equally, or perhaps more, important. I will offer an example of academic cooperation. Since Palestinians and Israelis want to feel equal as partners, neither the Palestinian nor the Israeli side would be willing to have the academic institute of the other side be responsible for coordinating a project, including the management of funds. But the issue is about much more than funds – it is about associating with the other side. For example, a Palestinian researcher would be reluctant to participate in an Israeli-funded project; as one Palestinian interviewee put it:

> I had an Israeli academic call and ask if I would join him on a proposal to an Israeli foundation, but I refused. If I did [join him], then I would be coded as working for the Israelis in my society. Instead, I suggested we apply with the same proposal to a German foundation, which did end up funding the project.[40]

Summary and Conclusions

Drawing from the social network understanding of social interaction, I have presented empirical scenarios of what is needed to rebuild trust between Israelis and Palestinians. I have suggested that long-term projects supported by the international community are one important strategy for the buildup of trust between Israelis and Palestinians. These projects lock in the dyadic (contentious) tie for a long-term commitment. Nevertheless, several questions remain a challenge.

First, we already have evidence that some projects which took place since the Oslo agreement of 1993 have failed. For example, many of the People-to-People efforts which sprang up as a result of Annex 4 of the Oslo agreement have significantly decreased in face of the last al-Aqsa *Intifada*.[41] This decrease is a natural outcome of the objective and subjective difficulties which occur when an active war between Israelis and Palestinians breaks out. First, constraints are imposed as a result of the war – such as movement of individuals from one area to another. At present, for security purposes Israelis are prohibited by law from traveling to Palestinian areas, and Palestinians are reluctant to cross to Israeli-controlled areas; therefore, their journey now entails hours of waiting in roadblocks and days of uncertainty about the permits. Second, subjective perceptions about the other's society play an important role in the decision to travel to the other's side. Despite these difficulties, ongoing People-to-People efforts seem to be flourishing and renewing energy when any possible hopes for peace emerge, as they did immediately following the death of Chairman Arafat. However, even in these efforts the role of the international community is of paramount importance.

For large-scale cooperative projects to succeed at the Government-to-Government level, there must be real and public monetary incentives for cooperation, a structured accountability for progress with clear, timely, achievable and measurable outcomes for actors at the periphery and – more importantly – for Israelis and Palestinians. Moreover, it is argued that indeed the projects conceived since the Oslo agreement that failed to reach their stated goals did in fact create social capital and public goods which have been predominantly overlooked.[42] These have increased the level of trust for participants themselves, and I would argue that in time of possible peace, the social capital that resulted from the (otherwise failed) projects will provide the first basis on which to connect the two societies.

For the Government-to-Government level project to take place, there first has to be a realistic, supportive leadership at the political level. For example, Israelis and Palestinians have dealt with water management issues since the Oslo agreements. However, many times Israelis suggested projects which would have created real advantage and assistance in water management for Palestinians but they were stymied by Chairman Arafat for one political reason or another. As suggested by an Israeli water commission delegate who continuously works with his Palestinian counterpart:

> At one point we were discussing the issue of water desalination. We both agreed that it is an important issue. I asked for their data, [and] he brought me the data, such as population growth and all the other relevant data. We did the research, found out about their needs and how we would be able to plan together. At one point he returned and told me to get off the topic. I asked, "Why?" [and] he told me that he was told to get off the topic. Every month I asked – "Let's talk about it" – he said, "I can't." It was stuck at the political level – namely, from what I understood – Arafat. Now I hope that things will change.[43]

Another challenge to the success of the proposed model is the possible egoistic interests of the peripheral actors that could act as a deterrent to success. To illustrate this point, one could argue that actor A in Figure 7.4 is the United States, who for egoistic reasons has an interest in keeping Israelis and Palestinians apart, thereby enjoying a structural advantage. To deal with this challenge, one should consider that the public good produced by the overall network (and considered in the planning of the network) must be valid for all participants of the network, and benefits must be fairly shared. Namely, there must be real (economic as well as other) interests that are great enough for each of the international participants from their egoistic point of calculations. On the more abstract level, in the case of American and/or Chinese interests, bringing Israelis and Palestinians to a better place should have a clear and inarguable benefit for that actor, such as the reduction of international terrorism. While the benefit of any projects based on this model must clearly be of long-term benefit to both the Israelis and the Palestinians, the clear interests of the peripheral actors over the long term must also be carefully taken into account.

Most research and analysis of the Israeli Palestinian conflict has focused on the dyadic level – the Israel–Palestinian relationship.[44] In this chapter I suggest that this tie should be considered in the context of a larger network of actors. I apply our understanding of the characteristics of trust and its association with an arrangement of actors in a network. The model assumes rational actors and does not account for more ideological motivations.[45]

The accounting of micro-level dimensions of the Israeli–Palestinian conflict, though of critical importance, is not the focus of this chapter and lies beyond its scope. Rather, I suggest a macro-level approach precisely designed to move beyond the daily effects of destructive actions on the ground which seem to continually shape the situation in the Middle East. If actors who are experiencing these challenges understand that the overarching network is stable and working despite the daily challenges, then they will trust in the long-term survival of the network (their society) and its ability to face these challenges. The trust in the stability of the network, and the repeated positive interactions of Israelis and Palestinians as the core of this network, will create and reinforce a long-term, stable trust level between Israelis and Palestinians.

Yet a critical question remains – how to rebuild the trust level between the parties and how to avoid dependency of the peace process on particular individuals. As suggested in this chapter, the buildup of social capital – which is based on long-term infrastructural projects, NGO interaction, and People-to-People projects – answers these questions to some degree. My conclusion is that these efforts will also overcome the dependency on particular individuals whose own interests have until now steered the course of Middle East politics. The combined efforts of these three structural entities has the potential to supersede individualistic leadership, bringing the Middle East to a possible peace and making it a better place for all of its people.

Acknowledgment

I am in debt to Deborah Schlueter, Roger Leenders, Joseph Ginat, and participants of the Denver conference for their comments. Please refer all inquiries to Shaul Gabbay <sgabbay@du.edu>.

Notes

1   See Muzafer Sherif, *In Common Predicament: Social Psychology of Intergroup Conflict and Cooperation* (Boston: Houghton Mifflin Company, 1966) for an extensive pioneering discussion on inter-group deterrence.

2   W. I. Thomas, "The Definition of the Situation" in Jerome G. Manis and Bernard N. Meltzer (eds.), *Symbolic Interaction: A Reader in Social Psychology, 3rd edition* (Boston: Allyn and Bacon, 1978), pp. 331–36.

3   R. Ziegler, "Trust and the Reliability of Expectations," *Rationality and Society*, Vol. 10 (1998), pp. 427–50; Shaul M. Gabbay and R. Th.-A. J. Leenders, "Creating Trust through Narrative Strategy," *Society and Rationality*, Vol. 15.4 (2003), pp. 509–39; R. Hardin, "The Street-Level Epistemology of Trust," *Politics and Society,* Vol. 21 (1993), pp. 505–29; R. Hardin, "Conceptions and Explanations of Trust" in K. S. Cook (ed.), *Trust in Society* (New York: Russell Sage Foundation, 2001), pp. 3–39.

4   The issue of perception has been elaborated when "the psychological barrier" (Shalhabi, Ben Meir, 2004) has been discussed. In this chapter I propose a structural approach for how to tackle this "psychological barrier" inherent in people's perception. I propose a network approach for building (or rebuilding) trust between Israelis and Palestinians.

5   Shaul M. Gabbay and Amy J. Stein, "Embedding Social Structure in Technological Infrastructure: Constructing Regional Social Capital for a Sustainable Peace in the Middle East" in J. Wright (ed.), *The Political Economy of the Middle East Peace* Process (Boston and London: Routledge, 1999), pp.154–80; Illan Talmud and Shaul Mishal, "The Network State: Triangular

Relations in Middle Eastern Politics," *International Journal of Contemporary Sociology*, Vol. 37, No. 2 (2000), pp. 176–207.

6　See Shaul M. Gabbay and R. Th.-A. J. Leenders, "SCS: The Structure of Advantage and Disadvantage" in R. Th. A. J. Leenders and S. M. Gabbay (eds.), *Corporate Social Capital and Liability* (Boston and Amsterdam: Kluwer Academic Publishers, 1999) for the use of the terms 'Social Capital Management' "the purposeful alteration of social structure to fit players' goals," p. 491.

7　For an informative discussion on managing expectations and their effect on the Oslo outcomes, see R. L. Rothstein, "A Fragile Peace: Could a 'Race to the Bottom' Have Been Avoided?" in R. L Rothstein, M. Maoz and K. Shikaki, *The Israeli–Palestinian Process* (Brighton & Portland: Sussex Academic Press, 2002), pp. 1–30.

8　Shaul M. Gabbay and R. Th-A. Leenders, "SCS: The structure of Advantage and disadvantage" in R. Th-A. Leenders and S. M. Gabbay (eds.) *Corporate Social Capital Liability* (Boston and Amsterdam: Kluwer Academic Publishers, 1999), p. 3.

9　In this case the characteristics of a tie – trust – are the outcome. A critical question that is beyond the scope if this chapter is what comes first, the relationship and/or the characteristic of the relationship. For a pioneering comprehensive discussion on the "what comes first" issue on social networks in friendship ties, see Roger Th.-A. J. Leenders, "Evolution of Friendship and Best Friendship Choices," *Journal of Mathematical Sociology*, Vol. 21 (1997), pp. 133–48.

10　"Tie" vs. "structural form" approaches. See Shaul M. Gabbay and Roger Th.-A. Leenders, "Social Capital of Organizations, " in *Research in the Sociology of Organizations* (New York: JAI Press, 2001), pp. 1–20.

11　James S. Coleman James, *Foundations of Social Theory* (Cambridge, MA: Harvard University Press, 1990).

12　Mark S. Granovetter, "The Strength of Weak Ties," *The American Journal of Sociology*, Vol. 78, No. 6, pp. 1360–80; David Krackhardt, and R. Stern, "Informal Networks and Organizational Crisis: An Experimental Simulation," *Social Psychology Quarterly*, Vol. 51 (1988), pp.123–40; (Granovetter, 1973); Ron S. Burt, *Structural Holes: The Social Structure of Competition* (Cambridge, MA: Harvard University Press, 1992).

13　Shaul M. Gabbay, S*ocial Capital in the Creation of Financial Capital: The Case of Network Marketing* (Champaign: Stipes Publishing, 1997).

14　Roger Th.-A. Leenders, "Evolution of Friendship and Best Friendship Choices," *Journal of Mathematica Sociology*, Vol. 21 (1997), pp. 133–48.

15　It is important to note that the nature of the interaction is of significance. The interaction I am discussing here are of course assumed and important to be positive in nature.

16　See Harrison C. White, *Identity and Control: A Structural Theory of Social Action* (Princeton: Princeton University Press, 1992) for multiplexity of ties as forming identities.

17　A good example for the existence and sanctioning in deviating from these norms is in the Israeli Government's accusations that Crescent ambulances were used to smuggle weapons and deviating from the norms of organizations aimed at working to save lives, thereby enjoying prerogatives in searches.

18 See Klein in this volume.

19 Robert D. Putnam, "The Prosperous Community: Social Capital and Public Life," *American Prospect*, 13 (1993), pp. 35–42; James S. Coleman, *Foundations of Social Theory* (Cambridge, MA: Harvard University Press, 1990); Ron S. Burt, *Structural Holes: The Social Structure of Competition* (Cambridge, MA: Harvard University Press, 1992).

20 I am using the term actor for simplicity reasons assuming interest-driven actors who maximize benefit and minimize cost (Coleman, 1989; Burt, 1992).

21 This illustration assumes that the actors are similar and the only difference is the network.

22 This situation allows the actor to play C and B against each other (Burt, *Structural Holes*).

23 It is important to note that this theoretical analysis assumes that the interdependence among the three actors is equal or other alternative ties will inhibit the equal dependency of each on the network, creating an advantage to one.

24 Brain Uzzi, "The Sources and Consequences of Embeddedness for the Economic Performance of Organizations: The Network Effect," *American Sociological Review*, Vol. 61 (1996), pp. 674–98.

25 See the Geneva Accord for an example of progress at the informal level (Klein, this volume).

26 Abraham Maslow, *Motivation and Personality*, 2nd ed. (Harper & Row, 1970).

27 Also see Ginat and Altman in this volume for the challenge of a halt on violence from both sides, embracing the *hudna*.

28 David Schoenbaum, *The United States and the State of Israel* (New York: Oxford University Press, 1993).

29 Joseph Nevo and Ilan Pappe, *Jordan in the Middle East 1948–1988: The Making of a Pivotal State* (London: Frank Cass, 1994).

30 One also needs to consider the self-interests of each actor.

31 On water issues see Corr in this volume.

32 Shaul M. Gabbay and Amy J. Stein, "Embedding Social Structure in Technological Infrastructure: Constructing Regional Social Capital for a Sustainable Peace in the Middle East" in J. Wright (ed.), *The Political Economy of the Middle East Peace Process* (Boston and London: Routledge, 1999), pp.154–80.

33 Marshal Kaplan, *Planning for Peace: A summery Report of the Forum between Israel, Palestinian and U.S. Leaders* (Aspen, Colorado: Institute for Public Policy, Graduate School of Public Affairs, University of Colorado at Denver, 2003), p. 2.

34 Harrison C. White, *Identity and Control: A Structural Theory of Social Action* (Princeton, NJ: Princeton University Press, 1992).

35 Yossie Beilin, *The Path to Geneva: The Quest for a Permanent Agreement, 1996–2004* (RDV Books, Akashik Books, 2004).

36 A Palestinian Professor of Al-Quds University, Jerusalem – who is working on Joint projects with Professors of the Technion, Israel.

37 Israeli Professor working on joint projects with Palestinian Professors.

38 Interview with a Palestinian Professor of Al-Quds University, Jerusalem.

39 Israeli water commission delegate.

40 Ron Pundak, "From Oslo to Tabba: What went wrong?" in R. L. Rothstein,

M. Maoz and K. Shikaki, *The Israeli–Palestinian Process* (Brighton & Portland: Sussex Academic Press, 2002), pp. 88–113.

41 See Shaul M. Gabbay, "The Paradigmatic Clash: Rationality and Ideology in the Israeli–Palestinian Conflict," paper presented at Association of Israel Studies annual meeting, Arizona, 2005.

PART II

Learning and Making Use of the Past

CHAPTER 8

The Peace with Egypt: President Sadat's Visit Through 1977 Israeli Eyes

SHLOMO GAZIT

I was serving as Head of Israeli military intelligence branch during the November 1977 Sadat visit. Our particular sensitivity pertaining to a possible change in Egyptian policy notwithstanding, and despite the systematic tests begun by us in the form of periodic intelligence assessments (assisted by certain indications determined by us for this purpose), we did not envisage Sadat's initiative or his dramatic visit to Israel. About two months prior to President Sadat's visit to Israel in November 1977 we issued our periodic intelligence assessment, in which we referred to the "peace index" in Egypt, emphasizing that changes had in effect taken place, mainly in Egyptian semantics on the Israeli issue. These, however, were a long way away from indications of Egyptian readiness for peace with Israel, albeit an ongoing follow-up in this respect needed to be maintained.

Anwar Sadat first announced his plan to visit Israel to a group of US Congressmen visiting Cairo after first having visited Israel. During the group's visit to Israel they met with Prime Minister Menachem Begin, and I had in fact attended and delivered an intelligence briefing at that meeting. Begin had spoken of his striving for peace, appealing to the American Congressmen to convey to Sadat his (Begin's) readiness to travel to Cairo and hold peace talks there. More than anything else, this readiness evinced by Begin reflected the tragic paradoxical situation wherein Israel had to respond to every Arab initiative suggested whereas, on the other hand, no one was moved by the lack of Arab response to the offers made by us.

When the report of Sadat's intention to visit Israel was first published, we were at a loss as to how to understand it. At first, we thought it was some sort of public relations gimmick on his part, and that he had not the slightest intention of actually coming to Israel (yes, we were caught up in that concept and we were not ready to acknowledge the possibility of thinking the unthinkable!). It was not until two or three days later that we realized Sadat's stated intention was genuine.

In this chapter, I review specific events, discussions and meetings that occurred within the Israeli Government in which I was involved that I believe are important in considering Arab–Israeli relations since 1977 and today. The content comes from my personal papers. Related are the Motta Gur interviews, the meetings of the intelligence services on the Sadat initiative on the eve of his visit, portions of my summary of that meeting, the three papers written on the basis of the meetings, including possible Israeli reactions to the visit, and discussion with Prime Minister Menachem Begin about the pending visit. The purpose of this chapter is to describe the distrust, confusion, and suspicion that surrounded the announcement and subsequent visit of Sadat to Israel. Despite all the negative perceptions and risk involved, Sadat and Begin took the proverbial "leap of faith" in order to make an effort for peace and reconciliation. These two men and their courage should be seen as examples of how to reach peace in the present, despite all the detractors and negative perceptions emanating from both sides.

The Interview with Motta Gur Reveals Israeli Sincerity

Initially, one man who reacted with extreme doubt to Sadat's intention was Chief of Staff Motta Gur. Motta was about to pay a secret visit to Iran, and he had decided, on his own, to make the Israeli public believe that he was in Israel during the period of his visit. His plan, known only to his bureau chief, was to give an interview to Israel Har'el, a *Yediot Ahronot* correspondent at the time. The interview was to be published four or five days later, once Motta was already well into his visit to Iran. In this interview, he stated his evaluation that Sadat had no intention of proceeding to Israel and that the entire initiative was an act of deception on Egypt's part.

The interview was heavily headlined by the paper, and resulted in thoroughly upsetting the political system. Everyone interpreted it as a clear attempt to sabotage Sadat's initiative. The Prime Minister ordered Defense Minister Weizmann to instruct Motta Gur to return to Israel immediately. A grim talk took place between the two, and Weizmann went to Jerusalem intending to dismiss the chief of staff from his post there and then. Fortunately for the chief of staff, the defense minister's car was involved in an accident en route to Jerusalem, and Weizmann was injured. Thus the handling and intention of firing Gur were postponed.

Intelligence Assessment Talks on the Eve of the Visit

Things then moved at a dizzying pace. Once it was obvious that Sadat was in fact due to arrive in Israel, I held a multi-participant discussion in my office aimed at assessing Sadat's intentions and the possible outcome of the Egyptian move. This was an out of the ordinary discussion and, to the best of my knowledge, unique in its format and number of participants. In addition to the usual research group of Intelligence Branch officers, I invited people from the research branch of the Mossad, the research department of the Foreign Ministry, and academics from Tel Aviv University and the Hebrew University in Jerusalem. For added value, I also invited Aharon (Arele) Yariv, former Intelligence Branch chief and my former commanding officer.

To add a touch of melodrama, I opened the discussion by pressing the button of the tape recorder, from which resounded the Egyptian national anthem; these sounds would, in one week's time, accompany the beginning of the Egyptian President's historic visit to Israel! The meeting itself was fascinating. I consider it one of the most interesting discussions ever held in my office. It was divided into two parts: in the first half, comprising a larger forum, we made attempts to understand the Egyptian move; in the second half, restricted to a far smaller group, we endeavored to draw up our thoughts and considerations as to Israel's possible reaction to the Sadat initiative.

Content of Inter-Service Analysis of the Sadat Initiative as Recorded on November 16, 1977

Opening by Head of Intelligence Branch   These are historic days. I think this is the first ever meeting of an inter-service forum with representatives of all other research elements present, and it has been convened with good reason.

(After playing the Egyptian anthem) –

My first plan was to convene a discussion and posit: "Contrary to what people think – Sadat truly desires peace." However, given the brief time and the lack of relevant intelligence, I decided to convene a symposium instead – a gathering to discuss the subject, a sort of free for all.

Summation by Head of Intelligence Branch   Firstly, I enjoyed the discussion; and Efraim Kam's commendable opening on such a complex issue certainly contributed to the succinct and orderly presentation of all the options. Methodically speaking, such a forum deserves our time every so often. And I intend to distribute the minutes of the discussion.

Now to the gist of the matter, I would like to make one preliminary comment. Last night I met with an Orientalist – a non-Jew, Alan Wolfe, head of the Middle East desk at the CIA – and in the course of our conversation he mentioned an article published in *Foreign Affairs* by Fayiz Sayag to the effect that the entire conflict is made up not of two sides fighting each other, but that each side is caught up in its own individual complexities and trauma. Israel continues to live the trauma of the Holocaust, afraid of an existentialist threat that will destroy it, and the Arabs are enveloped in their own complexities of liberating themselves from imperialism, fearing a desire to regain control over them – and Israel is the tool of imperialism. Therefore, no solution of the conflict as a whole can or will be attained until its emotional, irrational aspect is resolved. And this cannot be done on the spur of the moment. It is a slow and lengthy process. On the other hand, it did not begin today – it dates back many long years. As early as 1965, Habib Bourguiba stood up in Tunis as the first Arab leader to propose peace with Israel. Let us recall how his initiative was received at the time; the boycott that was imposed on him then.

Several things happened after Bourguiba's proposal. The Six-Day War came and the Arab countries became directly involved, anxious to obtain something from us. Our new contacts with the Arabs in the territories created new openings; there were open bridges and understanding existed between us and Jordan – an understanding that deepened and strengthened in "Black September", when we rescued King Hussein from the Syrians. And then came the events in Lebanon.

This is not a process to be resolved in one generation, especially since the years go by and disappear into the past. Nonetheless, progress has been made and we are at a stage where the process is moving forward.

At this point I do not know what resulted from the Sadat initiative, but there has been a revolutionary change in one respect. A year ago, we began discussions on "signs attesting to peace." We said at the time that, on the one hand, it was difficult to spot signs that could be used as litmus tests, as it were; on the other hand, we agreed that developments at that point were mainly of a semantic nature. But what is happening now can no longer be termed semantics!

From the moment of Sadat's arrival here, we no longer have a case for claiming that we need proof of the Arabs' recognition of Israel, regardless of whether another war breaks out between the Arabs and us. (Bear in mind that countries fight one another despite the diplomatic relations prevailing between them.) By his visit, Anwar Sadat confers official recognition upon us. This is the understanding of Menachem Begin, of Jerusalem, and of the Knesset. What is behind Sadat's move? I, for one, believe that Sadat himself still does not know. The test of his initiative does not lie in the visit per se, but in the results that will ensue, and it is my assumption that Sadat is genuinely prepared for two options:

1   The first – he wants and hopes to return from Jerusalem with a tangible achievement.
2   The second – in the event that the talks fail, the idea is that this will expose a "wicked" and intransigent Israel.[1]

Even if he is pessimistic and holds out little hope regarding the first of the two options, he will have accorded us recognition.

Is it possible that he is traveling to Jerusalem with something positive to offer? I agree with what Harkabi said in this respect – that is not the responsibility of the Intelligence Branch. We are responsible for solely *checking out the other side*, albeit this will also greatly depend on Israel. *It invariably takes two to tango!* And Israel's actions – not merely from the ceremonial aspect, but where content is concerned and where the substantive issues come into play – will be of cardinal importance.

Here I agree with those who contend that Sadat has not yet said the last word, and that he may well surprise us when he addresses the Knesset. For instance: "I have appointed X as future ambassador to Israel. He is ready to move here in two months time, provided that progress is made and we reach an agreement." Or perhaps some other gimmick.

It is quite clear to me that Sadat cannot just hold a speech before the Knesset and then go home. He will meet with our top leadership; he will hold talks and will need to be clearer and more detailed in his proposals. All this, as stated earlier, also depends on us.

I do have certain questions:

Why is the Arab world so calm? I reject the claim that this is caused by shock as the only explanation. What is more, we are in possession of intelligence regarding the negative reactions of some Arab leaders, albeit they have said nothing in public.

How do we explain Assad's consent to Sadat's Jerusalem visit when he saw him in Damascus? Sadat's arrival in the Syrian capital in itself implies tacit consent to his initiative (incidentally, the issue may have arisen in a telephone conversation held by the two a week ago).

Perhaps Syria has no wish to add to Sadat's present dilemma, since he is already committed and cannot cancel the visit. A sharp denunciation or personal attack on him would only push him into reaching a separate agreement.

And perhaps Sadat's step in moving towards peace is so spectacular that it cannot be condemned without risking a totally anti-peace reputation? This would be a huge political gain for Israel.

A further reason – leaving for Jerusalem via Damascus could perhaps build a military option. Sadat talks to Assad and explains that the alternatives are either a political solution within Arab parameters, or that Egypt will join the war camp.

I cannot imagine that Egypt is planning a deception and preparing a military surprise for us from inside the Knesset Building. However, in the event of a crisis, the IDF will go on alert on the day following the visit. And yet, there is another way of perceiving this.

We have said that Sadat, on his own initiative, has been moving things forward. He is no Esther Shahamorov (Israeli Olympic athlete) having to jump a hurdle along 400 meters on the way to the finishing line. Sadat has made an about-face of 180 degrees, and is running straight for the tape, with no hurdles to bar the way. To save time and not waste it on "trivialities", he is taking the bull by the horns. Cutting time short is immensely important to him – he has decided that the year 1977 will be decisive.

The agreement signed with us two years ago – according to Sadat and the Intelligence Branch – expires in another year. Yet again, after taking such a step, he has saved himself a year, and, prior to the renewal of the UNDOF mandate on 30 November, he can tell Assad that there is no mandate and no agreement, and that he is in a state of emergency deployment. Will he do that? Who knows. But it is a possibility; it is not a surprise step as H-hour approaches, albeit it is certainly a new situation, on the verge of exploding into a crisis both in Israel and in the world. He has moreover stolen the show from the United States. They want a settlement and would like to prevent a war, but, all of a sudden, they make no more demands; also, they have a vested interest of their own. And the Nobel Peace Prize will go to Anwar Sadat and not to Jimmy Carter!

Where the Americans are concerned, Sadat's stands constitute complete alignment with Carter's positions. No arguments were waged over the borders or over the Palestinians; only on the meaning, the nature of peace. And here, too, he has gone all the way and perhaps even surpassed Carter.

He has taken a further step. We had been thinking in terms of "a portion of land for a portion of peace" and here comes Sadat and tells us: "I am handing you full peace on a silver platter." What about all the land we need to hand back? In order to bargain, he has gone all the way and is pressuring us. Thus whoever wishes to gradate our withdrawal over a 25-year period finds himself faced with a compelling counter claim. He has taken things all the way to the end, clarifying the two options: peace or war!

If it is to be peace, it mainly depends on us, and I must voice a warning about the shock to us in Israel should the move fail and end in naught, let alone the eventuality that Sadat has more to say to us and surprise us during his visit – things that could embarrass us even more. In the event of war – if no progress is made towards a settlement, we will abruptly find ourselves on the brink of a military confrontation.

Given one incidental aspect, two issues may possibly be raised today, during his visit to Damascus:

1   Aligning with Syria to find a solution for Southern Lebanon, in order to extricate the Syrian army.

2　　There can be no going to war while the Syrians are mired there; then everyone will pressure the PLO to pull back 10 km.

It is important also to emphasize this possibility, as it could signify the intention to wage an inter-Arab war.

In the longer term, it is difficult today to make predictions where the question of war/no war is concerned. However, a highly important layer has been added here on the road to peace – no longer can there be talk of "Israel the leper" or "Israel the monster." The effect left by the visit will remain even in the event of another war, and also after it.

Finally, there is the point reiterated yesterday in the Knesset – the under-tone of "respect him but suspect him". As the Intelligence Branch, we must underline this to the fullest. Mention was made of the various moves made in Egypt – moves that trouble us. But if we exacerbate these moves, matters could swiftly cross from one pole to the other, to the pole of war.

Analysis and Recommended Israeli Action

We issued three papers – one written by the Research Department and widely and normally circulated. This paper reflected the first part of our discussion: an analysis of the Egyptian move. Two further papers were written by me: the first was similar in content to the department paper, but (as was my habit from time to time) far shorter, in which the issues were sharpened, even if this was done at the expense of precise and cautious formulation.

The third paper was different; I had never issued such a paper before. It was an assessment of Israel's possible reactions and how Egypt was likely to respond to each of these. This third paper infuriated Prime Minister Menachem Begin: "Since when does the Head of Intelligence Branch tell the Government what to do?" I had naively assumed that given the prevailing extraordinary circumstances – when, for the first time since the establishment of the State, the greatest leader of the Arab world planned to come to this country to talk peace – Israel would not insist on formali-ties and would moreover be delighted to receive evaluations and recommendations prompted by our perception and understanding of Sadat and his initiative. In any event, there was no one to come to my defense at that time. The chief of staff himself was facing near-dismissal (quite possibly the reaction directed against me was caused to no small extent by the anger at Motta), and the minister of defense lay injured in hospital.

Under these circumstances, I had no choice. I complied with the Prime Minister's demand and requested all addressees to return the paper written by me, in order to destroy it. I have in my possession the summary of the discussion on this issue held in my office. It was my custom to make a note of all the main points of every important discussion, and I had been the speaker when we came to the summary; I had operated the tape recorder and was therefore able to render my summation word for word. The summary to the paper of recommendations reads as follows:

My Opening Remarks

At the previous intelligence assessment discussion, we said that Israel's stand would be an important component in the moves anticipated in the near future.

Hence my first question: What can Israel do to prevent Sadat's trip from ending in failure – without, of course, prostrating ourselves on the floor and agreeing to be "raped"? Point two, and this is the other side of the coin – if Sadat's initiative is about to fail, do we have anything to suggest – and if so, what – to prevent the onus of the resulting crisis from falling on our shoulders in all its severity? And I return to the basic assumption – in our struggle for US support – how do we conclude this chapter without causing the Americans to stand by Sadat?

Summation of the Discussion

1   I will not summarize anything at this stage. I have, however, received sufficient ideas and reasoning from you and I don't have much to add that is new.

2   Nonetheless, I would like to sharpen a number of points:

A.   To me, Israeli public opinion is of paramount importance. Sadat's visit will elevate the people of Israel to new heights, and it would be extremely dangerous later to plunge it into the deep pit of serious crisis and military confrontation. This may not fit Sadat's "horrible" prediction (if no understanding is reached), but it would be enormously problematic for us domestically speaking, and would also create a serious crisis for Israel with the Jewish diaspora. Therefore – we must manage the situation in a manner that will prevent such a crisis.

B.   We need to remember – there are tactics and there is strategy. We must on no account despair of the strategy – particularly because of the first point, the moral point. It is incumbent upon us to give our people the maximum sense that we have given peace a chance. We must on no account be small-minded and be seen as blocking the way to Sadat's generous heart.

C.   Concurrently, it is highly important to take the right steps on the tactical level.

D.   As far as possible, we need to preempt Sadat, to precede him, to come up with initiatives before he sets foot in Israel. If possible, we need to steal the limelight in which he planned to bask. We have the possibility to make gestures, and we should not wait to make them. For instance:

    i. A declaration on halting Israeli settlements until clarification of the Egyptian initiative is completed. And we will be the ones to determine the timetable in this respect.

    ii. A further gesture is possible on the subject of AMOCO and the oil surveys on the shores of the Bay of Suez.

Declarations such as those suggested here could well steal Sadat's thunder and gain points for us where international information is concerned.

E. I accept the stand presented here, namely that Sadat cannot be presented as a traitor to the pan-Arab cause. The struggle must be directed with an inter-Arab view, and our efforts must be aimed at seeing the other Arab leaders join the Sadat initiative, even if we would also be pleased to reach a separate settlement.

F. We need to play word games, particularly words that will have a major media impact.

G. My personal approach regarding the character of a lasting settlement with Egypt accords with the lines of June 1967, and I endorse the proposal and the formula of "a settlement based on the '67 borders", and the Panama Canal is a model that suits us. In other words, an agreement that will not be implemented from one day to the next, but will contain elements to be carried out only after a period of 30 years, or a similar, even longer timetable. The final target will, however, be agreed upon in advance.

H. This must also be a form of progress built layer upon layer, with a solution requiring a continued military presence, an agreement on leasing territory, etc. The most important point, in my opinion, was raised by Yehoshafat Harkabi. We need to insist on reciprocity, on the fact that Sadat's appearance in Jerusalem should naturally enable Menahem Begin to visit Cairo. Making such a claim and insisting thereon will give us some time; it will embarrass Sadat but, also, vice versa – making such a move will help to break the ice. In any event, I feel that we should hold back with this tactical gimmick until the very last moment, until the speech held to welcome Sadat at Ben-Gurion Airport.

I. As to the meaning of peace – if my words were not properly understood earlier, then obviously this visit is far from the solution. But Sadat's initiative has without doubt neutralized the case for us. We can no longer contend that we do not believe the Arab intentions.

J. Another important idea was raised here by Arele Yariv. This visit must not end as a onetime happening. True, even if it were to be a one-time move, it will still be a dramatic event that will leave its mark even if we were to find ourselves in yet another war. We must, however, endeavor to extract even more – we need to reach a process of ongoing contacts, of rapprochement and continuing drama.

K. The last point pertains to the United States. In this respect, I agree with Meir Elran, who suggested that we remain coordinated with the US – to a certain limit:

    i. Where Sadat is concerned, he needs to realize that the Americans do not have Israel in their back pocket. The US is without doubt a super-power, but not everything that is good for Washington is good for Israel or Egypt.

    ii. I do not rely on US ability to prevent the leaking of any tactical move made by us – thereby leading to its disruption and failure.

    iii. All in all, however, coordination is needed. We realize full well that we need to live with Washington for a long time to come!

Meeting the Prime Minister Prior to the Visit

Following the discussions held by us, I made an attempt to verify that the Prime Minister would indeed convene a cabinet discussion on the significance of Sadat's visit. It did not occur to me for one moment that the government would not hold such a discussion or attempt to shape a policy prior to the visit. I called Brigadier General Efraim Poran, the Prime Minister's military secretary every single day. He repeatedly assured me that he was pestering the Prime Minister on this subject.

The days passed and nothing happened. Then, on Friday morning (November 18, 1977), one day before the Egyptian President's plane would land in Israel, I received an urgent summons to proceed to Jerusalem for a discussion with the Prime Minister. I was informed that the chief of staff and the head of the Mossad (Yitzhak Hofi, known as Haka) had also been invited to attend, and that a helicopter was standing by for us at Sdeh Dov airport. I was certain that at last the Government was about to discuss the significance of the visit.

We found the Prime Minister's Bureau in uproar and confusion. Media figures from all over the world were milling about, as were *Beqez* technicians who were there to set up communications systems prior to the dramatic event.

We were invited to enter the Prime Minister's room. I was surprised to note that we entered his study and not the conference room. Two people were in the room – the Prime Minister and Deputy Prime Minister, Professor Yig'al Yadin.

I was astonished by Mr Begin's question, and was not prepared for it in the slightest: "As we all know, the Egyptian President is arriving tomorrow, and the Deputy Prime Minister has asked me anxiously whether this initiative is nothing more than a deceptive ruse prefacing an immediate Egyptian military offensive against us. What does the Chief of Intelligence Branch think?"

I was stunned, and needed a brief breathing space to collect my thoughts before answering: "While we have witnessed tension and alert status in the Egyptian army during recent days, no indication exists that this is an initiative for an Egyptian attack. The alert came about due to misunderstandings and misinterpretations of our activity in the Sinai and is also linked to the tension on the Libyan border. In short – there is no reason to fear a military surprise."

The Prime Minister directed the same question at the head of the Mossad, who replied: "As you know, we do not maintain close monitoring of military activity in Egypt. At any rate, so far as we know, I totally agree with the assessment of the Head of Intelligence Branch."

The question was then asked of the chief of staff: "After all, you have claimed from the outset that the whole initiative is an act of deception. What, then, is your evaluation as to what lies in store for us tomorrow?" And Motta, who was feeling most uncomfortable at this point, also said that he agreed with my assessment.

Then the Prime Minister turned to Yig'al Yadin – "What do you recommend under these circumstances?" And Yadin, without batting an eyelid, said – "I suggest giving instructions for the immediate mobilization of two armored divisions."

The three of us tried to protest; I said that I considered this as harboring the risk of a political catastrophe. It would be interpreted as planned sabotage on our part of an Egyptian effort to reach a peace agreement with us.

Both the chief of staff and the head of the Mossad joined me in their reservations over this idea. But the Prime Minister summed up: "I will not make a decision on this matter here and now. Since the Deputy Prime Minister is currently also the acting Minister of Defense, I leave it to your (plural) consideration. Whatever you agree with him will be acceptable to me."

Yadin added: "We will in any case meet this afternoon at five, and we can discuss it again then."

We returned to the waiting helicopter and asked the pilot to land us immediately at Tel Hashomer Hospital; we wanted to ask for Ezer Weizmann's help.

We found Ezer lying in bed, all of him bruised and bandaged, one leg suspended in a cast. We explained what had happened, and asked him to intervene – "Save us from those madmen in Jerusalem," we requested.

Weizmann phoned the Prime Minister there and then, informing him that although he was confined to a hospital bed, he was still among the living and understood what had occurred; he requested that no decision be taken without first obtaining his consent. And that settled this problem.

I do not know what Menachem Begin's intention was. Was he in fact prepared, in such fateful circumstances, to leave the decision on mobilizing reserves to Professor Yadin, without taking into account any additional considerations? That is exactly what his decision could have meant.

At the time, I was very angry that the Prime Minister had failed to initiate a prior discussion to assess the coming visit. As time passed, I changed my mind. I saw him repeat the same stratagem eight months later, on the eve of the Israeli delegation's departure for the Camp David talks. Albeit the government was convened for a discussion on that occasion, but this consisted mainly of a presentation of the data that had been prepared for the delegation prior to its departure – without any debate or attempt to firm up any stands. After that, I think I understood what he had meant. Begin did not want to tie his own hands by making arbitrary decisions before the talks began. He realized that it would have been impossible to convene the government without its making such decisions.

Note

1   Some two years later I was working at Harvard University's Center for International Affairs. A colleague of mine was Ambassador Takhsin Basheer, formerly the right hand of Gamal Abdel Nasser and, subsequently, of Sadat. We talked a great deal about that period, and Takhsin told me that Sadat had called him just before leaving for Jerusalem and had made clear that he had no idea what kind of message he would bring back to Cairo. He instructed Takhsin Basheer to plan an extensive information campaign, in which Sadat would blame Israel for the failure of his trip.

CHAPTER 9

Normal Relations without Normalization: The Evolution of Egyptian–Israeli Relations, 1979–2006 – the Politics of Cold Peace

ELIE PODEH

March 26, 2004 marked the twenty-fifth anniversary of the Egyptian–Israeli peace treaty – the first formal agreement signed between Israel and an Arab country – yet no official ceremonies were held either in Israel or Egypt to celebrate this event. The fact that such an important occasion passed unacknowledged was a true indication that something indeed was awry in Egyptian–Israeli relations. According to article three of the treaty, the "normal relationship established between them [Egypt and Israel] will include full recognition, diplomatic, economic and cultural relations, termination of the economic boycott and discriminatory barriers to the free movement of people and goods."[1] Although some of these provisions were implemented along the years, the peace between the two countries, as a whole, largely remained frozen or "cold" – a term often used in Israeli public discourse.[2] While the academic terminology is more nuanced with regard to these relations – hostile peace,[3] distrustful relations,[4] peaceful confrontation[5] – all terms reflect nevertheless a significant measure of coldness.

Cold peace is a situation characterized by the absence of war and threats of force. According to Benjamin Miller, it is typified by five features: first, the underlying issues of the conflict are in the process of being moderated and reduced, but are not fully resolved. Second, the existence of revisionist groups in one or more of the regional states. Third, there are formal agreements but relations are conducted mainly through inter-governmental agencies with strong limitations on non-governmental activity. Fourth, there exist contingency plans that take into account the possibility of war. And, finally, there is a conscious attempt to moderate the level of conflict through negotiations and security and crisis-prevention regimes. Miller concludes that in a situation of cold peace "there is still a danger of the use of force in the longer run despite the formal diplomatic relations between the parties."[6] The Israeli–Egyptian treaty, according to this definition, is indeed a cold peace; yet several additional features, unique to this relationship, have dictated its "warmth" level. In general, however, though their bilateral relations have moved along a "cold-warm" continuum, they could usually be placed near the cold end.

This chapter aims at assessing the reasons that led to the cold peace and unraveling the mechanisms enabling its endurance. Conceivably, problems in bilateral relations emanate from difficulties on both sides. The focus here, however, is on Egyptian behavior, while Israel's contribution to the cold peace will be only briefly discussed. It is surprising that in spite of the importance of the subject for Israeli–Arab relations, there has been no comprehensive study of this experiment.[7]

The main argument posited here is that warm relations with Israel are not a domestic or regional necessity for Egypt. In many ways, a warm peace is a liability rather than an asset. The treaty is part of a package deal in which Egypt enjoys formidable economic and financial assistance from the US and the West in general, necessary to alleviate the internal socioeconomic burden. Moreover, the resulting stability allows for greater Arab and Western investment. Consequently, Egypt has had no incentive to move from cold to warm peace – a move that may threaten its domestic stability and regional standing. Thus, the cold peace strategy has been a deliberate and calculated policy meant to achieve certain political gains; it was not a vague process of trial and error, as claimed by Itamar Rabinovich.[8] Change in Israel's relations with the Palestinians and Syria may warm Israeli–Egyptian relations but the structural constraints, in my view, would hamper a dramatic change.

In broad terms, the cold peace is the outcome of three Egyptian constraints. First, it is a bilateral agreement that collides with the multilateral nature of the Arab regional system in which Egypt has been playing a pivotal role. Put differently, the Egyptian self-perception of Arab leadership constrains its maneuverability since it has to adopt certain policies – particularly with regard to the Palestinian problem, the core of Arab politics – which are bound to alienate Israel. In a situation in which most Arab states still eschew formal recognition of Israel, greater Egyptian involvement in Arab politics *ipso facto* means a narrow interpretation of the peace treaty. Moreover, any scheme (particularly if initiated by the West) that may threaten Egypt's perceived leadership (while elevating that of Israel) is bound to raise Egyptian antagonism.

Second, from an ideological perspective there is a clash between Egyptian and Israeli identities. Egyptian identity includes Arab and Muslim elements, while Israeli identity has Jewish and Zionist components. None of the elements of the Israeli identity seem to impede peaceful relations with Egypt (except, perhaps, for a minority advocating the creation of Greater Eretz-Israel). Though the local territorial dimension in the Egyptian identity is dominant, the Arab and Muslim components may pose a problem: pan-Arabism sees Palestine as part of the Arab homeland, while Islamic thinking sees Palestine as a sacred Muslim land. Both ideologies, at least literally, are committed to its liberation from its Jewish-Zionist usurpers. President Anwar al-Sadat's success in temporarily insulating the Egyptian identity from its Arab and Islamic influences facilitated the peace treaty. Yet, the recent reinvigoration of the Islamic component once more poses a barrier to warmer Israeli–Egyptian relations.

The psychological barriers created by the transmission of negative perceptions of the "other" added a third constraint responsible for the cold peace. The media, the education system, literature, art, and even historiography perpetuated the negative image, which was crystallized during long years of conflict. With the signing of the peace treaty no serious attempt was made to change ingrained perceptions by providing balanced information or by confronting anti-Israeli and anti-Semitic propaganda. This was mutually destructive since Israeli perceptions of Egypt were heavily influenced by the image Egyptians were believed to have of Israel.[9]

As a result of these constraints, Egypt opted for the strategy of a normal peace, which was interpreted in Israel as cold peace. In Arab terminology, there exists an important difference between "normal relations" (*'alaqat tabi'iyyia*) and "normalization" (*tatbi'*). The former means a state of non-belligerency, while maintaining minimal – no more than the necessary – diplomatic and economic contacts. It precludes normalization as stipulated in the peace treaty, but supports specific, one-timed measures necessary for the promotion of a certain policies or interests.[10] In contrast, normalization means a higher degree of relations in all spheres, particularly in the non-political fields, such as economy, tourism and culture (a situation more equivalent to the term "warm peace"[11]).

The fact that Egypt is a hierarchical state and society means that most activity is vertical, that the state is able to enforce its will on society and that links with other states tend to be on the official level.[12] This means that in the absence of a networked civil society, the government can use all state agencies (such as media and education) to promote its policies. Thus, in order to explain the reasons for the cold peace it is necessary to analyze Egypt's official behavior, in light of the constraints mentioned above. What follows is an attempt to deal with each constraint in greater detail. But first a short historical note is due.

Historical Note

The history of Egyptian–Israeli relations from war to peace in the twentieth century is not the subject of this essay.[13] Suffice here to say that since 1979, the peace treaty has been fully upheld by both sides, even during periods of crises, such as the Lebanese War (1982) and the two Palestinian uprisings (1987–91; 2000–4). In many ways, the treaty was a positive precedent, as it proved to be stable, durable, irreversible and duplicable.[14] According to another view, the peace is not fully stable, as the parties do not entirely exclude the possibility of using military force or even the threat of it. Yaacov Bar-Siman-Tov argued, therefore, that peace is in a transitional stage towards stabilization.[15] Whether fully or partially stable, Israeli–Egyptian relations have been considered cold, though the level of "coldness" has fluctuated along the years. Relations between 1979 and 2006 can be divided into six sub-periods:[16]

1   *1979–82:* Relatively warm ties, reflected in 52 agreements signed on various bilateral issues, characterized this period. These agreements were meant to signify the essence of normalization, though eventually most of them were not implemented after Sadat's assassination (October 1981). In spite of the positive effect of Israel's withdrawal from Sinai (April 1982) the Lebanon War (June 1982) soured relations.
2   *1982–92:* Cold relations as a result of domestic and regional pressures on Egypt following the Lebanese war, which led, inter alia, to the recalling of its ambassador. Further reasons for the cool ties: Egypt's desire to return to the Arab world, the failure of the autonomy talks and the dispute over Taba (resolved in 1988).
3   *1992–96:* The 1993 Oslo agreements and the regional economic conferences improved the regional atmosphere, leading to Egypt's growing cooperation with the Yitzhak Rabin government.
4   *1996–2000:* The collapse of the Oslo process and the election of the right-wing Benjamin Netanyahu government in Israel once more soured relations. The rise of Ehud Barak in 1999 improved the situation only temporarily.
5   *2000–2004:* The outbreak of the second Palestinian *Intifada* led to an almost complete freeze of relations. The Egyptian ambassador is recalled.
6   *2005–?:* Signs of improvement in the political (the release of the Israeli detainee 'Azzam 'Azzam and the return of the Egyptian ambassador) and economic (the signing of the Qualifying Industrial Zone, QIZ)

spheres in light of changes in the regional and international arenas. (US President George W. Bush's reelection; Yasser 'Arafat's death and official end of the *Intifada*; Israel's Disengagement Plan and withdrawal from the Gaza Strip). Hamas's election led to an escalation in Israeli–Palestinian relations, resulting in greater Egyptian diplomatic involvement.

This periodization shows that concrete political events were primarily responsible for the fluctuations in relations. Yet, even during periods of relative warmth, Israeli–Egyptian relations suffered from structural problems, ensuring their freeze at a certain level. In the words of Bar-Siman-Tov: relations "never transcended a minimal security and political cooperation that was required to maintain the peace."[17] The next section will analyze these structural constraints by focusing on three clusters: the political–strategic dimension; the economic sphere; and cultural aspects.

The Political–Strategic Dimension

Egypt's Place in the Arab World

Egypt's Arab identity began to crystallize in the inter-war years (1919–39). During this period, Egyptians became increasingly aware of their cultural and linguistic affinity with the Arabs. With independence in 1936, Egypt began playing a growing role in the emerging Arab system – a process that was reflected in the establishment of the Arab League in 1945 and the placing of its headquarters in Cairo. This attested to the fact that Egypt was a leading Arab state, if not actually *the* leader. Over the years, Egypt's central position in the Arab system was based on some tangible assets, such as military and human capabilities, and some intangible ones, such as geo-strategic location, regime legitimacy, domestic stability, pan-Arab ideology, cultural centrality, charismatic leadership, as well as self-perception of Arab leadership. Each of these attributes weighed differently along the years, yet their existence, coupled by a willingness to make use of them by various methods of influence, ensured Egypt's central position in the Arab system. The Israeli–Egyptian peace treaty in 1979 led to a temporary exclusion of Egypt from the Arab world, but since Iraq's invasion of Kuwait in 1990 Egypt returned to play a leading Arab role.[18]

One of the results of the peace treaty was Israel's growing involvement in regional affairs. While in the past it was regionally ostracized and boycotted, in the post-1979 period Israel could affect, and even set the agenda, of regional politics. Moreover, a regional system dominated militarily and economically by Israel could jeopardize Egypt's perceived leading role. Consequently, the latter acted to forestall such a development. The Israeli–Egyptian competition, or the desire to maintain a certain balance of power, manifested itself at least twice: during the negotiations of the Arms Control and Regional Security (ACRS) multilateral group in 1992–95, which also dealt with the issue of the Israeli nuclear capability and the review of the Non-Proliferation Treaty (NPT) in 1995; and the dialogue over the vision of the New Middle East or the concept of the Middle Easternism (*al-sharq awsatiyya*).

I The ACRS Talks and the Nuclear Issue

Following the international peace conference in Madrid in 1991, several multilateral groups were established, chief of which was the ACRS group, which included Israel, twelve Arab states and over 30 parties from outside the region.[19] Egypt believed that the nuclear issue must be on the ACRS agenda, including Israel's commitment to sign the NPT. At the root of the Egyptian demand was the argument that in spite of the peace treaty, Egypt's national security was threatened by Israel's nuclear superiority. "No other country in the world," the Egyptian strategic thinker 'Abdel Moneim Sa'id 'Ali said, "can be dependent on the good intentions of a former adversary." He further argued that in the absence of nuclear balance in the area, no mutual deterrence was possible as in the case of the Cold War. In such a way, deterrence was dependent on the decision of the monopolistic state (Israel).[20] This logic led President Hosni Mubarak to propose in April 1980 to transform the Middle East into a zone free of weapons of mass destruction (WMDFZ) – a proposal formally submitted to the UN in April 1990.[21]

During the ACRS talks, Egypt insisted that all parties in the region should adhere to the NPT. In late 1994, it escalated the campaign to obtain Israel's signature and ratification of the NPT. The immediate reason for that policy was the convening of the NPT review and extension conference in April 1995, which seemed to be the last Arab opportunity – perhaps with the support of the US – to pressure Israel. The fact that the peace process progressed rapidly at that time raised fears in Egypt that it would be left behind and that the conflict would be resolved without the nuclear issue addressed. Thus, beyond security considerations Egypt's primary concern was related to the regional order: the distribution of power and influence in the post-peace Middle East period. In other words, Egypt's leading position was jeopardized.[22] Eventually, in late 1995, the ACRS talks were suspended so that they would not adversely affect Israeli–Egyptian relations further.

The dispute over the nuclear issue and NPT reflected the duality of the relations: the existence of a strategic dialogue, but which led to the break-down of the talks in an acrimonious way. Thus, Emily Landau concluded,

Egypt developed an ongoing interest in maintaining this rivalry with Israel as a source of power and influence, but at the same time both were interested in continuing the dialogue and not jeopardizing the peace treaty.[23] 'Abdel Moneim Sa'id 'Ali defined it somewhat differently, arguing that the tension between Israel and Egypt on that issue stemmed from divergent hidden agendas concerning the future of the Middle East.[24]

2 Middle Easternism

In 1991, following the Iraqi invasion of Kuwait, a new thinking emerged in the Arab world, mainly among Egyptian intellectuals. Appearing in the wake of a crisis that fundamentally shook the Arab world, the new thinking envisaged a new Middle East – comprising the Arab states, Israel, Turkey and Iran – as a major political arena, replacing the old, and what seemed outdated, notion of the Arab system. The idea of Middle Easternism (*al-sharq awsatiyya*), as it came to be known, gained momentum with the Oslo Accords (1993) and the Middle East Economic Conferences (1994–95), which seemed to transform Israel's place in regional affairs.[25] The publication of and wide exposure given to a book on the New Middle East by Israel's foreign minister, Shimon Peres, was interpreted as proof of Israel's desire to play such a prominent role in the new system.[26]

The Arab debate over this concept reflected a genuine fear of Israeli hegemony due to its powerful economy, advanced army and technology, nuclear capability and its close ties with the US. Most of the Arab intellectuals favoring this concept emphasized that Israel should keep a low profile in the new system. The idea of an Israeli hegemony in a Middle Eastern system was particularly menacing for Egypt, since it was bound to undermine its aspirations for leadership.[27] From an Egyptian perspective, therefore, the logical response was to slow down the normalization process with Israel. In this connection one might understand why Mubarak viewed with apprehension Israeli moves in the Gulf and North Africa, which stood to dwarf Egypt's economic and political role in the Arab world (see also the Economic Dimension, below).[28]

Domestic Opposition

The existing literature has largely ignored or underestimated the internal reasons for Egypt's cold peace. Yet, there are strong undercurrents that disapprove the treaty for ideological and/or political reasons. The Muslim Brotherhood – the largest and most organized Islamic organization – as well as more radical fundamentalist groups, such as *al-Jama'ah al-Islamiyya* and *al-Jihad*, have consistently preached against Israel and Zionism, which – in their view – usurped Palestine. Though the Islamic groups cannot form parties based on religious ideology, Islamic members occupy seats in parliament on an independent basis and further their ideology. The strengthening of the Islamic forces in parliament following the November 2005 elections, increasing from 17 to 88 (23% of the seats), makes it even harder for the regime to ignore their voices. Moreover, Islamic representatives control most of the trade unions, as well other state and civil society associations. The opposition against Israel on Islamic grounds is closely associated with a measure of solidarity with the Palestinians (see below) and a conviction that Israel was born in sin (see below). All this amounted to a heavy burden on the regime, whose legitimacy has often been questioned by these groups. While the regime has harshly fought against the threats posed by the Islamic groups (sometimes by violent means), it has allowed a measure of anti-Israeli activity as an outlet for the expression of grievances. In other words, the regime did not curb Islamic rhetoric and activity against Israel since they indirectly strengthened its legitimacy. And though it proclaimed that the Islamic activity is a reflection of political pluralism in Egypt, Mubarak's authoritarian regime could have easily prevented this activity, but found it useful for its purposes.[29]

The Palestinian Problem

Observers and academics have repeatedly argued that the Palestinian problem has been the single most important issue adversely affecting Israeli–Egyptian relations. According to this argument, there is a strong linkage between the two issues and only a solution to the Israeli–Palestinian conflict can bring a real warming in Israeli–Egyptian relations.[30] Historically, as a leading Arab state, Egypt has felt a strong commitment to and expressed certain responsibility for the Palestinian problem. This was manifested in 'Abd al-Nasser's policy during the 1960s, as well as Sadat's attempt to address the issue in the Camp David Accords, in September 1978. The fact that these leaders eventually concentrated on Egypt' problems made the Palestinian issue all the more important, at least rhetorically, in its foreign policy. In addition, the fact that each aspirant for Arab leadership was compelled to show commitment to, and solidarity with, this core issue of Arab politics meant that Egypt had to display a rigid attitude *vis-à-vis* Israel and the US on that issue.[31]

In the two Palestinian uprisings Egypt found itself between the Arab/Palestinian hammer and the Israeli anvil. Since the sympathy of the Egyptian people was in favor of the oppressed Palestinians, official policy reflected the public mood. Indeed, a poll that may reflect larger trends in society showed that intellectuals of all ideological inclinations felt responsible for the plight of the Palestinians.[32] It seems that the Palestinian problem epitomized their perception of Israel: born in sin, serves Western interests and eager to expand in the Middle East. Thus, during the second

Intifada the Egyptian ambassador was recalled and relations were almost frozen. In an attempt to halt the deterioration in Israeli–Palestinian relations, Egypt offered its good offices to the parties, but these mediation efforts usually failed. Recently, Israel's Disengagement Plan has brought a certain rapprochement with Egypt, reflected in the release of alleged spy 'Azzam 'Azzam, the signing of the QIZ and the return of the Egyptian ambassador. In this respect, these developments indicate that taking actual steps in favor of the Palestinians does indeed create a better atmosphere in Israeli–Egyptian relations.

More broadly, it is argued that Israel's behavior with respect to certain Arab affairs was responsible for the cold peace. In this connection one might refer to the following events: the failure of the autonomy talks (1981), the bombing of the Iraqi nuclear reactor (particularly as it came immediately after a Begin–Sadat meeting, 1981); the invasion of Lebanon (1982); the massacre at Sabra and Shatila (1982); the bombing of the PLO headquarters in Tunis (1985); the first *Intifada* (1987–91); the deportation of Hamas activists (1992); the opening of the Western Wall tunnel (1996); and the second *Intifada* (2000–4).[33] These events, according to this argument, forced Egypt – with its Arab identity and desire to lead the Arab world – to adopt an anti-Israeli policy.

The Economic Dimension

Warm relations between states often rely on mutual economic interests. Following the treaty, Egypt and Israel signed a trade agreement, which was formally approved in May 1981. Structurally, however, both countries can ignore each other economically: for Israel, Egypt is a small and unsophisticated market; for Egypt, Israel is too technologically advanced. In contrast to Jordan, for example, Egypt does not need direct economic relations with Israel in order to improve its economy.[34] Moreover, since the Gross Domestic Product (GDP) per capita in Israel is higher than that of the four surrounding Arab states (Israel = \$19,790; Egypt = \$3,520; Syria = \$3,280; Jordan = \$3,870), the prospects for Egyptian–Israeli close economic relations is remote.[35] It should be emphasized that a main Egyptian motivation for signing the treaty derived from the prospects of massive US assistance and Western–Arab investments.[36]

Indeed, Egypt's imports from Israel have been negligible, and its exports only slightly higher due to the sale of oil (see Tables 9.1–9.2). Though Egypt and Israel trade through third parties as well, the overall trade has not been significantly different from the numbers cited below.[37] Except for oil, Egyptian–Israeli trade includes agricultural products and equipment, textile, fertilizers, electronics and chemicals. Interestingly, however, in spite of the low level of bilateral trade, in the 1980s Israel was the largest regional trader with Egypt (including oil) and second or third, after Saudi Arabia and United Arab Emirates (if oil is excluded). This low level of Arab trade was due to the fact that Egypt was partially boycotted by the Arab countries and because its trade was directed mainly at the US, Europe and the Far East.[38] In the 1990s, Egypt increased its trade with Arab countries (mainly with Saudi Arabia), though this sector still commanded less than 10% of its overall trade.[39]

Table 9.1 Egypt's trade with Israel (in US Dollars)

Exports (including oil)	Imports	Year
182.3	1.0	1980
549.3	9.8	1981
443.2	69.0	1982
391.6	68.1	1983
369.0	63.7	1984
462.0	15.0	1985
230.1	59.0	1986
140.2	26.9	1987
145.8	28.2	1988
163.1	22.4	1989
167.9	40.6	1990
369.1	4.3	1991
187.6	13.0	1994
173.6	23.3	1995
343.6	36.7	1996
314.1	41.9	1997
133.8	19.5	1998
186.9	22.3	1999
266.0	23.9	2000

Sources: IMF, Direction of Trade Statistics Yearbook, various issues (Washington, DC); Arab Republic of Egypt, Ministry of Trade and Industry, official website (http://www.economy.gov.eg).

Table 9.2 Israel's Trade with Egypt (in US Dollars) (without oil)

	1997	1998	1999	2000	2001	2002	2003	2004
Exports	54.9	53.4	54.4	58.9	47.1	26.2	26.4	23.6
Imports	30.4	17.9	20.4	20.7	20	20.3	22.3	36.2

Source: State of Israel, Central Bureau of Statistics, Foreign Trade Statistics Quarterly, various issues (Jerusalem).

In addition to the bilateral trade, there have been several mutual industrial and agricultural projects in Egypt. Thus, for example, the Israeli Delta and Bagir textile factories established plants in Cairo. By 2005, this industry, which employs directly and indirectly some 9,500 Egyptian workers, exported products to the US and Europe in the amount of $80–90 million.[40] Also, on the basis of the agricultural agreement signed in March 1980, Israel established two demonstration farms (in 1983 and 1987), on the Nile Delta, aimed at transferring know-how, technologies and advisory services, particularly in the field of cultivation of arid zones. In this connection, Israel supplied a modern irrigation network, pesticides, fertilizing systems, seeds, etc. In addition, several thousand Egyptian University graduates received training in related fields in Israeli academic institutions.[41]

Yet, the low levels of Egyptian–Israeli bilateral trade and the small number of joint ventures did not stem only from economic constraints or structural incompatibilities. Indeed, though the Egyptian parliament abolished the Arab Boycott over Israel, in practice there has been an informal boycott, encouraged and implemented in various ways by the government. These deliberate bureaucratic impediments have caused despair among private businessmen on both sides.[42] After reviewing some of the difficulties in Israeli–Egyptian trade relations, Ann Lesch concluded: "The competitiveness of their products, administrative and financial restrictions on foreign trade and politically based constraints combined to inhibit contacts."[43] In addition, various elements in Egyptian civil society, such as trade unions and other professional associations – many of which are controlled by Islamists – have acted tirelessly to impede warmer economic relations. Thus, the bilateral trade – a major sign of normalization – became a political instrument in the hands of the Egyptian government.

Yet, when the government saw advantages in specific economic enterprises, it would go a long way toward implementing them. The recent gas deal and the establishment of the Qualifying Industrial Zone (QIZ) are cases in point. In July 2005, the Israel Electric Corporation signed a long-negotiated deal with an Egyptian Gas Company, EMG, to deliver 40 billion cubic meters of natural gas (with an option for another 10 billion) over 20 years, in the amount of $2.5 billion. For that purpose an underwater pipeline is to be laid from al-Arish to Ashqelon by the end of 2007.[44] Apparently, the idea of laying this project was raised already in the early 1990s, but mainly bureaucratic – and not political – problems on both sides impeded its realization.[45] The deal was financially attractive to Egypt, but it also blocked the much-discussed possibility of a similar deal with Qatar for the supply of gas to Israel. This deal opens the door for Israel to become integrated in the future in the pan-Arab gas pipeline network.

More recently, in December 2004, Israel, Egypt and the US signed the QIZ agreement – along the lines of the Israeli–Jordanian QIZ. It allows Egypt to export products to the US duty free, as long as 35% of the product is jointly Israeli–Egyptian and that the Israeli component constitutes at least 11.7% (it is only 8% in the Jordanian QIZ) of the total. It is expected that as Israeli–Jordanian trade substantially increased (from $15 million in 1998 to $132 million in 2004), Israeli–Egyptian trade will increase at least in the same proportion. But the main gain for Egypt is the expected increase in US–Egyptian trade. As Jordanian trade to the US jumped from $50 million in 1998 to $1 billion in 2004, Egypt's exports to the US surely may exceed this sum. In addition, the QIZ agreement was expected to add some quarter of a million jobs in the Egyptian textile and clothing industry.[46] By signing the QIZ agreement Egypt, in fact, followed the Jordanian lead – not a common feature in inter-Arab relations. Yet, the advantages attached to this agreement in terms of the Egyptian economy overshadowed the blow to its prestige. The improving political atmosphere facilitated the signing of the QIZ agreement. Yet, it seems that the immediate incentive was the Egyptian fear of its products being exposed to tough competition as a result of the US lifting of the quota system on textiles and garments from China and India in January 2005. Even some vehement criticism from opposition circles (mainly for the Israeli connection) in parliament could not prevent the signing of the agreement, which both the president and government perceived as advantageous economically.[47] This agreement showed that in spite of the differences and gaps between the two economies, a wide spectrum for economic cooperation does exist.[48]

Undoubtedly, the gas and QIZ agreements are the most significant developments in Egyptian–Israeli relations since the signing of the peace treaty.[49] Their importance lay not necessarily in the economic realm (though it is not insignificant) but in its political repercussions. These agreements, in which both sides can lose, should they be suspended, may ensure the stability of relations in periods of political crisis (as was the case with the supply of Egyptian oil during the Lebanese War and the *Intifada*).

The Psycho-Cultural Dimension

The Israeli–Egyptian cold peace is also a result of a psycho-cultural chasm. According to Raymond Cohen, each side is "imprisoned within the confines of its own habits, traditions, language, and most important, assumptions about the way people think and behave."[50] This, Cohen concludes, leads to a kind of dialogue between deaf people. But the existence of cultural differences does not inevitably lead to alienation, fear, animosity and dislike. Cultural differences can be mitigated, negotiated and discussed, but in the Egyptian–Israeli context they are mainly perpetuated. The psychological component is perhaps the most important dimension here, transmitted through the use of socialization instruments such as the media and the education system.

Both Egyptians and Israelis have shared negative images of the other. Developing and sustaining such images in international protracted conflicts is not uncommon: both laymen and decision-makers acquire them through various socialization processes and channels. Quite often these processes lead to demonizing the enemy and consequently to miscommunications and misperceptions.[51] To be sure, the signing of a peace treaty cannot eradicate ingrained negative images. The limited polls taken in Egypt on the subject demonstrate that the psychological barriers are very much in place.[52] Therefore, only a long, arduous effort, mainly initiated from above, can demolish this psychological wall. The Egyptian government, however, has not taken such an effort. In 1983, Marie-Christine Aulas argued, "cultural relations have proven the most resistant to any form of collaboration."[53] This conclusion is still valid at present.

The "Original Sin"

Mustafa Khalil, a former Egyptian prime minister, told Israeli President Yitzhak Navon in 1981: "You are a foreign people in the region with no historical rights. We had no choice but to accept you in a region which is wholly Arab, live peacefully with you and even have good neighborly relations – but not beyond that."[54] A staunch supporter of the peace treaty, Khalil was voicing a typical and oft-repeated Egyptian dictum: that Israel was born in sin; that the Zionists-Jews wrongfully usurped Palestine; and that the Palestinians were deliberately expelled.[55]

The almost unanimous belief in Egypt that Israel is a sinful creation resulted from a protracted campaign in the media and the education system. Unfortunately, leading Egyptian intellectuals often express anti-Israeli and even anti-Semitic positions. Though no systematic study has been carried out on the Egyptian media and literature, there are enough examples to show that Israel has often been depicted as an illegitimate entity, and that the peace treaty has reflected merely an acknowledgement of this lamentable reality. At the same time, Egyptian history textbooks convey a clear message: though peace is a necessity and within Egypt's interests, and though Egypt is playing a leading role in this process, Western imperialism illegitimately established Israel.[56]

Undoubtedly, the historical perception that Israel was sinfully created has contributed significantly to the maintenance of the cold peace. These images would be eradicated only after a long socialization process. Meanwhile, supporters of peace can overcome their cognitive dissonance by adopting the notion of "entitlement" – first used by the Palestinian intellectual Constantin Zurayk. According to this thinking, sinful as they are, the Israelis have worked so hard to be what they are that they deserve it.[57] This sophisticated thinking, however, does not seem to be shared by many Egyptians. In this connection, it is claimed that Israel must redress the grave historical injustice that accompanied its establishment (a reference to the solution of the refugee question).[58]

The Education System

The education system is an important socialization instrument in developing national identity. In fact, the education system is highly important within the process of nation building. States which are engaged in protracted conflicts use the education system to mobilize their citizens and strengthen the legitimacy of the regime. In this regard, textbooks, and history textbooks in particular, play a significant role in developing the collective memory of the society, which is a necessary component of the national identity. According to the French sociologist Maurice Halbwachs, "every group develops the memory of its own past that highlights its unique identity *vis-à-vis* other groups. These reconstructed images provide the group with an account of its origin and development and thus allow it to recognize itself through time."[59] The process of molding a nation entails the "building" of a collective memory, which necessitates rediscovering, reconstructing or even fabricating the national past. This past includes myths, symbols and other shared memories that provide maps and moralities delineating a psychological barrier between "we" and "they."

In the Egyptian case, the "other" was the Jew or, more specifically, the Zionist. In the pre-1967 period, Egyptian history textbooks were replete with de-humanizing and de-legitimizing labels of Israel and the Jews. The post-1967 period – particularly since the signing of the Egyptian–Israeli peace treaty – saw some improvement: the historical narrative was less chauvinistic but still did not accord legitimacy to Israel, though it recognized the state and supported the peace treaty. In my study of Egyptian history textbooks I concluded that they "create in the mind of the student a dual reality: on the one hand, recognition of the importance of the peace with Israel (which involves a tacit recognition of Israel); and on the other hand, rejection of the legitimacy of the Zionist enterprise."[60] In other words, the textbooks fortify the prevalent Egyptian (and Arab) notion that Israel is an illegitimate entity in the region.

Another problem inherent in the Egyptian textbooks is the absence of any reference to the Holocaust. Surely, to get acquainted with the Israeli psyche it is necessary to learn Jewish history. In addition to the old history of persecutions and isolation, becoming acquainted with the Holocaust (*shoah*) is important for understanding Jewish fears of annihilation and encirclement. The need for "universalizing the Holocaust," however, does not exist in Egypt, or in any other Arab country, for that matter.[61] On the contrary: the subject has either been ignored or denied. To sum up, instead of using the education system to foster peace education and a climate of reconciliation, the younger Egyptian generation has been exposed to negative stereotypes, as well as distorted and biased information on Israel. In such a climate it is not surprising that anti-Semitic views are articulated and absorbed by the average Egyptian.

The Media

The negative images of the Jews and Israel are also carried out through all media channels: radio, television, the Internet and the press. Even the government-owned media – and not only the opposition's – has been replete with anti-Semitic statements. The subordination of the media to the Ministry of National Guidance means that these oft-repeated statements cannot be a coincidence.[62] For some, this was tantamount to a "hate industry," taken under official patronage.[63] The anti-Jewish references include citations from the *Protocols of the Elders of Zion* – a publication of wide circulation. In addition, many racist terms are used to depict the Jewish nation; according to one study, "Jews are constantly perceived as incorrigibly and hopelessly corrupt, evil, greedy, immoral, intriguing and unconcerned with anyone but themselves." It further contends that this negative image of the Jews often entails the screening of "facts" and outright fabrication of "data" that fit this image.[64] In times of crises, comparisons have been made between Israeli leaders and soldiers with the Nazis.[65]

Political anti-Semitism has continued unabated in the Egyptian media to the present. A cursory reading of the official *al-Ahram*, the religious weekly *'Aqidati* (part of the official *al-Gumhuriyya*) and the opposition papers, *al-Wafd* and *al-Sha'ab*, reveals that the Egyptian media continue to transmit anti-Semitic messages. These messages include the following elements: the demonization of Israeli leadership; the Jews as possessing certain negative traits and characteristics (often depicted in degrading caricatures); the power of the Jewish lobby – a phenomenon validating the authenticity of the *Protocols of the Elders of Zion*; and Holocaust denial.[66] The fact that some of these messages are published in the government-owned mainstream press confers validity to the allegations in the eyes of the common people. Even if the regime does not initiate these expressions of hatred, the very fact that it does not halt them (at least in those that are controlled by the government), indicates their endorsement. Perhaps the publication of this kind of press serves the regime as a possible outlet for the public grievances. The result of these attacks, wrote Dan Pattir, is that "an entire generation [of Egyptians] has come of age since the 1979 peace treaty being exposed to the same negative presentation of Jews and Israelis."[67]

Conclusions

The Egyptian–Israeli peace treaty is one of the most significant achievements in the realm of the Arab–Israeli conflict, allowing both countries certain political and economic gains. From the Israeli vantage point, the treaty proved to be durable, duplicable and to some extent also stable.

Though some claim, in response to Egypt's recent military buildup, that the peace treaty is reversible, the chances of a renewed military confrontation between Israel and Egypt seem slim at best.[68] But the cold nature of the peace, at least in Israeli eyes, soured the taste of achievement and contributed to the endurance of feelings of animosity, suspicion and even hatred on both sides.

In March 2005, Muhammad 'Assem, the new Egyptian ambassador, arrived to Israel after this seat was vacant for four years, during the years of the *Intifada*. His arrival, in the wake of a Palestinian–Israeli cease-fire, and following the signing of the QIZ and gas agreements, seemed to herald a new, promising beginning in Egyptian–Israeli relations.[69] These developments indicate that Egyptian–Israeli relations are dynamic, fluctuating according to domestic, regional and international developments. Indeed, Egypt seems to be willing to inject more substance to the relations, but normalization or warm peace is still very much beyond the horizon.

The present study contends that the structural problems existing between the countries inhibit the warming of their relations to the desired end (at least according to the Israeli definition). In fact, a situation of normal relations without normalization has perfectly suited Egypt in its relations with Israel. Steps taken in the direction of the latter were temporary, contingent and conditional. A retreat, however, from normal relations to a complete freeze is unlikely unless a new round of Arab–Israeli hostilities begins. Even then, the recent signing of the economic agreements may ensure that the economic interests would mitigate the military–political tension.

Observers tend to predict that Israeli–Egyptian relations will substantially improve once the Israeli–Palestinian conflict resolved. Though such a development would surely improve relations, this argument ignores the other structural problems that would impede a dramatic change. Peace with Israel is a necessity for Egypt, allowing it to effectively deal with its chronic demographic and economic problems through the US financial support as well as Western and Arab investments. As Egypt perceives itself as the leader of the Arab states, Israel poses a regional challenge, either by its economic or military superiority. Their strategic imbalance – reflected in the realm of the nuclear issue and many economic indices – places Egypt in an inferior position *vis-à-vis* Israel, creating *ipso facto* a situation of competition. In addition, the importance of the domestic factor on Egypt's external behavior should not be underestimated: as long as parties and organizations unwilling to recognize Israel pose a serious challenge to the regime's legitimacy, its ability to warm relations with Israel will be circumscribed. The fact that most of these parties and organizations are driven by Islamic ideology, which considers Palestine as a sacred Islamic territory, makes it difficult for the regime to ignore them.

In addition to these structural problems, the psycho-cultural differences pose another obstacle in the way of warming relations. As long as Egyptians continue absorbing distorted information on Israel, tinged by prejudice and negative stereotypes, in the media and the education system (as well as other socialization instruments), the cold peace will be maintained. Even if the Egyptian government becomes aware of these adverse effects, embarking on a campaign of correcting these malfunctions (and at present there is no sign of it), the change will occur only in later generations. For Bar-Siman-Tov, reconciliation is the most difficult aim to achieve because "it asks for a deep cognitive change, a real change of beliefs, ideology and emotions not only among the ruling elites but also among most if not all sectors of both societies."[70] Lessons of 1979–99 indicate, in his opinion, that the Egyptian–Israeli peace cannot develop into a stable peace.[71] A similar forecast can be predicted with regard to the temperature of Israeli–Egyptian relations: between cold and lukewarm but not warm.

Following the present analysis, the steps the Egyptian side should take in order to improve relations are self-evident. Yet, Israel may also contribute to this process by revealing more sensitivity to Egypt's domestic and regional constraints. In other words, Israel should be careful not to antagonize or embarrass Egypt's perceived regional standing but rather attempt to cooperate with it, particularly in the Israeli–Palestinian arena. Israel's willingness to allow the stationing of a token Egyptian police force along the Egyptian–Gaza border as part of its Disengagement Plan (in breach of the treaty) in August 2005 is a case in point. Other possible areas for cooperation between Israel and Egypt are their mutual concern of Islamic fundamentalist terrorism, Iran's nuclear capability and its drive for regional preeminence.[72] Such cooperation would improve Israeli–Egyptian relations, signaling that Israel is indeed in the Middle East and not an external player that happens to be geographically located in this region.[73] Such thinking and behavior may bring some changes in the Arab position toward Israel's role and place in the area. In sum, though there are structural impediments to the attainment of a warm Israeli–Egyptian peace, nevertheless there are certain measures that can be taken by both sides to extricate these relations from their cold nature.

Notes

1   Walter Laqueur and Barry Rubin, *The Israeli–Arab Reader: A Documentary History of the Middle East Conflict* (New York: Penguin, 1984), p. 616.

2   The first to coin this phrase, according to journalist Smadar Peri, was Boutrus Boutrus-Ghali, Egyptian Deputy Minster of Foreign Affairs and later UN Secretary. See her postscript to his book, *Egypt's Road to Jerusalem: A Diplomat's Story* (Tel Aviv: Yediot Aharonot, 1998), p. 410 [in Hebrew].

3   Shawn Pine, "Myopic Vision: Whither Israeli–Egyptian Relations?" *Israel Affairs*, Vol. 3 (1997), p. 332.

4   Kenneth W. Stein, "Continuity and Change in Egyptian–Israeli Relations,
    1973–97," *Israel Affairs*, Vol. 3 (1997), p. 305.
5   Itamar Rabinovich, *Waging Peace: Israel and the Arabs 1948–2003* (Tel Aviv:
    Dvir, 2004), p. 202 [in Hebrew].
6   Benjamin Miller, "The Global Sources of Regional Transitions from War to
    Peace," *Journal of Peace Research*, Vol. 38 (2001), p. 203.
7   For some studies that dealt with certain aspects, see Shimon Shamir, "Israeli
    Views of Egypt and the Peace Process: The Duality of Vision," in William B.
    Quandt (ed.), *The Middle East: Ten Years after Camp David* (Washington: The
    Brookings Institution, 1988), pp. 187–216; Ehud Yaari, *Peace by Piece: A
    Decade of Egyptian Policy toward Israel* (Washington, DC: The Washington
    Institute for Near East Policy, 1989); Fawaz A. Gerges, "Egyptian–Israeli
    Relations Turn Sour," *Foreign Affairs*, Vol. 74, No. 3 (May–June 1995), pp.
    69–78; Kenneth W. Stein, "Continuity and Change in Egyptian–Israeli
    Relations, 1973–97," *Israel Affairs*, Vol. 3, Nos. 3–4 (Spring–Summer 1997),
    pp. 296–320; Ann Mosely Leach, "Egyptian–Israeli Relations: Normalization
    or Special Ties?" in Ann Mosely Leach and Mark Tessler, *Israel, Egypt, and
    the Palestinians: From Camp David to Intifada* (Bloomington: Indiana
    University Press, 1989), pp. 61–85. Particularly disappointing is a recent article
    by Yoram Meital, "Peace with Israel in Egypt's Policy," in Joseph Ginat,
    Edward J. Perkins and Edwin G. Corr (eds.), *The Middle East Peace Process:
    Vision Versus Reality* (Brighton: Sussex Academic Press, 2002), pp. 140–50.
    The most valuable analysis of the peace is found in Yaacov Bar-Siman-Tov,
    "Israel–Egypt Peace: Stable Peace?" in Arie M. Kacowicz, Yaacov Bar-Siman-
    Tov, Ole Elgstrom, and Magnus Jerneck (eds.), *Stable Peace among Nations*
    (Lanham: Rowman and Littlefield Publishers, 2000), pp. 220–38.
8   Rabinovich, *Waging Peace*, pp. 199–200.
9   On the role of images in international relations there has been vast literature.
    Surprisingly, few studies deal with the role of images in the Arab–Israeli con-
    flict. For an analysis of Israeli perceptions of Nasser, see Elie Podeh,
    "Demonizing the Other: Israeli Perceptions of Nasser and Nasserism," in Elie
    Podeh and Onn Winckler (eds.), *Rethinking Nasserism: Revolution and
    Historical Memory* (Gainseville: University of Florida Press, 2004), pp.
    72–99.
10 When the Saudi Crown Prince 'Abdallah offered his initiative to end the
    Arab–Israeli conflict, in February 2002, he talked about the normalization of
    relations between Israel and the Arab states in return for full Israeli withdrawal
    from the Occupied Territories. The Arab states, particularly Syria, insisted on
    the term "normal relations" rather than "normalization." Elie Podeh, *From
    Fahd to 'Abdallah: The Origins of the Saudi Peace Initiatives and Their Impact
    on the Arab System and Israel*, Gitelson Peace Publications 24 (Jerusalem: The
    Harry S. Truman Research Institute for the Advancement of Peace, 2003), pp.
    21–22, 42.
11 Miller, "The Global Sources," p. 203. In his typology, Miller suggests also
    "normal peace" as a possibility between "cold peace" and "warm peace".
    There is no attempt here to suggest that Israeli–Egyptian relations fall within
    Miller's "normal peace" category. The Arab use of the term "normal relations"
    is closer to Miller's "cold peace" category.

12 Shaul Mishal and Nadav Morag, "Trust or Contract? Negotiating Formal and Informal Agreements in the Arab–Israeli Peace Process," *International Negotiations*, Vol. 5 (2000), p. 528.

13 For some studies, see Howard M. Sachar, *Egypt and Israel* (New York: Richard Marek Publishers, 1981); Yoram Meital, *Egypt's Struggle for Peace: Continuity and Change, 1967–1977* (Gainesville: University Press of Florida, 1997).

14 Sa'ad Eddin Ibrahim, in a round table discussion, "Twenty Years of Egyptian–Israeli Relations," The Moshe Dayan Center for Middle Eastern and African Studies and the Kaplan Chair for the History of Egypt and Israel, Tel Aviv University, December 22, 1999, p. 60.

15 Bar-Siman-Tov, "Israel–Egypt Peace," p. 221.

16 On the historical evolutions of relations, see Joseph Alper (ed.), *What Went Wrong? Summary of the Proceedings of an Arab–Israeli Workshop convened to assess the peace process since Madrid* (Tel Aviv: American-Jewish Committee, 1998); Stein, "Continuity and Change," pp. 296–320.

17 Bar-Siman-Tov, "Israel–Egypt Peace," p. 220.

18 On Egypt's central role in Arab politics and Egyptian perceptions of this phenomenon, see Elie Podeh, *The Quest for Hegemony in the Arab World: The Struggle over the Baghdad Pact* (Leiden: E.J. Brill, 1995), pp. 8–38; Fouad Ajami, *The Arab Predicament: Arab Political Thought and Practice since 1967*, updated edition (Cambridge: Cambridge University Press, 1992), pp. 89–167. In contrast to the prevailing premise, Egypt was not politically and economically ostracized in the Arab world following the peace treaty, see Elie Podeh and Onn Winckler, *The Boycott That Never Was: Egypt and the Arab System, 1979–1989*, Durham Middle East Papers, 72 (Durham: 2002).

19 Most of the information on the ACRS talks is based on the following: Emily Landau, Egypt and Israel in ACRS: Bilateral Concerns in a Regional Arms Control Process, Memorandum No. 59 (Tel Aviv: Jaffee Center for Strategic Studies, 2001); *idem.*, *Arms Control in the Middle East: Cooperative Security Dialogue and Regional Constraints* (Brighton & Portland: Sussex Academic Press, 2006), pp. 90–159; Shai Feldman, *Nuclear Weapons and Arms Control in the Middle East* (Cambridge, MA: MIT Press, 1997), pp. 205–42; Dalia Dassa Kaye, "Madrid's Forgotten Forum: The Middle East Multilaterals," *The Washington Quarterly*, Vol. 20 (Winter 1997), pp. 167–86.

20 "Twnety Years of Egyptian–Israeli Relations," p. 153.

21 Feldman, *Nuclear Weapons and Arms Control*, p. 226.

22 Ibid., p. 222; Landau, Egypt and Israel in ACRS, pp. 24–26.

23 Ibid., p. 52. Kaye wrote that Egypt's position generally supports regional inclusion of Israel, but in a nuanced and complex way." See "Madrid's Forgotten Forum," p. 182.

24 Abdel Moneim Sa'id 'Ali, "Twenty Years of Egyptian–Israeli Relations," p. 69.

25 On this concept, see, for example, Lutfi al-Khouli, *Arab? Na'am, wa-Sharq Awsatiyyun Aydan* [Arab? Yes, but Middle Easterners Too] (Cairo: 1994); Nabil 'Abd al-Fattah, "al-Arab wa-Nizam al-Sharq al-Awsat dhat al-Tashkil" [The Arabs and the Emerging Middle East Order], *al-Siyasa al-Duwaliyya* (January 1993), pp. 46–69. For further information, see Avraham Sela, *The*

Decline of the Arab–Israeli Conflict: Middle East Politics and the Quest for Regional Order (Albany: SUNY Press, 1998), pp. 339–40, and notes 42–43; Elie Podeh, "Rethinking Israel in the Middle East," *Israel Affairs*, Vol. 3 (1997), pp. 289–90.

26 Shimon Peres, *The New Middle East* (New York: Henry Holt and Company, 1993).

27 Sela, *The Decline of the Arab–Israeli Conflict*, p. 340; Rabinovich, *Waging Peace,* p. 200. See also Ephraim Dowek, *In Spite of All Peace* (Tel Aviv: Yediot Aharonot, 1998), p. 153 [in Hebrew].

28 Bar-Siman-Tov, "Israel–Egypt Peace," pp. 231–34; Zvi Barel, "Who Threatens Mubarak's Hegemony?" *Ha'aretz*, April 5, 2000. The fear of Israeli hegemony was prevalent even before the inception of the New Middle East concept. See, e.g., Muhammad Sayyid Ahmad, *After the Guns Fall Silent* (Jerusalem: The Harry S. Truman Research Institute, 1976), p. 72 [in Hebrew, originally published in Arabic].

29 For a short reference to this, see Rabinovich, Waging Peace, p. 200. Bar-Siman-Tov's excellent article ("Israel–Egypt Peace") completely omits the domestic considerations. See also Magdi Khalil, "Egypt's Muslim Brotherhood and Political Power: Would Democracy Survive? *Middle East Review of International Affairs (*MERIA), Vol. 10 (March 2006); Muhammad Abdel Salam, "Bewildering Elections: Two Steps Forward, One Backward on the Way to Egyptian Democracy," *Arab Reform Brief* (February 2006), <http://www.arab-reform.net>.

30 See the proceedings of a recent (June 2005) Israeli–Egyptian academic conference, Michal Sela (ed.), *Israeli–Egyptian Economic Relations: On the Doorstep of a New Era?* (Tel Aviv: the Institute for Diplomacy and Regional Cooperation, 2006).

31 On the importance of the Palestinian issue in Egyptian policy, see Moshe Shemesh, *From the Nakba to the Naksa: The Arab–Israeli Conflict and the Palestinian National Problem, 1957–1967* (Sede Boker: The Ben-Gurion Research Institute, 2004) [in Hebrew]; Boutros-Ghali, *Egypt's Road to Jerusalem*, p. 410.

32 Dina Guiguis and Anas Anani, "Peace, Peace Process and Normalization: Egyptian Intellectuals Who Reject Israel's Superiority Complex in the Region," *Palestine–Israel Journal*, Vol. 7 (2000).

33 Stein, "Continuity and Change," pp. 305–6.

34 Gil Feiler and Ephraim Yaar, in *Twenty Years of Egyptian–Israeli Relations*, pp. 126, 138.

35 UNDP, Human Development Report 2003 (New York: Oxford University Press, 2003), pp. 237–39, table 1.

36 For the reasons that prompted Egypt to sign the treaty, see Gad Gilbar and Onn Winckler, "The Economic Factor of the Arab–Israeli Peace Process: The Cases of Egypt, Jordan and Syria," in Elie Podeh and Asher Kaufman (eds.), *Arab–Jewish Relations: From Conflict to Resolution? Essays in Honor of Moshe Ma'oz* (Brighton & Portland: Sussex Academic Press, 2006), pp. 190–209.

37 According to Dowek, this indirect trade amounts to $25 million annually. See his *In Spite of All Peace*, p. 236.

38 For data, see ESCWA (UN Economic and Social Commission for Western

Asia), External Trade Bulleting of the ESCWA Region, Vol. 7 (New York: 1994), p. 68, table 5.

39   For data see Ibid., Vol. 10 (New York: 2000), pp. 73, 86.

40   Dov Lautman, Chairman of the Board, Delta-Galil Industries, *Israeli–Egyptian Economic Relations*, pp. 59–62.

41   This information is based on several Israeli Foreign Office reports.

42   For the administrative restrictions and impediments, see Dowek, *In Spite of All Peace*, pp. 231–47. Some of these restrictions are still in operation according to Egyptian and Israeli businessmen according to the proceedings of the conference on Egyptian–Israeli economic relations (see note 30).

43   Ann Mosely Leach, "Egyptian–Israeli Relations: Normalization or Special Ties?" in Mosely Leach and Tessler, *Israel, Egypt, and the Palestinians: From Camp David to Intifada*, p. 72.

44   *Ma'ariv*, July 14, 2005; Eli Ronen, Director-General of the Ministry of Infrastructures, *Israeli–Egyptian Economic Relations*, pp. 74–77.

45   Nimrod Novik, Senior Vice President, Merhav Group, ibid., pp. 68–73.

46   On the agreement, see a brief of the Israeli Ministry of Industry, Trade and Labor, <http://www.moit.gov.il>. See also Yair Shiran, Director of International Agreements and Trade Policy, Ministry of Industry, Trade and Labor, Israeli–Egyptian Economic Relations, pp. 53–56. On the Jordanian case, see Joseph Nevo (ed.), *Neighbors Caught in a Maze: Israeli–Jordan Relations before and after the Peace Treaty* (Tel Aviv: the Yitzhak Rabin Center, 2004), pp. 189–230. [in Hebrew]; Shimon Shamir (ed.), *Israel–Jordan Relations: Projects, Economics, Business* (Tel Aviv: The Institute for Diplomacy and Regional Cooperation, 2004).

47   Niveen Wahish, "Enter QIZ," *al-Ahram Weekly*, December 16–22, 2004; *The Jerusalem Post*, December 14, 2004.

48   For some ideas of this cooperation, such as "border trade" and "input sharing," see *Twenty Years of Egyptian–Israeli Relations*, pp. 106–7. Tareq Heggy talked of the drawing of an "investment map," and Gil Feiler spoke of the need to privatize peace (pp. 118–19, 125).

49   This was also the position of Ehud Olmert, the then Deputy Prime Minister and Minister of Industry, Trade and Labor. See his lecture, *Israeli–Egyptian Economic Relations*, pp. 45–48.

50   Raymond Cohen, *Culture and Conflict in Egyptian–Israeli Relations: A Dialogue of the Deaf* (Bloomington: Indiana University Press, 1990), p. 7.

51   See note 9.

52   Gerges, "Egyptian–Israeli Relations Turn Sour," p. 74.

53   "The Normalization of Egyptian–Israeli Relations," *Arab Studies Quarterly*, Vol. 5 (1983), p. 234.

54   Quoted in Dowek, *In Spite of All Peace*, p. 377.

55   See, e.g., Sayyid Ahmad, p. 76; Sa'ad Eddin Ibrahim, *Twenty Years of Egyptian–Israeli Relations*, p. 89; and Tahseen Bashir, in ibid., p. 84.

56   On the positions of intellectuals, see Fouad Ajami, *The Dream Palace of the Arabs: A Generation's Odyssey* (New York: Pantheon Books, 1998), Chapter 5. For a unique Egyptian criticism of these positions, see Amin al-Mahdi, *The Other View*, translated from the Arabic by Marcel and David Sagiv (Tel Aviv: Hakibbutz Hame'uhad, 2001), [in Hebrew]. Regarding the textbooks, see Elie

Podeh, "Recognition without Legitimization: Israel and the Arab–Israeli Conflict in Egyptian History Textbooks", *Internationale Schulbuchforschung* (International Textbooks Research), Vol. 25, No. 4 (2003), pp. 371–98.

57 This logic was used by Sa'ad Eddin Ibrahim, in *Twenty Years of Egyptian–Israeli Relations*, p. 89.

58 Guirguis and Anani, "Peace, Peace Process and Normalization."

59 Quoted in Y. Zerubavel, *Recovered Roots: Collective Memory and the Making of Israeli National Tradition* (Chicago: Chicago University Press, 1995), p. 4.

60 Podeh, "Recognition without Legitimization," p. 393. See also Arnon Groiss (ed.), *Jews, Christians, War and Peace in Egyptian School Textbooks* (Jerusalem: Center for Monitoring the Impact of Peace, 2004). For the way Israeli history textbooks have depicted the Arab side, see Elie Podeh, *The Arab–Israeli Conflict in Israeli History Textbooks* (Westport, CT: Bergin and Garvey, 2002).

61 This was the title of an article published by the Lebanese Hazim Saghieh and the Tunisian Salah Bashir, Hebrew version in *Ha'aretz*, February 21, 2000. On the Arab representation of the Holocaust, see Meir Litvak and Esther Webman, "The Representation of the Holocaust in the Arab World," *Journal of Israeli History*, Vol. 23 (2004), pp. 100–15; *idem.*, "Perceptions of the Holocaust in the Palestinian Public Discourse," *Israel Studies*, Vol. 8 (2003), pp. 123–40.

62 For the workings of this ministry, see Dowek, *In Spite of All Peace*, pp. 113–25.

63 See, e.g., Reuven Erlich (ed.), "'Hate Industry' in Egypt under Official Patronage," Information Bulletin No. 7 (Herzliya: Intelligence and Terrorism Information Center, January 2003).

64 Raphael Israeli, *Peace in the Eye of the Beholder* (Berlin: Mouton Publishers, 1985), pp. 360–61. See in this connection also Rivka Yadlin, *An Arrogant Oppressive Spirit: Anti-Zionism as Anti-Judaism in Egypt* (Oxford: Pergamon Press, 1989); *idem*, "Arab Anti-Semitism in Peaceful Times – The Egyptian Case," *Nativ*, Vol. 3 (January 1990), pp. 20–25, [in Hebrew].

65 Stein, "Continuity and Change," p. 309.

66 For some examples, see *al-Ahram*, July 17, 2002, 4, August 15, 2002, October 28, 2002, 6 November 2002. In contrast, see Usama al-Baz's articles in 23–25 December 2002, which was published as a response to the TV series "A Knight without a Horse," which included many anti-Semitic symbols and messages. On that episode, see Andrew Hammond, *Pop Culture Arab World! Media, Arts, and Lifestyle* (Santa Barbara, CA: ABC-CLIO, 2005), p. 68. I would like to thank Mrs. Neta Marmur for monitoring the Egyptian press during 2002.

67 Dan Pattir, "Arab Demonization of Israel and the Jews," *Justice*, No. 27 (Spring 2001), p. 23. The author brings different examples for this kind of anti-Semitism, see pp. 21–25. See also Israel Landers, *Ma'ariv*, February 16, 1990.

68 See, e.g., Pine, "Myopic Vision: Whither Israeli–Egyptian Relations"? *Israel Affairs*, Vol. 3 (1997), pp. 321–34; Dan Eldar, "Egypt and Israel: A Reversible Peace," *Middle East Quarterly*, Vol. 10 (2003), pp. 57–65. Here lies an important question of why and to what end the Egyptians need to modernize their army? In my opinion it is a mixture of the following reasons: to maintain Egypt's Arab leadership role; to defend the regime from domestic – primarily Islamic – opposition; to defend the country against a threat coming from either

Sudan or Libya; and as a possible deterrent against Israel, with its superior military equipment. See the debate on this issue in *Ha'aretz*, Reuven Pedatzur, September 19, 2005; Reuven Pedatzur, September 19, 2005; Yuval Shteinitz, December 4, 2006; Yoram Meital, December 12, 2006.

69 *Al-Ahram Weekly*, No. 731, 24 February–2 March 2005.

70 Bar-Siman-Tov, "Israel–Egypt Peace," p. 237.

71 Ibid., p. 236.

72 Rami Ginat, "Egypt and Its Involvement in the Disengagement Agreement Process: Strategic, Regional and International Aspects," *BESA Perspectives*, No. 9 (September 2005).

73 See in this connection, Elie Podeh, "Israel *in* the Middle East or Israel *and* the Middle East: A Reappraisal," in Podeh and Kaufman, *Arab–Jewish Relations*, pp. 93–113.

CHAPTER 10

Israel–Egypt: What Went Wrong? Nothing

SHLOMO GAZIT

Allow me to begin with the conclusion – the only thing that did go wrong in the implementation of the Israeli–Egypt peace agreement was the collapse of the illusions of all those that believed that signing the bilateral treaty will lead to a new relationship between the two countries – a warm and very close relationship. It did not happen nor were there any real possibilities for it to materialize.

Egyptian–Israeli peace never took off. Most of the culpability for this rests on Egyptian shoulders. Egypt was the only party that might have adopted a different attitude and policy, a policy of genuine peace, of coexistence and warm relations. The people in Israel hoped and wanted to see a new era in the relations between the two nations and an end to hostilities. Israel, however, did not have the means to impose its will on the Egyptians.

But Israel, is also to be blamed for various decisions and steps that contributed to the dreary relations between the two nations, steps that contradicted the interests of co-existence. Nevertheless, the results would have been the same were Israel to have acted differently.

Egyptian reservation and reluctance to allow closer relations has characterized all levels of interaction. President Mubarak, at the top political level, has refused to visit Israel since he took office in 1981, and the Egyptian leadership, without exception (and not only the political leadership), adopted the same policy of boycotting Israel. The most regrettable boycott is that of Egyptian academics.

In the last 23 years Cairo has twice recalled its ambassador in Israel. Most of the time Egypt was represented in Israel with a "chargé d'affaires." At the very same time, the Israeli ambassador in Cairo was almost completely isolated and boycotted. Economic relations are conducted on the lowest possible level. If we examine tourism, not only do we not see any Egyptian tourists in Israel, there is no third-party tourism combining visits to both countries, tours that would be the most obvious combination. Egyptian media is extremely hostile to Israel. There is not one single positive word, only false stories designated to portray Israel and Israelis in the ugliest colors.

The relations between the two countries have known ups and downs during the last 23 years. These ups and downs influenced and reflected changes in the region, in Egypt itself, and also reflected Israeli confrontations in Lebanon and with the Palestinians. Yet, even during the best of times, mutual relations never really warmed-up. Furthermore, they never went beyond a few symbolic gestures, with no intention to change the basic shape of relations between the two parties. These ups and downs were always at the governmental level. They had no impact on the Egyptian people at large, and the government made no attempt to change public feelings towards Israel.

The conclusion is quite obvious – nothing actually went wrong with the bilateral peace. Simply stated, we should not have had any illusions and non-realistic expectations about what would materialize following the formal relations.

As related in chapter 8, I was serving as Head of Israeli military intelligence during President Sadat's historic visit to Jerusalem, and it was my responsibility to present to the cabinet our intelligence assessment. Once we learned of the coming visit, we had a fundamental argument with Prime-Minister Begin and his cabinet. We differed on four points:

1   Our assessment was that Egypt would not accept an agreement unless it included a complete Israeli withdrawal behind the former 1948 international border;
2   We claimed that Egypt would not agree to any continued Israeli presence in the Sinai (neither military nor civilian) once the agreement had been implemented;
3   We thought that Egypt would insist that the bilateral peace treaty would be part of a comprehensive Arab–Israeli peace that would encompass all borders between Israel and its Arab neighbors, including the Palestinians;
4   And last, we thought that there was no chance to develop close co-existence between our two countries, at least as long as all aspects of the Arab–Israeli conflict had not been resolved.

The first two points dealt with the characteristics of the bilateral agreement. The two last points, however, dealt with the future relations between our two countries, which are presently the base of our discussion. Unfortunately, we at military intelligence, proved to be right. I shall discuss the challenge in two parts. In the first part we shall deal with the basic Egyptian position towards Israel and its right of existence in the region. We shall review in the second part the ups and downs of the relationship in the last 24 years.

Egypt did not change its basic attitude towards Israel after and because of Sadat's visit, after the signing of the peace treaty or in the 24 years that have passed since then. Egypt had never accepted Israel's existence as a sovereign state in the region. Egypt – like all other Arab countries – still views Israel as an alien element from a religious, cultural, linguistic and political point of view. They believe that Israel has a clear mission to serve as a modern form of Western imperialism that wants to dominate the Middle East and the third world by spreading the western way of life and dominating Arab economies.

A part of this deep and basic negation of Israel – of its very existence and of its ideological goals – according to Arab conviction is that one cannot ignore two generations of Israeli–Arab wars and the humiliating military defeats Arab armies suffered from the tiny Israeli state. This caused a most serious Arab and Egyptian complex. This humiliation and severe damage to Egyptian pride has been caused by the inability of the Arab "Goliath" to overcome little Israeli "David."

A visit to the beautiful Panorama museum in Cairo clearly demonstrates this problem. The museum was designed to commemorate the great victory of the Egyptian forces that crossed the Suez Canal in October 1973 and occupied its eastern bank. The visitor to the museum leaves with the clear impression that the War of Ramadan (what Israelis refer to as the Yom Kippur War) ended two days later, on October 8. Not a word about what happened later, i.e. of the Israeli counter-crossing of the canal, of the Egyptian Third Army being surrounded and cut-off, nor of the Egyptian call for a cease-fire after just 16 days, with Israeli forces well established in "Africa," just 100 kilometers from Cairo.

As long as we do not see a change in the Arab–Egyptian views as to Israel's character and goals, there is no real chance to transform the cold and formal peace into a warm relationship and to see true co-existence between the peoples. We observe three ideological groups encompassing the great majority of the Egyptian people that totally reject Israel's existence.

1   The ideology of the Islamist group places Islam at the center of Egyptian life. For its proponents, the religious common denominator comes before the Arab–nationalist ideology.

2   The political ideology and goal of the Nasserite group is to unite the Arabs of the Middle East and to free the region from Western imperialism and from the Western Way of life. The Nasserites believe that Israel serves as the spearhead of this penetration.

3   Last come the promoters of the Egyptian nationalist ideology. Their aspiration is to ensure Egyptian supremacy in the Arab Middle East. They view Israel as a competitor striving to assume the leading role in the area. Egypt paid a heavy political price for its separate peace with Israel. It generated a painful confrontation with all other Arab parties. Egypt lost its position of leadership, the offices of the Arab League were removed from Cairo, and diplomatic relations were severed. It is no wonder that Cairo believes that its relations with Israel are a handicap to its endeavors to regain its central leadership position in the Arab World.

This brings us to the second part of my essay. General developments in the region as well as the decisions and acts of the two parties have their impact on the level of peace and cooperation between Egypt and Israel.

I would like to begin with Israel's negative contribution in this domain. Israel is guilty and responsible for three sins. First and foremost was its abuse of the Egyptian expectation to see the bilateral agreement as the first phase and as a lever to other future agreements, in accordance to Arab claims, that would bring an end to the Arab–Israeli conflict. Second, Israel had initiated various unilateral acts that embarrassed the Egyptians and damaged their position in the Arab world. Last, these involuntary acts hurt Egyptian pride.

I have already mentioned, in chapter 8, the argument that Israeli military intelligence had a serious disagreement with Prime Minister Begin and the cabinet as to President Sadat's position and goals. The 1978 Camp David agreement had two parts. The first dealt with the details of the bilateral peace treaty, while the second part created an agreed framework on how to solve Israel's conflict with all other Arab parties. The most important element was the decision to initiate full Palestinian autonomy in the West Bank and in the Gaza Strip that would bring a final Israeli–Palestinian settlement within five years.

The Israeli government in the 1980s, headed by Mr. Begin, had no intention to seriously negotiate peace with Syria or with the Palestinians. The Israeli government's position was that "Israel can only offer peace for peace." Rather than seeking peace with Palestine and Syria, Prime Minister Begin decided to annex formally the Golan Heights, which required a special Knesset Resolution. As to the Palestinians, Israel did join talks with Egypt and the United States on local "full autonomy," but what Israel offered was "autonomy to people with no autonomy to land." Moshe Dayan, the Israeli Foreign Minister at the time, resigned from the cabinet once he realized that Begin had no intention of reaching an agreement with the Egyptians on the Palestinian problem. Shortly afterwards, Ezer Weitzman, the Minister of Defense, also resigned for the same reasons. This brought to an end the second part of the Camp David agreement.

Israel's second sin was taking unilateral steps and actions with no consultation with the Egyptians; steps that the Egyptians considered to be clear Israeli insults and affronts. The Israeli government, immediately after signing the accords, initiated a plan of massive implantation of new Israeli settlements both in the West Bank and the Gaza Strip. The government thought that its chances of retaining these territories were not possible unless they were justified by a high number of settlements and settlers. In 1977, when the Likud party came to power, the Jewish settler population numbered some 5,000 men and women. Twenty-five years later the present number is around 250,000. This has been a clear negative message to the Egyptians who were waiting to see full Palestinian autonomy that would lead to a final settlement in accordance to the Camp David accords.

Another Israeli defiant act for the Egyptians was the War in Lebanon (1982). Hardly two months after completing the withdrawal from Sinai, when hopes were high that time was ripe to capitalize on the fruits of peace, Israel launched the war, occupied an Arab capital, and forced both the PLO leadership as well as Syrian forces out of Lebanon. Right or wrong, Egyptians became convinced that Israel signed its peace treaty only in order to have a free hand along its northern border.

Israel's third sin was its insensitivity towards Egyptian pride. Prime Minister Begin had shown his insensitivity already during the mutual peace talks and negotiations in 1979 when he insulted the Egyptian Foreign Minister and Head of Delegation in Jerusalem calling him "Young-man." The members of the Egyptian delegation were totally insulted and President Sadat ordered the delegation to return home, thus freezing the talks.

Some 18 months later, in May 1981, President Sadat met Prime Minister Begin in Sharm el-Sheikh. The meeting took place just one week prior to the Israeli air strike against the Iraqi nuclear reactor near Baghdad. Mr. Begin did not realize what would be the consequences of such timing. Arab public opinion suspected that the Israeli attack had been coordinated with the Egyptians and that Sadat gave his blessing to the attack.

Yitzhak Shamir, who replaced Mr. Begin as Prime Minister and as head of the ruling Likud party, admitted publicly in regard to the peace talks held in Washington with the Syrians and the Palestinians, following the Madrid international conference (1991), that he would have continued these futile negotiations for another 10 years, but with no intention to reach an agreement.

Later, after the Oslo Declaration of Principles and during the euphoric days of the Palestinian peace process, Shimon Peres, the Israeli Foreign Minister and later Prime Minister, spoke again and again of the "New Middle East" and of the economic cooperation that would be in the interest of both sides. The Arab party was convinced that these expressions were manifested Israeli intent to dominate the Arab world through its economic ventures. The Rabat economic conference that followed, where hundreds of Israeli businessmen attended, was regarded as further proof of this Israeli plan.

With respect to Egyptian negative actions after signing the Israel–Egypt peace treaty, we saw their ambassador in Israel recalled in 1982 because of the war in Lebanon. A new ambassador had been appointed only after the Oslo Declaration of Principles, eleven years later the Egyptians again recalled their ambassador at the beginning of the al-Aqsa *Intifada*. Israel's main complaint is directed against the Egyptian media, which is highly controlled by the government. The Egyptian media portrays Israel and its Zionist history in a perverse way. Most damaging are the anti-Semitic TV dramas.

There are hardly any Egyptian–Israeli joint economic projects, and the very few are all in the Cairo area operating almost in the "underground". Most international conferences held in Cairo are closed to Israeli participants, and even at the Cairo book fair there is no place for books from Israel.

Israelis resent that Egyptians held an Israeli citizen in prison eight years under false accusations of "spying." Israel also cannot forgive the Egyptians for keeping their eyes closed and doing literally nothing to prevent the smuggling of weapons from Sinai into the Gaza Strip. Israel is convinced that if the Egyptian authorities so decided, they could greatly diminish or possibly even stop the smuggling of weapons into Palestine.

As previously mentioned in the opening remarks, the last 24 years cannot be characterized as "a peace-process that went wrong." Rather, the lack of peace between Egypt and Israel has been the direct outcome of the basic positions of both parties during the negotiation of the agreement. Indeed, both parties have contributed and added obstacles along the road, but what has happened could and should have been foreseen.

CHAPTER 11

Jordan–Israel Relations: A "Lukewarm" Peace

JOSEPH NEVO

When looking back at the trials and tribulations of the decade-long Jordan–Israel peace, it is definitely more successful and more fruitful than its predecessor, the Egyptian–Israel one, in every given aspect. Indeed, the so-called "de facto peace" (that predated the conclusion of the formal treaty) provided Jordan–Israel relations with a rather advanced starting point; yet the expectations of the late King Hussein and of the late Prime Minister Yitzhak Rabin are still far from achievement. By and large the Israeli–Jordanian peace can be depicted as a lukewarm one that has not fulfilled Jordanian expectation. In this chapter we will endeavor to survey and explain the reasons.

The major obstacles have been cultural and perceptual gaps and a lack of knowledge and understanding between the two societies. This yielded many misconceptions, a disregard of sensitivities, mistrust and suspicion on the one hand, and unrealistic expectations on the other hand.

Most Israelis have perceived Jordan differently, and more favorably, than they have viewed other Arab states. Their perception of Jordan has stemmed from several factors. First, it has been generally believed that Jordan and Israel share common interests, and common apprehension about militant Palestinian radicalism, aimed, as the Israelis suspect, against both. Second, King Hussein, like King Abdullah I, exercised a more balanced attitude towards the Jewish state than his Arab counterparts. Finally, Jordan's withdrawal of its claim to the West Bank removed the major territorial and political bone of contention between Jordan and Israel, and paved the way to solidifying their practical understandings and formalizing their tacit, de-facto peace. After the peace treaty was concluded, however, this attitude became somewhat counterproductive. Most Israelis have taken Jordan for granted as their most sympathetic and friendly neighbor. They have failed to understand that most Jordanians have felt uncomfortable, personally and collectively, by this Israeli attitude. Most of them did not feel the same way towards Israel, not to mention the fear that amiable ties with Israel might harm Jordan's relations with other Arab countries.

The Israeli public was not prepared for the impact of the bilateral encounter. The lessons of the Egyptian–Israeli peace were practically ignored. On the Jordanian side, too, sufficient educational and media measures were not taken to prepare the ground for the political and ideological shift that the peace with Israel would reflect. Not only were the Jordanians not prepared for relations with the Israelis, the notion of peace with the Jewish state contradicted what they had hitherto been taught and believed. A Jordanian scholar wrote:

> The peace came upon the citizens of Jordan by surprise . . . after about eight decades during which they were taught about the hostile and aggressive nature of Israel; nothing was changed in school curriculum with regard to the Arab–Israeli conflict. They were neither prepared nor explained how to refer to the State of Israel and the Israeli society after the conclusion of the peace treaty. Decisions were imposed on them and they were forced to quickly digest them.
>
> It was not easy to put aside eight decades of indoctrination according to which Israel was an evil colonial imperialistic state and society – and to treat it as an ordinary society. Even for me, an academic who spent 17 years in Europe, it was difficult to accept that decision.[1]

An additional factor that made peace with Israel hard to accept was the Palestinian one. About half of Jordan's population is of Palestinian origin, and for them it was even more complex to endorse such a peace agreement. Indeed, negotiations for a Jordanian–Israeli peace-treaty officially began only after the mutual recognition between Israel and the Palestinian Liberation Organization, a recognition that was reflected in their joint declaration on principles and the historical handshake between Prime Minister Yitzhak Rabin and Chairman Yasser Arafat on the White House lawn in September 1993. Still, many Palestinians opposed that agreement. Later on, when political negotiations between Israel and the Palestinian National Authority reached an impasse, and particularly after the outbreak of the al-Aqsa *Intifada*, opposition to Israel and to the peace treaty increased among many Jordanians (Palestinians and non-Palestinians alike).

Despite all that has been mentioned above, the attitude of Jordanian society towards peace with Israel was not monolithic. A public discourse regarding the pros and cons of that peace began shortly after the treaty was signed and continues to flourish. This issue was more extensively discussed around the anniversary of the peace treaty, particularly at the time of the fifth and tenth anniversaries in 1999 and 2004 respectively.

The main advantages of the peace as perceived not only by its supporters but also by political analysts in Jordan can be summarized as follow:

1   The major benefit of peace is peace itself, the end of conflict, tension, violence and suffering.
2   Jordan enjoys, after almost five decades of a state of war, the demarcation of internationally recognized borders.
3   Jordan is no longer seen by Israel as a substitute homeland (*al-watan al-badil*) for the Palestinians. (Many Jordanians suspected that the transformation of their country into a Palestinian state, an idea not uncommon among right-wing circles in Israel, was the intention of the Likud governments.)
4   These first three "benefits" have relieved Jordan of severe economic, political, military and psychological burdens, and have enabled the kingdom to concentrate on pressing domestic issues.
5   Jordan has gained important new water resources.
6   In the first years after the peace treaty was concluded there was an improvement of the economic situation: a tourism boom, the writing-off of foreign debts, and increased foreign investment and financial aid.
7   Unique export opportunities have opened up as the US granted free trade access to Jordanian goods under the scheme of the Qualified Industrial Zones (QIZ). The new projects in these zones also created new jobs that somewhat contained the mounting unemployment rate. The products from those Zones increased Jordan's exports to the US from $13 million in the late 1990s to $420 million in 2002 and to over $1 billion in 2004.
8   The peace treaty has extracted Jordan from the isolation and the economic plight it plunged into as a result of its stand during the Gulf war.

On the other hand, the disadvantages of the peace as depicted by Jordanian observers are more complicated and can be divided into three categories. The first category concerns the immediate impact of "the fruits of peace" on the economic welfare and the standard of living of the Jordanian population.

1   The state has been the primary beneficiary of the material and economic advantages of peace. Benefits are felt less by the general population, except the workers of the tourist industry and in the QIZ.
2   The peace treaty created expectations that have not materialized. This has caused disappointment and bitterness.
3   Obstacles and limits set by Israel on trade between Jordan and the Palestinian Authority.

The second category concerns the impact of peace on Jordan's domestic life.

1   The peace treaty had a negative impact on freedom and democracy in Jordan. It slowed the political liberalization process that began in 1989, and political freedom has regressed since 1994. Claims were made that the most controversial legislation, namely the press and publication law and the election law, were designed to curtail any criticism and opposition to the peace with Israel, and thus constituted a retreat from the freedoms that were restored after 1989.
2   The peace treaty may prevent Jordanians of Palestinian origin from adequately pressing their "legal and historical claims" against the State of Israel. Moreover Jordan may become a permanent dumping ground for Palestinian refugees.

The third category of negative issues exceeds the narrower bilateral aspects of the peace treaty. They refer to Israel's "bad behavior" and reflect solidarity with the Palestinians, and broadly with pan-Arab sentiments.

1   The peace treaty allows continued Israeli aggression against Palestinian, Lebanese and Syrian lands.
2   Israel maintains an arrogant, superior, and apartheid-like attitude towards Palestinian and Arab rights.
3   No substantial progress has been achieved in Palestinian–Israeli negotiations; on the contrary, they have worsened.
4   The peace treaty has damaged Jordan's, and Jordanians', position in the Arab world.
5   For those who believed that Israeli–Arab relations were a zero-sum game, the peace was perceived as an Israeli victory and an Arab surrender.

The Jordanian public was roughly divided into three groups regarding peace with Israel. One section was ready to approve it, either because they believed it was good for Jordan, or they would personally benefit from its "fruits." Such a hope was rather common in Jordan in the immediate wake of the conclusion of the peace accord. The late King Hussein repeatedly iterated the term "the fruits of peace" as an incentive for the public to support his policy. In doing so, he probably created some exaggerated expectations by people that their own economic situations would be considerably improved in a matter of weeks. When rapid economic improvement did not materialize, many felt deceived. Nevertheless, some Jordanians did find work in Israel or in Israeli affiliated projects.

Another group may be depicted as "moderate nationalists" who were ready to acquiesce to peace provided that Israel would make certain political concessions, such as withdrawing from the West Bank and the Gaza Strip and allow for the establishment of a Palestinian state.

The third group however, the most vocal and influential in Jordan's political sphere, rejected any ties with Israel, and was reluctant to acknowledge the legitimacy of the Jewish state, regardless of its political behavior or whatever concessions Israel may have made. This group consisted of Islamists and pan-Arab nationalists whose major source of political power derived from the professional associations that they controlled. During the 1970s and 1980s, in the absence of parliamentary elections and active political parties, the professional associations filled the political vacuum and became a semi-recognized channel of political activity. When parliamentary life and party politics reemerged as a result of the political liberalization presented in the late 1980s and early 1990s, the associations spearheaded the struggle against peace and normalization with Israel. They adhered to this agenda in order to remain politically powerful and relevant, while the government endeavored to channel their activity back into the professional realm.

The scope and effectiveness of these associations' activity are a major reason why the peace has remained between governments and not transformed into peace between peoples. The associations's Council is a coalition of 14 professional associations with a membership of over 120,000. These professional associations, often headed by Islamists, have controlled essential aspects of Jordan's private and public sectors, and have enjoyed the support and organizational infrastructure of the Islamic movement in Jordan. The fact that many of their constituencies are Palestinians adds another dimension to their popular power. They have managed to mobilize tens of thousands of people to attend their anti-normalizations rallies, marches, and demonstrations.

The constitutions of most associations strictly prohibit any ties with Israel or Israelis. Infringement of those rules carries severe sanctions. Jordanian law allows most professionals to practice only if they are members of the relevant association. Expulsion of a member might result in a loss of employment and career. The most telling instance is the case of three Jordanian journalists who visited the University of Haifa in September 1999 as guests of the Jewish–Arab Center. After the visit, they found themselves on the point of being dismissed from their jobs. It was not until after they had publicly repented and government pressure was applied to their association, that the association's decision to dismiss them was eventually revoked.

The Council of Professional Associations' anti-normalization committee published, at least twice, intimidating "black lists" of Jordanian individuals and organizations that supported normalization, even though the government opposed their publication. Moreover, it seems that the public difference in attitude between King Hussein and his son Abdullah (at least in his first years on the throne) regarding the peace, unintentionally played into the hands of the anti-Israeli opposition.

King Hussein repeatedly underlined his commitment to *peace* with Israel, and King Abdullah reiterated his commitment to the *peace treaty*. However, the first Jordanian cabinet, formed in March 1999 after Abdullah's ascendancy, was that of Abd al-Ra'uf Rawabda, and contained not a single minister who was involved in either the peace treaty or the peace process. It did, however, have among the newcomers two leaders of professional associations, including the figurehead of the Associations' anti-normalization committee.

The gap between the two kings' attitudes to normalization was even wider. Hussein considered normalization as the essence of the peace treaty, and refused to regard normalization as a hostage of Israel's good behavior, or as a lever to pressure Israel to grant more concessions to the Palestinians – as many advised him to do. Abdullah, on the other hand, did not promote normalization and left discretion to individuals and organizations on whether or not to visit Israel or cooperate with Israeli colleagues and counterparts. Anti-normalization forces welcomed this attitude. Later on, however, King Abdullah signaled to the anti-normalization forces, in various ways, to limit their opposition to normalization.

One has to bear in mind that normalization with Israel is a much more sensitive issue than the peace treaty. Many among those who may have acquiesced to a formal peace as a matter between the two governments vehemently oppose normalization, which they regard as a direct threat to Arab tradition, culture, and even religion. On the eve of the conclusion of the peace treaty in 1994, 66% of publicly polled professionals in Amman supported peace talks with Israel. Less than half of them however were in favor of economic normalization, and a far lower percentage was willing to interact with Israel.

On the other hand, Jordanians who were (and still are) willing to visit Israel, despite the aforementioned difficulties and anti-Israeli atmosphere – and they are not few – have been sometimes discouraged by the bureaucratic obstacles laid by the Israeli embassy when they applied for a visa. Israeli authorities were indeed facing a dilemma over this issue. On the one hand, visitors from Jordan have been appreciated and welcomed. On the other hand, due to security and economic constraints, the Israelis thoroughly check visa applicants. They fear not only infiltration by terrorists or other security risks, but also illegal immigrants from Jordan. The number of Jordanians with illegal status (most of whom are of Palestinian origin) in Israel, is estimated to be in the thousands.

Israeli bureaucratic blocks have also hampered private and public endeavors for bilateral joint projects or joint ventures. Some of these obstacles have nothing to do with attitudes towards Jordan but are the result of "normal" Israeli bureaucratic foot-dragging. Some Israeli economists and entrepreneurs recommended the novel idea of an Israeli–Jordanian common international airport in Aqaba, or between Eilat and Aqaba. The idea was discussed in bilateral meetings among experts and the project was said to contain tremendous economic advantages for both parties. This idea has yet to materialize, not only because of bureaucratic constraints, but also because of hesitation by decision makers on both sides. Reasons for the hesitation include mutual suspicions and fear (primarily in Jordan) of unfavorable reaction from both domestic sectors and the larger Arab world.

The Present Situation and What Can Be Done to Improve It

The current situation is understandable considering the political reality, especially when compared to Israeli–Egyptian relations. The Jordanian government has not discouraged bilateral relations or restricted Jordanian citizens who wish to visit Israel or work with Israelis. The same applies to Israelis visiting or working in Jordan. Jordanian government representatives reiterate time and again that peace was – and still is – a strategic choice of Jordan.

On the occasion of the 10th anniversary of the Jordanian–Israeli peace treaty in October 2004, there were about 30 articles in the Jordanian press regarding the issue. They expressed a variety of opinions and comments, revealing Jordanian public awareness, of and interest in, the relations with Israel.

The economic ties between the two countries are ongoing. Mutual visits are constantly taking place, albeit in low profile, and so are cooperation and coordination between government officials in matters of common interest such as water and security.

What is needed and what has to be done to facilitate a warmer peace?

1   A change in the regional political atmosphere. Stabilization of the situation in Iraq and a political settlement for the Israeli–Palestinian conflict can create a better environment for the improvement of bilateral relations. As many Jordanians put it, Israel should recognize Palestinian rights, but not at the expense of Jordan.
2   A mutual recognition that peace is not a zero-sum game.
3   A greater awareness by Israel and the Israelis to Jordanian apprehensions regarding Israel's alleged intentions of turning Jordan into a Palestinian state, economically dominating Jordan, and turning Jordanian society into a bridge between the West and the Arab world that threaten Jordan's traditional and cultural values.
4   Israel should establish a national authority to discuss, in cooperation

with Jordan, all issues relevant to mutual relations. For example, one issue that the authority should address is simplifying visa procedures for those Jordanians wishing to visit Israel, while still safeguarding its security and economic interests. Such an authority should also survey all potential joint projects and give priorities to the viable ones.

5   A more active Jordanian policy, rather than the current passive one, regarding ties with Israel.
6   The weakening of the ability of the professional associations and other anti-normalization forces actively to preach and act against ties with Israel. This can be done, of course, only as a part of a comprehensive government policy to curb the involvement and interference of the professional associations in political matters.

Recently there have been some indications of a decrease in the associations' political power. Among the Jordanian visitors to Israel in 2004 and 2005 were a considerable number of members of professional associations. As noted, these associations formally prohibit their members from visiting Israel, and therefore it seems that either the associations' leadership or their constituencies are ignoring those "violations".

Moreover, Jordanian Interior Minister Samir Habashneh declared that the professional associations should focus on their own internal matters and refrain from interfering in politics. Political views should be expressed through other channels i.e., political parties. The minister warned that the government would no longer tolerate associations that have transformed themselves into platforms for ideologies considered harmful to the state and to its relations with other countries.

It is still unlikely, even if all necessary changes and developments were to occur, that Israel–Jordan relations would assume what one could term "Scandinavian style" neighborly relations. There will always remain forces that will refuse to accept Israel on ideological or religious grounds. However, the aforementioned recommendations may decrease the influence of those forces, and create a mainstream that will approve, or at least acquiesce, ties with Israel with varied levels of participation.

Note

1   In late 2006 trilateral discussions began between Jordanian, Israeli and Palestinian working groups regarding the old–new idea of the constructing of a canal between the Red and the Dead Seas, and this quote comes from those meetings.

CHAPTER 12

The Jordan–Israel Peace Process: How Can We Rebuild Trust and Replace Despair and Division?

RATEB MOHAMMAD AMRO

The Process as a Whole since Madrid

The convening of the Middle East peace conference in Madrid in 1991 was a direct reaction to international and regional developments that had altered the strategic environment of the region. The United States directed its diplomatic power towards a negotiated settlement to the Arab–Israeli conflict. The time was ripe for realizing this strategic goal. Both the Arabs and Israel had to enter the process, which was packaged as a feasible mechanism that took into account the concerns and interests of both parties.

The Madrid peace conference, and its aftermath, the Washington talks, represented a departure from the long-held Arab position of negotiating collectively in order to reach a comprehensive peace settlement. Ideologically, both Arabs and Israelis publicly acknowledged the territorial, as opposed to existential, nature of the conflict. The Arabs were willing to accept Israel's right to exist within clearly defined borders. Israel indicated its willingness to renounce its claim to parts of what some of its Zionist founders declared the Land of Israel. Israelis remain hostage to what many Arabs describe as an unrealistic and anachronistic obsession with security. On the Arab side, many are driven by the belief that Israel has to make the concessions because it is the aggressor who has humiliated them.

Since 1991 when Arab and Israeli negotiators began talks in Madrid, considerable "achievements" have been made. Jordan and Israel signed a peace treaty in 1994. The treaty came almost one year after the Palestinians and Israelis reached the Oslo interim agreement.

Jordanian–Israeli Relations

Following the successful conclusion of the peace treaty between Jordan and Israel in 1994, relations between the two countries proceeded in what promised to be a positive direction. Bilateral agreements covering a wide range of subjects were signed. Significant issues such as borders and security cooperation were tackled bilaterally in good faith. The mood in both countries was one of optimism.

Jordanian society has not yet seen the promised dividends of peace. Jordanians were initially led to believe that peace would produce a considerable improvement in their economic situation. At the macro level, the Jordanian economy has improved, but people are frustrated because they can see little reflection of the peace on their daily lives. The lack of sufficient peace dividends has made the peace treaty less popular in Jordan and has pushed pro-peace forces towards defensive positions.

Immediately after signing the peace treaty, the mood in Israel was very positive. People believed peace with Jordan could be genuine. However, the mood in Israel grew negative after realizing the intensity of the Jordanian anti-normalization campaigns. Israelis failed to understand the extent to which Jordanian–Israeli relations were affected by developments in other area. Jordan's commitment to a comprehensive regional peace is not solely rooted in altruism. It is a matter of national interest and security, dictated by realistic considerations.

Jordanians could not wholeheartedly engage in peaceful relations with Israel while Israel continued to occupy Arab territories and oppress other Arab people. Jordanian intellectuals refused to visit Israel to explain Jordan's needs and concerns, which could have led to a better understanding of Jordanian internal considerations.

The peace between the two countries was often described as warm. This might have been a correct assessment at the beginning of the peace, because the relationship between the late King Hussein and the late Yitzhak Rabin was one of mutual respect and trust. However, with the victory of the Israeli right wing in May 1996 the situation began to change. Tensions between the two countries started to develop and to be visible.

Despite the conclusion of agreements designed to encourage economic cooperation between the two countries, the volume of trade between Israel and Jordan has been low. On the heels of the 1994 Israeli–Jordanian peace treaty, the United States and Jordan began encouraging meetings among Israeli and Jordanian businesspersons. The US logic was simple: creating Arab–Israeli business links encourages and strengthens the private sector, which is a natural supporter of peace and a bulwark against radicalism. To provide incentives for these exchanges, US officials offered the Qualified Industrial Zone (QIZ) program. Jordan's exports to the US rose from less than $20 million in 1999 to over $1 billion by 2006. Many jobs have been created in the QIZs, with a reported 70 % of the jobs going to women. The success of the QIZ program is crucial, since it was the foundation of the more ambitious US-Jordan Free Trade Agreement. Under the FTA, tariffs between the two countries will be phased out over a ten-year period.[1]

Key Foreign Policy Issues

Palestinian Track

How does the Palestinian track affect Israeli–Jordanian relations? Given that the Middle East is a volatile region, Jordan attaches high importance to a comprehensive solution to the Arab–Israeli–conflict. The dangers of escalation of violence in Palestinian territories are not limited to Jordanian–Israeli bilateral relations but extend to Jordan's domestic and national interests. The continuation of the dangerous current situation has regional implications that could undermine previous accomplishments. For Jordanians, the crisis in Palestine is very near. From some areas of Jordan you can see the lights of Jerusalem illuminating the night sky. Everyday the people of Jordan know the suffering that is taking place in Palestine, and experience the destructive regional impact of the conflict.

Jordan has been a leader in the search for peace. For decades, Jordan has taken the risks that peace requires. Jordan is committed to helping achieve a real resolution and has a genuine interest in advancing the peace process, especially on the Palestinian–Israeli track. Jordan views the lack of peace as both an external and an internal threat. Hence, the establishment of an independent Palestinian state is in Jordan's strategic interests. Final status issues have far-reaching implications for Jordanian security and Jordanian–Israeli bilateral relations, as detailed below.

1. Jerusalem

The issue of Jerusalem is of great importance for both sides. In the peace treaty, Israel recognizes Jordan's special links to the Muslim shrines in Jerusalem. Jordan would like to preserve the religious status quo in the Old City. For the Arabs in general and the Jordanians and Palestinians in particular, East Jerusalem is part of the Arab territories occupied in 1967 to which Resolution 242 applies. The Jordanian government insists that Jerusalem has to be the capital of the Palestinian state. However, the Jordanians are willing to consider the possibility of Jerusalem (both east and west) remaining a united and an open city for both sides, with clear demarcation of Palestinian and Israeli sovereignty lines.

Israeli governments have refused this. They have insisted that Jerusalem will not be divided again, that it is the capital of Israel, and that no sovereignty other than that of Israel will be allowed. In Israel this has been the national consensus since 1967. However, many Israelis argue that there is a crack in this national consensus. Jerusalem, according to this new thinking, could serve as a capital for the two states and there should be creative thinking with regard to solving the conflict over it. Mainstream Israelis understand that they cannot be occupiers of another people. A Palestinian capital in Eastern Jerusalem would be matched by an Israeli capital in Western Jerusalem. This is the unavoidable road to peace.

2. Refugees

Jordan hosts the largest number of Palestinian refugees outside Palestinian territories (more than 1.57 million Palestinian refugees living in Jordan were registered with UNRWA in 2001 out of a population of approximately five million Jordanians). The high number of Jordanians of Palestinian origin whose relatives live and suffer in the Palestinian territories makes Jordan particularly sensitive to the daily events and tragedies that occur in these territories. The historic, social, and political relationships that have strongly bound Palestinians and Jordanians places the Palestinian–Israeli conflict at the top of Jordan's political priorities as one of its most critical national interests.

This situation underlines the urgency and absolute necessity for the Kingdom to be fully and aggressively engaged in the pursuit of a peaceful settlement to the Palestinian problem as it has been throughout more than five decades since its independence. The refugee problem, a vital Jordanian concern and interest, is considered to be one of the country's most important issues in the final status negotiations. Jordan hosts 41% of Palestinian Refugees and 90% of Displaced Persons (DPs).

Jordan's legal standing, interests, and legitimate concerns should not be ignored. Jordan cannot be expected to consent to unacceptable solutions on refugees and DPs, or to enforce such solutions on its citizens; it must therefore have a central role in the political and economic settlement of this problem, which should recognize the right of refugees and DPs in Jordan to return and be adequately compensated.

3. Settlements

Jordanians believe that settlement activity is the main obstacle to peace. According to international law, all settlements are illegal. Various Israeli governments have built settlements in order to create political facts on the ground that would lead to a gradual absorption of more Palestinian land.

A continuation of such activity in any manner hinders the prospects for the emergence of a viable Palestinian state, thus threatening the prospects for a peaceful solution to the Israeli–Palestinian conflict. In addition, Israeli settlements place intolerable burdens on Palestinian movement and development while depriving the Palestinian people of important land and water resources.

Jordanians believe that sustaining pre-existing settlements will have serious negative implications not only for the Palestinians but for Israel as well. If settlements are not dismantled, Israel will face increased difficulty in guaranteeing its own security. Furthermore, demographers estimate that the Arab population in Israel and the territories will exceed the Jewish population by 2020.

Therefore, Israel's dismantling of its settlements is of utmost importance if Israel is to preserve its Jewish character and democratic nature by making way for the creation of an independent and viable Palestinian state.

4. Security: Suicide Bombings and Political Assassinations

From a political and moral point of view, the targeting of Israeli civilians is to be abhored. But the whole spectrum of security issues needs to be addressed, including Israel's targeted political assassinations. This latter policy will only lead to further escalation, violence, and instability in the region. In addition, Israel's Separation Barrier Wall, which cuts deep into Palestinian territories, is illegal and needs to dismantled.

Security cannot be used as a pretext for depriving millions of Palestinians from getting essential food and medical services. Israel has to realize that its approach is unacceptable; it results in excessive use of force, which in turn fuels and deepens hatred and replenishes the wellspring of violence. Dialogue is the only way to end the regional tension, find a just solution to the occupied territories issue, and establish an independent Palestinian state.

5. Gaza Pullout

Jordan welcomes the Israeli dismantlement of Jewish settlements and withdrawal from the Gaza Strip as a step in the right direction. The Gaza withdrawal should not be a replacement of the Roadmap but very much a part of it. Jordan insists on a clear commitment by Israel to all three phases of the Roadmap, and Israel's coordination not only with the Palestinians, Egypt, and Jordan but also the four co-sponsors of the Middle East Roadmap peace plan – the United States, the European Union, the United Nations, and Russia.[2]

How Can We Rebuild Trust to Replace Despair and Division?

Rebuilding trust and replacing despair and division is easier said than done, and I do not think that those who are not directly involved in the conflict can fully understand how much it takes to break this pattern, to be the first one to hold out a hand to the other side, and perhaps even to face a potential friend instead of the hereditary enemy. The solution is not an abstract concept, but a durable peace that both the Israeli and Palestinian governments will accept. Additionally, the governments of the other Arab countries should also endorse and contribute to the process.

But peace is not just the responsibility of governments – it is the responsibility of all of us, and we all have to contribute the best we can to a peaceful solution. People-to-people relations since December 2000 are no longer working. We who believe in peace must now succeed, not only for the sake of those who are suffering from this relentless cycle of pain and violence, but also for the sake of the world we live in, a world that is indivisible, a world that must achieve peace and justice if it is to be open and free.

The process starts with trust, and trust starts with respect. Respect will only come if occupation and killing cease; if the two sides no longer ignore each other's views and aspirations; and once the protagonists give each other the right to live in peace. Palestinians, Jordanians, Israelis and others are entitled to the inalienable right to life, liberty, and pursuit of happiness.

Is this achievable? I believe it is – the roots of success go back deep in our culture. Today the eyes of the world are on our region, and again the issue of trust is paramount – it is about words and commitments. People around the globe are debating about who can be trusted, and how long they can be trusted. It is no exaggeration to say that millions of lives are at stake, yet while our attention is being focused in one direction, the real trustbuster may lie somewhere else.

For half of the 20th century and now, into a new era, the Arab–Israeli conflict has brought instability and danger, not just to the region but also to the whole world. Like acid, it has eaten across the pages of history. What is left is the record of failure, both moral and political. It is time to open a new volume and write a new future. Such a peace must include at a minimum, for three million Palestinians, a commitment to rebuild their shattered infrastructure; it must provide security for Israelis and Palestinians alike. Only then will extremists on both sides be deprived of the support that keeps violence alive.

After all the progress at the negotiating tables – and there have been successes – the reality remains. A deadly cycle of violence and years of hostility have stalled regional development. Millions have been left to believe that the powerful West is indifferent, or worse, that despair, hatred, and division have helped extremists recruit for global campaigns of terror.

Clearly a lasting peace in the Arab–Israeli conflict is a core requirement for peace in the region. But we must go further; we must offer real hope to the young minds of today. To accomplish this, we must devote ourselves, individually and collectively, to building better futures for our people.

Assuredly, the conflict remains central to the Middle East and to the world. No other conflict has cast such long shadows on our globe, been used to cause such division, or promoted such bitterness. The time has come to put a stop to the long and hateful cycle of violence. The 21st century has opened billions of minds to the possibilities of a better life – one of freedom, prosperity and hope.

This brings the discussion to a second regional challenge, the challenge of development. The region needs to put its energy into development not conflict. Arab states have young populations. Within the next few decades, the overwhelming majority of our people will have been raised and educated in a world where democracy, human rights, and market economies are the norm, and they will not accept less for themselves. Meeting those expectations will require structural change. Arab economies must increase if they are to absorb the expanding labor force. Growth is also essential in meeting important social goals such as reducing poverty, improving the quality of life, and enhancing health, to name a few.

Reports show that per capita income has actually shrunk in Arab countries during the last 20 years. One of every five Arabs lives on less than $2 a day, and in the labor force, one of seven is unemployed. Youth, who constitute more than 60% of the population, are especially vulnerable when they lose hope. They can turn to apathy or violence. Perhaps most importantly, we need to rebuild trust – the foundation for a civil society that is open, modern and responsive.

The contours of a historic reconciliation are before us. It involves a two-state solution, in which an independent Palestinian state lives in peaceful coexistence alongside a secure and recognized Israel, within the 1967 frontiers, with full normalization between the Arab countries and Israel.

The parties, their neighbors, and the region cannot do it alone. The international community has a crucial role. To achieve a just and lasting peace requires a collective international alliance for peace and stability, but daring diplomacy is what the present crisis needs. A clear road to a stable lasting peace now exists, with clear committed leadership from the United States and Europe. A majority of Palestinians and Israelis will choose coexistence and peace. Both of these people share a commitment to peace and stability; they share respect for human dignity and security. It is now paramount that they share the leadership in achieving these values. It is time to act, and time to succeed. We look to ourselves to create our own future, but our friends around the globe can also make a vital contribution. When the international community supports those of us who are engaged in reform, when it supports development, it helps create a climate of justice and hope – the necessary environment for security in the region and around the world.

Those of us who live in the Middle East share a special heritage. From our soil, the Levant, faith in One God, the united beliefs of Judaism, Christianity, and Islam took root and spread across the world. What is taking root in the Middle East today can also impact the world. If we succeed – and success will require all of us – this may be a century in which billions of people have access to the world's promise. Those who believe in peace must stand together. For those who want to rebuild the bridges across borders, let this be our monument of lasting good; let it be a testament to those who lost their lives; let it be the victory of humanity.

What I think is most needed right now is for all the international civil organizations that are not directly involved in the conflict to take a neutral position, stop the condemnations, and instead use their strength to put pressure on both sides in order to build peace and trust between the two people – the sooner the better. Violence creates violence – hatred leads to more hatred. This evil spiral has to be broken by brave people – people on each side of the conflict who have the courage to overcome the evil pattern that has characterized the area for so long, in order to make a new beginning, one in which confidence and the will to compromise are given the seat of honor.[3]

Conclusion

Peace between Arabs and Israelis will mean the culmination of two different processes. For the Israelis, it is the crowning jewel in a series of victories, which started with the establishment of the Jewish state in parts of historic Palestine and are finally ending with the Arabs' political and diplomatic recognition of its right to exist. For the Arabs, peace will mean a final defeat, recognizing it and accepting to live with its consequences.

The Middle East peace process has reached a serious impasse. Structural problems inherent in the step-by-step approach may require rethinking the mechanisms of negotiations. New initiatives, particularly on the Palestinian–Israeli track, could offer the only way for saving the process. The fear is that the focus would be on maintaining the process regardless of results. Violence (as a result of Palestinian frustration and further deterioration in the economic conditions in the West Bank and Gaza) could continue.

What is needed is a newfound sense of energy from the US administration on Middle East peacemaking and the determination of the administration and the President to commit fully to supporting the

Israeli–Palestinian process and finding a true peace. The seriousness of such commitment and involvement will be judged on whether the United States is prepared to put pressure on Israel as well as on the Palestinians. At the same time, the role of the United States is critical and indispensable in complementing and sustaining the efforts of Arab states towards achieving an end to violence and movement towards political talks. There is compelling evidence that without sustained and active American leadership the situation on the ground in the Palestinian Occupied Territories continues to deteriorate.

The Palestinians and the Israelis have in principle accepted the emergence of two states west of the River Jordan. Yet they remain reluctant to make all the necessary concessions for reaching a final agreement. Third-party help is needed. Jordan and Egypt should, and can, play a constructive role in facilitating the talks and saving the process from collapse. Europe should not restrict its involvement to the economic sphere. It can make important political contributions to the negotiations.

In conclusion, Jordanian–Israeli relations are stable. But their further development is linked to progress on other tracks. For Jordan, the achievement of comprehensive peace is a matter of national security. The improvement of Jordanian–Israeli relations depends on the progress in the peace process as a whole. The potential for joint projects between the two sides is high. But even though Jordan is eager to develop its relations with Israel, its national interests, inter-Arab position, and domestic public opinion make the development of relations beyond a certain limit extremely difficult before a comprehensive peace is achieved in the region. It is time for the Middle East to enter a new era. Globalization and the spread of democracy have necessitated major changes in policy priorities and in inter-regional relations. The development of a network of regional institutions addressing issues of common interest can create a degree of inter-dependence that will protect and support the peace.

Jordanians maintain that the only viable course for addressing the Palestinian–Israeli question lies in the resumption of the peace process as a whole from the point where it stalled and within the agreed frameworks, which include complete Israeli withdrawals from all Arab territories occupied in 1967 (including the Palestinian, Syrian, and Lebanese territories) and the establishment of the independent Palestinian state, with East Jerusalem as its capital, pursuant to relevant Security Council resolutions, especially 242, 338, 425 and United Nations Security Council Resolution 1397.[4]

Notes

1   "Peace Process," report by the staff of the Center for Strategic Studies, March, 2004, University of Jordan, Amman, Jordan.

2   "Peace Process in the Middle East," report of the Ministry of Foreign Affairs, May, 2004, Hashemite Kingdom of Jordan.

3   "Peace between Jordan and Israel," reports by Rateb Amro, Horizon Strategic Studies Institute, Amman, Jordan.

4   "Middle East News," *The Jordan Times New Paper,* Monday, January 27, 2003, p. 2.

CHAPTER 13

What Went Wrong in the Middle East Peace Process? The Jordanian–Israeli Relationship

MOHAMMAD AL-MOMANI

What Justifies this Question?

After more than a decade since the signing of the peace treaty between Jordan and Israel, observers and analysts are convinced that enough evidence is available to assess the success and viability of the treaty. The need for assessment was motivated by the lack of warm peace, which was highly expected and emphasized before and during the declaration of the treaty. Although no one could describe the peace between Jordan and Israel as "cold", similar to that between Egypt and Israel, the optimal declared goal was a warm and genuine peace. Simply stated, the declared goal has not taken place.

Another factor that justifies the question "what went wrong?" is the belief that Jordan–Israel relations had the potential to grow and flourish and be a model to similar bilateral relations between Israel and other neighboring states. It was believed that peace between the two countries had the potential to spread all over the Middle East due to Jordan's credibility among many Arab countries, its often balanced political behavior, and its relatively educated public that holds more socio-political liberal ideas than many other Middle Eastern societies.

Any peace assessment between Jordan and Israel must distinguish between two major levels of analysis: government and people. There is a drastic difference between these two levels. Many would rate government-to-government peace and relations as highly successful and, at certain periods of time, warm; it deserves an 8 out of 10 to use a scale of 1 to 10. A good example of the positive interaction between the two governments is the Qualified Industrial Zones (QIZ) that are creating a state of complex interdependence which provides an opportunity to institutionalize peace, as both countries' interests are highly connected and indeed interdependent.[1] The QIZs have constituencies in each country that are very sensitive to maintaining strong bilateral relations. Israeli investors became the best force to pressure their government and lobby for Jordanian interests as they coincide with their own interests. The same logic could be applied to the Jordanian beneficiaries of interactions with Israel, including thousands of individual workers.

On the other hand, this peace has not been actualized in other societal levels. People-to-people peace had often been poorly rated and could be assigned a 2 out of 10. Psychological barriers, often emphasized as significant in promoting conflict and hindering peace, still exist between the two peoples and little improvement had been noticed on that front.[2]

Reasons for the "Lukewarm" Peace

In light of the deteriorating peace status between Jordan and Israel, it is legitimate to search for the reasons affecting the level of, and how to lessen, their negative effects. These reasons can be categorized as international, regional, and domestic.

International Reasons

Peace between Jordan and Israel was always sensitive to American politics and American presidents' agendas. During the last period of the Clinton Administration the focus was on the Israeli–Palestinian track as President Clinton viewed it as the core of the conflict. While this is probably true, it did take the focus and pressure away from efforts to advance other bilateral peace agreements. Other peace parties in the region felt that the destiny of their relation with Israel is conditioned and subject to a Palestinian–Israeli peace and therefore lost their enthusiasm to a warm and sustainable peace. In addition, Clinton's intensely engaged approach came at the least favorable time when his presidency was about to end. Any peace attempt or commitment would have needed to be continued by the incoming president, and that did not happen, as was expected. Both parties understood that the late start by Clinton, and his impeachment proceedings, undermined his ability and credibility to pressure and to nurture a final peace settlement. Second, Clinton's intensely engaged approach gave the Palestinians and Israelis the sense that they were in optimal negotiation positions and they could gain more if they prolonged the negotiations. Clinton's attempt not only was unsuccessful but it also created an environment for an escalation of violence that makes it very hard for others in the region to advance the peace agenda. Peace was no longer a strategic priority.

Clinton's successor, President George W. Bush, on the other hand, adversely affected the regional peace with the exact opposite approach to that of President Clinton: a disengagement approach. Bush came with a clear doctrine of not committing the prestige of the American president unless parties in the region were ready to make peace. Bush clearly believed that an intense engagement policy was a mistake, but it did not take him long to discover that disengagement was equally wrong. He ended up pursuing a middle ground policy in what could be described as a "reluctant engagement policy". Bush had a fairly convincing logic, especially to the American public, that if peace partners are not ready to make concessions, then it should not be the United States' role nor is it in the United States' best interest to force them into peace. Such peace will be unauthentic and too fragile to sustain.

The result of President Bush's approach to the Middle East peace process was the regionalization of the conflict as opposed to the internationalization of it. States in the Middle East felt that the United States – the international mediator with acceptance and credibility among all conflicting partners, and the state that initiated the peace process and guided it – is no longer willing to play that role. Taking international mediation and pressure away was very damaging to the peace spirit, and the parties approached the peace settlement with the pure sense of traditional political calculations and interests.[3] Peace as a value was no longer looked at as a moral goal in itself. States wanted material gains.

Regional Reasons

Several regional reasons created a general negative environment and undermined any talk of peace. The hostile environment to peace harmed the liberal views and agenda, which were already weak and scattered in the Middle East. Liberalism as consistent with peace was aggressively questioned and indeed attacked.[4] The societal price that the pro-peace forces had to pay became increasingly high, which silenced such forces and yielded the floor to radicalism.

For Arabs, the war in Iraq made relations with Israel unpopular as nationalistic and anti-western views were exceptionally high. Based on the "rally round the flag effect," people and political forces will unite and support their previously hated rulers and ideologies when attacked by a foreign force.[5] This is exactly what the war on Iraq did to the region and across most societies. The war, with the many controversies surrounding it, shifted many segments of societies in the region to the extreme right and left, which tended to belong to the anti-peace camps.

The *Intifada*, without exploring its reasons and morality as both parties have completely conflicting views regarding this, had the same political effect on the peace values and process. In Jordan's case, the *Intifada* was far more influential than the Iraq war in terms of Jordan's willingness to advance peace and relations with Israel. What makes the *Intifada* far more influential in the domestic and foreign policy of Jordan is the demographic nature of the Jordanian society. The country, with its high percentage of citizens of Palestinian origin, found it increasingly difficult to talk about peace and friendship with Israel with all the violence that took place and was aired daily on TV screens.

Violence in the West Bank is not only a political and societal issue, but also an individual matter that many take very personally and, indeed, are affected by it at the family and personal level. People die in the West Bank and funeral homes open in Jordan, indicating the high degree of family connections between Jordan and the West Bank. The phenomenon was intensified due to the media revolution that the Middle East has been living through. Satellite TV stations and the World Wide Web made information more accessible and its flow unstoppable, including scenes of violence and conflict, which further antagonized people and increased the level of hatred towards Israel. People were angered to the degree that one of the immediate demands they made to their governments was to cut diplomatic relations with Israel, which would hurt these governments' own national interests. These demands at some point reached a very dangerous level that could have caused a full-scale regional war. There were calls for war against Israel or to open borders to those wanted to attack Israel.

The other major regional factor that inhibited the declared goal of a warm peace between Israel and Jordan is the inherited traditions of the widespread negative and hateful feelings toward Israel. It was not easy for Jordan or any other Arab countries to challenge public opinion, conventional wisdoms, and values that people have held dear for decades. People had been preparing for the coming battle that would bring justice and revenge from the enemy state, which is characterized in their literature by all kinds of evil characters.

Domestic Reasons: Israel

The democratic nature of the Israeli governments and the different views and approaches of political parties to peace with Jordan gave that peace a fluctuating character. In principle, all governments that came after the peace treaty was signed with Jordan kept their peace commitments and obligations; however, the degree of engagement and the temperature of that peace varied greatly. It was hard for both countries, given their international reputation and interests, to back out of their international obligations to the peace treaty. However, Binyamin Netanyahu's government, for example, felt that they could get better gains from Jordan on its signed obligations in the peace treaty. As a result, his government reluctantly delivered on Israeli treaty obligations and hampered progress in other areas between Jordan and Israel of importance to Jordan. For instance, Netanyahu at some point allowed intelligence operations on Jordanian soil that angered the late King Hussein who was a strong force for peace and a supporter of those who spoke openly about it.

There were other Israeli governments that genuinely believed in warm peace and were willing to take necessary steps to advance that peace. For such governments, the biggest strategic interest was a warm and lasting peace with neighboring countries, including Jordan. The Israeli government most often cited as a true seeker of peace with Israel's neighbors is that of the late Yitzhak Rabin.

Peace between the two counties was also subject to two conflicting mentalities: the "realist distribution of power mentality" versus the "positive sum" game and "absolute advantage" mentality. It was a well-known fact that the power distribution favored Israel when the peace treaty was signed, but many political forces, especially in Jordan, did not believe that this was the decisive factor and spirit that guided the whole process. If Jordan believed that power was the main factor guiding the peace process, it would have thought much more before entering into a peace deal. The belief among many Jordanians, including the decision makers and top leadership, was that peace is a positive sum game whereby all partners would benefit from the fruits of the peace. The country entered the peace process with the spirit of absolute gains and not relative gains, which made it a genuine peace seeker and a credible partner.

Several forces in Israel, on the other hand, thought that it was naïve and politically incorrect to ignore historic facts such as Israel's repeated victories in war; and the fact that Israel was the stronger partner in the peace equation. The belief was that other peace partners, including Jordan, must cope with these realities and make the appropriate concessions; or else, they would get little from the strong and victorious Israel. The clearest example of this kind of thinking was again the Netanyahu government, which acted under the most classic principles of realism and followed its main guidelines closely.

While this kind of thinking is perfectly consistent with political realism, it was not at all helpful to the advancement of the peace process or the creation of a warm peace.[6] The focus on how much one could gain over the others increased and highlighted the differences among the peace partners; it also created an unfriendly atmosphere for interactive relations. This attitude affected many segments of Israeli society and further radicalized them and their image towards the peace process. It was a strategic mistake to manage the peace process and treaties through a realist view. The values of peace and treaties naturally fall under the spirit of idealism, positive sum, and absolute gain.[7] Second, the realist approach and calculations, by many standards, were not well done and often short-sighted. Israel had a great interest in a warm and lasting peace at the strategic level, even if it came at the expense of tactical or short-term gains.

Domestic Reasons: Jordan

Societal factors were often fatal to Jordan's declared goal of a genuine and warm peace. The society has strong and persistent forces that have committed themselves to fighting peace and to overcoming all obstacles to the peace process. The efforts of the opposition forces turned out to be easier than expected as they found a fertile public filled with hostile feelings and hatred towards Israel.

Years of education and preparation of Arabs for a "just war" helped the anti-peace forces. When peace became the norm, war sentiments and war-related teachings persisted. Calls for war and preparation for the coming "just battle" persisted in the media, as well as in text and non-text books, after the peace treaty was signed between Israel and Jordan, which fueled a public debate about the teaching of war in Jordan. The compromise was to include such teachings in history but to teach equally about the values of peace and harmony, and about the new era of peace and friendship with Israel. This was done only at official and governmental level institutions because it was not possible to impose the program on private groups. The private media, for example, continued with strident pro-war teachings. People were more comfortable with the media tone and consequently the media's influence over social education grew dramatically. The Jordanian media was also re-enforced by the influential regional media with its strong pro-war tone.

Another societal factor that adversely affected warm peace was a phenomenon that might be called "opinion leaders fear". Public opinion leaders are supposedly the ones who shape the values and attitudes of the public; however, in many Middle Eastern countries it is the other way around. Public opinion leaders are often scared to counter prevailing public opinions. They therefore tend to agree and confirm public convictions rather than to confront or change them, even if they are wrong. Educated and informed thinkers should be shaping societal values and challenging what they consider erroneous public opinions. If not, society will divert from progress and distance itself from advancing world civilization. However, many opinion leaders are not willing to confront public convictions that they consider to be wrong because of the high social price they might pay. Given the fact that Middle Eastern societies are not individualistic societies, the price of challenging public convictions can be exceptionally high.

Many Jordanians did not feel the need for a warm peace; consequently, they were not ready to make major moves, sacrifices, or adjustments to help advance peace. Jordan has been living under relatively prosperous standards and most citizens live in far better economic conditions than other countries surrounding Israel. Jordan has also been living under a high degree of security and stability, and average citizens took their security for granted. In fact, most Jordanians would see violence, which mainly took place in the West Bank and Gaza, only on TV screens (just like people in Tokyo or New York). Many Jordanians did not view peace as needed to improve their lives and standard of living, since they were already living under decent and acceptable conditions.

The demographic context of Jordan's society presented itself as another obstacle to optimal peace. Jordanians of Palestinian origin, more than anyone else, found it very difficult to accept concessions made to Israel because of their personal and direct experience with the conflict. Many had previously devoted themselves to the destruction of the enemy state. Many of these citizens still identify themselves as Palestinians or Palestinian refugees who have unfinished business with the occupier, Israel. At another level, many educated Palestinians believe that Jordan should not make any concessions unless the Palestinian Authority agrees. They view the Palestinian Authority as most related to the conflict and as having the biggest say on how it should be resolved. They felt it was unwise of the government to ignore the sentiments of a great segment of society by pursuing a warm peace. The Jordanian government had to take into account the attitudes of the nation's large number of Jordanians of Palestinian origin in order to ensure an acceptable degree of stability in the country.

Jordanian Reasons: The Elite

The Jordanian elite, when asked why a warm peace has not happened, often answers that Israel's words of peace and friendship have not complied with its actions. This view is highly influenced by the intense media coverage of violence in the West Bank and Gaza, which often shows unarmed Palestinians fighting the well-armed Israeli army. The elite do not analyze the immediate reasons behind this violence, and the majority views suicide bombings as a legitimate technique of retaliation against the aggressor. They regard Palestinians' violent behavior as the natural consequence of Israel's actions (which is the exact opposite of what Israelis think). Few elites understand that this is a "chicken and egg" question, and that politicians have often used violence as a negotiation tool to maximize their gains.

The elite also notes that coldness in peace is the natural result of "injustice." They believe a great injustice has been done to Arabs and the Palestinians, and for warm peace to become a reality, justice must prevail. Justice for them is clear and undisputed and they do not accept any version of justice other than theirs. They discount the fact that justice is a relative term and differs across peoples and cultures; consequently, what is just for the Palestinians or Jordanians is not necessarily viewed the same by the Israelis. In fact, the Israelis have their own version of justice that addresses their own history and grievances. Also, in politics and negotiation, reaching a settlement takes precedence over the issue of justice, and the priority should be to issues of concession and compromise. What the whole Middle East peace process is trying to accomplish is not justice (as we do not know what justice is), but rather to create a peaceful mechanism to solve disputes and, indeed, to transform conflict into peace.

At the elite level, there is a medium level leadership crisis that is the result of weak civil society, which is a major supplier of leaders to societies. Leaders who could support peace were hard to find. Many in Jordan made a career out of blaming Israel and the United States for all societal ills, a position attractive to the politically uneducated and inexperienced public. Conversely, during some periods it was literally political and social suicide to side with Israeli and US policies, even if they were moderate and favorable. Conspiracy theory was popular, advocates of balanced views were unwelcome and often characterized as unfaithful to the principles, values, and rights of Arab nations and Islamic civilization.

Jordan has a weak pro-peace elite and a strong anti-peace one, which is the natural result of the historical evolution of the conflict. What makes the competition between the two camps unfair is the tremendous help the anti-peace movement gets from any political mistake of the peace advocates and from the regionally biased media with its strong pro-war stance. The pro-peace elite has to depend solely on their own performance and credibility. This elite made a strategic mistake. Peace was marketed negatively by emphasizing that Jordan had no other option but to agree on the offer presented. Peace was not marketed because of its intrinsic value, or because it was the right and natural thing to do; but rather because it was the only option and also because of the prosperity that would come as a result of peace. Prosperity never came and other countries chose other options than peace, and they survived. It was a missed opportunity to educate the public and establish a genuine belief in peace as a universal value.

What Could Be Done?

Assessing the problem and admitting its existence is the number one step toward treating it. Something did go wrong as optimal peace has never been achieved. Many solutions and mechanisms could be suggested. From a macro- and long-range point of view, liberalizing the Middle East could be the most effective and strategic mechanism for establishing the values of peace and coexistence, and for enhancing genuine and warm peaceful relations among nations and societies in the region. This can be supported by empirical and theoretical evidence that throughout history, democracies tended not to fight each other. There have been very few wars out of the thousands of wars fought that were between democracies. This is a powerful insight in political science with enormous implications.[8]

At the same time, we all are aware that the prospects for peace between Israel and Palestine do not at this time seem to have been advanced by the democratic election of the Hamas government in Palestine. Nevertheless, Middle Eastern societies and political behavior are expected to follow the democratic path.[9]

The situation between Hamas and Israel is a prime example of why there is a need to support and empower liberal and pro-peace forces directly and indirectly. Such forces are receiving little support from governments that have signed peace treaties. Governments in the Middle East could help liberal and pro-peace forces in their countries in a variety of ways. The minimum level of support would be verbal political support of peace in general, and the acknowledgment of favorable consequences and results.

International players can supply much needed moral support for peace and guidance to liberal and pro-peace groups and to governments. International players could help by providing political forums for pro-peace forces. Peace seekers could benefit by interacting with international peace supporters and from international views about peace. When pro-peace forces meet, they know and learn more about each other's grievances and aspirations.

Regional governments and international players' efforts to promote the value of peace and the peace process should focus on two main areas: the press and education. By all measures available, these two venues are the most powerful and effective in terms of influencing changes in the different societies. Winning the battle for change and reform in these two areas would automatically mean winning it at the societal level as a whole. What is needed is an environment that allows for the pro-peace alliance to grow and for pro-peace voices to be heard in the media and influence the educational process. Only then can we have public opinion leaders who would be ready to take risks to speak out about their pro-peace views; and only then will we have a generation that values and promotes peace.

Notes

1   J. David Singer, "The Level-of-Analysis Problem in International Relations," *World Politics*, Vol. 14, No. 1 (1961), pp. 77–92.

2   James A. Schellenberg, *Conflict Resolution: Theory, Research, and Practice* (State University of New York Press, 1996), Chapter 3.

3   Ibid., Chapter 10.

4   Immanuel Kant, *Perpetual Peace* (1795).

5   Ole R. Holsti, *Public Opinion and American Foreign Policy* (Ann Arbor: The University of Michigan Press, 1999).

6   Manus Midlarsky, *Handbook of War Studies* (Ann Arbor: University of Michigan Press, 1989); John A. Vasquez, *Classic of International Relations,* 3rd ed. (New Jersey: Prentice-Hall, 1996).

7   Schellenberg, *Conflict Resolution*, Chapter 8.

8   Michael W. Doyle, "Liberalism and World Politic," *American Political Science*

Review, Vol. 80 (4) (1986), pp. 1151–69; Zeev Maoz and Bruce Russett, "Normative and Structural Causes of Democratic Peace, 1946–1986," *American Political Science Review*, Vol. 87(3) (Sep. 1992), pp. 624–38; George Sorensen, *Democracy and Democratization: Process and Prospective in a Changing World (Dilemmas in World Politics)*, 2nd ed. (Boulder, CO: Westview Press, 1998).

9   Theoretically, the picture is less clear as we do not know yet what is it about democracies that give them the tendency toward peaceful resolution of conflicts. The most common explanation is that democracies have complex political structures, which often slow the decision of war. Also, democracies, because they have elected decision makers who are sensitive to voters, tend to invest and pay specially attention to voters' desire for prosperity. These characteristics of democracies have made them very reluctant to take the decision to enter expensive wars. It also made them prosperous (Sorensen, ibid.).

CHAPTER 14

Creative Measures Needed for a Peace Accord Between Israel and Syria

UZI ARAD

When one looks at the Syrian case one finds some good and bad news. The good news is that the Syrian issue has been less plagued by the kind of problems that have afflicted the Palestinian case. The Palestinian issue, which will be addressed later, has been extremely and heavily burdened by emotions, political overtones, fads, self-serving positions, and problems with the media. It is thick with theater, to the point of almost obscuring some obvious realities. In the Syrian case people do not have much difficulty with the facts, and the picture is much clearer. Not everything may be known, but what is known is quite consistent, and this should be helpful. There is less rhetoric and emotion, and the ingredients are clear.

Impediments to Clear and Timely Communications

The critical aspect of the Syrian–Israeli relationship is that its failure to progress to an agreement is due to unsuccessful management, lack of creativity, or, to use the terminology of the authors of the US Congress Commission's September 11, 2001 Report, due to a "failure of imagination." Interestingly, Shlomo Ben Ami discusses intelligence and failure, or inability, to see peace indicators. Sometimes one also needs imagination to see opportunities and grasp new options. I will argue that the Syrian case suffered from these kinds of failures – mismanagement and lack of creativity.

The context for negotiations with the Syrians is typified by difficulties that are not present in the Palestinian case. For example, if there is one thing that we do not lack in the Palestinian context, it is channels of communication. What we actually have is an embarrassment of choice, as there are many official and semi-official, overt and covert tracks. I do not remember another case in which societies were dialoging with so many points of contact. That has not been the case with the Syrians. With the Syrians we have consistently had a structural problem, not only of an ability to communicate and understand, but often there were shortages, sheer problems of passing messages and being able getting to talk. This has been the case, and continues to be the case, even though there are some channels of communication and contacts.

Furthermore, activating channels of communication has become part of the issue. The Syrians have made it a condition that you pay a price to enter into communication with them. At the time that I was more involved with this, during Netanyahu's premiership, Syrians levied a cost just to begin talks. Netanyahu was not willing to pay a political price just for the pleasure of talking with the Syrians, and had to go through an indirect approach of using emissaries, which is much less efficient, and causes the loss of a great deal of clarity. The very act of establishing communication was made part and parcel of the process.

The second impediment to negotiations with the Syrians has been the Palestinian obstacle. Had there been no Palestinian channel maybe more attention would have been focused on the Syrian option. But because the Palestinian case presented itself in full force again and again, as far as the Syrian issue is concerned, the Israeli–Palestinian negotiations have become an obstacle, and it remains an obstacle to this very day. Let us assume, by way of pure example, that there had been no Palestinian issue. I would say that the degree of interest that both sides would have devoted to the Syrian issue would have automatically been greater. So these are interesting differences that come to mind when you reflect on what went wrong in both the Syrian and Palestinian contexts.

The Need for Imagination and Creativity

One manifestation of the failure of imagination in seeking a solution is an implicit assumption that something went wrong in previous attempts to reach a solution. What follows from that is that we draw "lessons," and then once we determine those lessons, we apply them to make things better. There is an assumption of continuity here that is misplaced. Maybe there are more differences in the present situation, as related to the past, than there are similarities, and therefore the "lessons" may not apply. And, maybe some of the answers are not there, so what is the point of trying to learn lessons? In fact, we may have to unlearn some lessons, if we want to allow some space for creativity and imagination.

Let me draw your attention to some major differences with the past. A great deal of effort has been devoted to describing the good and hard work of four Israeli Prime Ministers (PMs) who dealt with former Syrian President Hafez al-Assad. Israeli former PM Rabin worked a great deal and made some progress toward negotiations and agreements. Former PM Peres, in his very brief term, also gained some ground toward an agreement. Former PM Netanyahu, in an indirect fashion, accomplished some important things. And then there was PM Barak who made a concentrated effort to achieve an accord. These four were followed by former PM Sharon and now PM Olmert. Today, the accomplishments of the first four Israeli Prime Ministers are almost irrelevant to further negotiations with Syria. This is one aspect of the discontinuity on the Syrian side.

Another aspect of discontinuity is that we now have a new Syrian leader, and no one should assume that Assad junior resembles Assad senior. There are many things that suggest that we are dealing with a different type of protagonist. So the protagonists have changed.

We have to look also at the United States, which is always an interested party. Over the last decade we had the Clinton administration, and now we have President Bush, who has a jaundiced view of Syria, and that is also a factor of change. What can one do about that? As we analyzed the legacy of the last decade, it appears now as ancient history.

We are now in the first decade of the twenty-first century, and it is a different context. Very significant and influential things have happened in the region and outside the region. I do not want to talk about this in the terms of being the post-Arafat, post-Assad, post-Saddam, post-Sharon Middle East, but it is a very different Syria. And it is also a different Israel, in many aspects. One regional constraint that worked until 2000 on Israeli policy regarding the Syrian issue, which is no longer there, is the fact that Israel no longer has a presence in southern Lebanon. Once we evacuated unilaterally from Lebanon, the character of the Lebanese constraint on Israel's negotiating position became different, and it is even more changed after the 2006 Israeli–Hezbollah/Hamas conflict.

So, if you add up all these differences, you come to the conclusion that we need to look at things completely afresh. Since the present is different, the question therefore is: are we going to revisit the old negotiating positions that have been presented and proposed without success, or are we going to think about a new approach, one that would give both greater coherence to the present circumstances, and might have a greater chance for a success?

With Syria, the territorial issue has always been central. It appears that no maps have been presented in previous negotiations; a fact that allows some flexibility of reflection. The point has been made repeatedly about Barak's insistence that when the territorial arrangements on the Golan Heights are considered, a strip of land on the east shore of Lake Tiberius – east of the 1923 boundary line established by the French and English – is a necessity for Israel. To achieve this, one has to look more creatively at future options if we are to resume negotiations.

I would like to propose a negotiating proposal that could be construed as an improvement in negotiations through greater creativity, and is not divorced from precedents and realities. This relates to Israel maintaining a presence on the Golan, either using new concepts of presence or sovereignty, or using the "new" mechanics (or options) of a potential land swap. Credit should be given to the Palestinian–Israeli context for the origin of this option.

In the Israeli–Palestinian context no one could conceive of an exact return to the 1967 line. Consequently, the idea that has surfaced was that if Israel were to retain some territory to the east of the line, this could be offset by an Israeli concession of land elsewhere. The mention of such a swap makes sense. The details may vary, but everyone can understand that this broadens the maneuvering margins that exist. A land-swap concept was codified into the Clinton proposals of 2000, and thereby given legitimacy. The concept later appeared in the privately negotiated Geneva Accord. Other proposals for final-status territorial agreements suggest all kinds of bilateral Israeli–Palestinian land swap concepts.

The idea of a land swap has become an option that now has merit in the Middle East. Again, in the Israeli–Palestinian context the creative idea of a bilateral swap has evolved into a trilateral swap possibility. Most noteworthy is the proposal floated by some Israeli professors about ceding Egyptian land to Gaza, so as to broaden Gaza's space, in return for which Israel would cede to Egypt land in the Negev. When you think creatively, you notice that once you increase the number of parties, the amount of creativity that can be introduced into this concept increases exponentially. This mechanism of a trilateral land swap also becomes interesting in the Israeli–Syrian context: Israel might retain a strip of land, a few miles wide, parallel to the 1923 boundary line, which would provide for the protection of Israel's water supply, give Israel high ground for security purposes, and would keep to the minimum the relocation of Israeli residents of the Golan.

There is another creative idea worth considering. President George W. Bush suggested in a letter to Prime Minister Sharon the possibility that Israel might retain settlement blocks in the West Bank and Jerusalem because of the reality of large Israeli populations there. Recognition of such facts on the ground might also apply to the Golan with respect to the city of Katzrin, which represents a similar settlement block. So, when you add up Israeli needs to protect the water, for elevated ground for security, and the demographic reality of Israelis settled on the western part of the Golan, one can conceive of the contours of a territorial swap.

Now, if Syria still wants to regain all the territorial mileage that it lost in 1967 (and Syria would not have to go back to the 1967 line – Egypt never went back to the 1967 since it relinquished Gaza), you could incorporate into the swap arrangements land that has been negotiated between Jordan and Syria, so that Jordan would cede the equivalent amount of land along its border with Syria, and Israel in return would cede some land to Jordan south of the Dead Sea. All this could introduce greater flexibility, for Israeli–Syrian negotiations as well as in the Palestinian–Israeli context.

Before one can entertain such ideas for renewed negotiations, there is a major obstacle to be addressed. Professor Moshe Ma'oz has suggested that there is procedural flexibility in the Syrian overtures, but that we do not know how much substantive flexibility there is. That has to be probed. I second the suggestion that the extent of the Syrian substantive flexibility be explored, either through backchannels, or overtly; and that this should be done in concert with the United States, because of the wider issues of the region involving Lebanon, Iraq and Iran.

What is a necessity, before such probes with Syria are undertaken, is a Syrian act against terrorism. If it were not clear before, it is evident since the 2006 war of Israel with Hezbollah and Hamas, to both American and Israeli eyes, that Syria continues its indirect complicity and support of Hezbollah and of Palestinian terrorists, who are being directed by their leaders from Syria. Syria's role in this war makes this the most serious obstacle to any immediate examination of the options for negotiations with Syria.

But there is hope: the United States and Israel should continue to probe Syria about a peace settlement, if it were to divorce itself from supporting terror, Hezbollah and its connection to Iran. Following these steps and the resumption of negotiations, there will be a need for more flexibility and creativity. This could give hope for productive negotiations.

CHAPTER 15

After the Lebanon War: Can Israel Rebuild Trust with Syria, Lebanon, and Palestine?

MOSHE MA'OZ

Deterioration of Arab–Israeli Relations

The July–August 2006 devastating war between Israel and Hezbollah, the Hamas victory in the January 2006 Palestinian elections, as well as the unresolved Palestinian problem – all these factors have contributed in recent years to further deteriorate Arab–Israeli relations. Hezbollah's military gains, despite its noticeable losses in the battles against the formidable IDF, have signified to many Arabs that Israel is not invincible and possibly can be defeated by utilizing Hezbollah-type guerrilla rocket-launching tactics. This notion is particularly relevant to militant elements in the Hamas movement that now controls the Palestinian Authority (PA).

To be sure: since its ascendancy, Hamas, despite continuous pressures and inducements, has refused to accept the three conditions of Israel and the international community for peace negotiations: recognizing Israel, acknowledging previous PLO–Israel political agreements, and renouncing terrorism, not to mention abolishing the Hamas charter that calls for Israel's elimination. Apparently, this militant policy has been led by Khalid Mashal, the head of Hamas political bureau, who resides in Damascus and may be influenced by the Syrian regime.

As it happened, Syria's president, Bashar al-Asad, has rejected Israeli and American requests to deport Mashal and close Hamas offices in Damascus. Nor has he agreed to stop supporting Hezbollah's military operations against Israel. Bashar has depicted both Hamas and Hezbollah as "national liberation movements not terrorist movements."[1] And although publicly suggesting to renew peace negotiations with Israel without preconditions, Bashar has also uttered harsh anti-Israeli/anti-Jewish remarks, and effusively praised Hasan Nasrallah, Hezbollah's leader. Damascus has continued to supply long-range rockets to Hezbollah that were used in the 2006 war against Israel. In the aftermath of this war, Bashar warned Israel that if the Golan is not returned to Syria through political negotiations, Syria might use military power. This stern warning (which was followed later on by peace suggestions) stemmed possibly not only from Hezbollah's "victory" and the strong backing of Iran, but also from the weakening posture of the United States in Iraq.[2]

Bashar has perhaps attempted to exploit the widespread anti-Israel rage in Lebanon and other Arab countries following Israel's devastating attacks on civilian targets in Lebanon (as well as in the Gaza Strip). These attacks have also contributed to blurring the Shi'i–Sunni divide among many Arabs, as well as hurting the prestige of the Sunni Arab leaders in Egypt, Jordan and Saudi Arabia, who had tacitly expected Israel to crush Shi'i Hezbollah, Iran's ally. Bashar probably aims at using these developments to win domestic legitimacy, regain influence in Lebanon, and for greater emergence as a pan-Arab leader – a unifying figure between Sunnis and Shi'is.

In sum, these critical developments in the Middle East during 2006 – Hezbollah's "victory," Hamas' ascendance, Syrian and Iranian belligerency – may lead to more anti-Israeli hostilities and, in a worse-case scenario, to another war between Israel and Syria, Hamas and/or Hezbollah.[3]

The crucial question now is what can Israel do to prevent such scenarios from occurring, and to try to improve relations and rebuild trust with Syria, Lebanon and the Palestinians.

Israeli Positions and Options

The 2006 Lebanon war has hardened, or radicalized, the position of many Israeli Jews, like the attitude of many Arabs. The uninterrupted barrages of Hezbollah rockets (some 4,000) into northern Israel, and the unimpressive performance of the Israeli Defense Forces (IDF) in southern Lebanon have rekindled concerns regarding Israel's high vulnerability to rocket attacks from adjacent territories (the West Bank, for example), as well as increased Islamic and Arab hostility to Israel. These Israeli concerns have been reflected in the growing support among Israeli Jews for right-wing parties, such as Netanyahu's Likud and Lieberman's "National Unity" (the later of which joined the Olmert government). Yet, other Israelis, including cabinet ministers, have advocated the resumption of peace negotiations with Syria, with the Palestinians, as well as reaching a political settlement with Lebanon. Additionally, Prime Minister Olmert has expressed a desire to re-open conditioned-talks with a united Fatah–Hamas Palestinian government.

The Syrian Option

On its face the Syrian option still seems to be the most promising. In the best-case scenarios, peace with Syria will entail the end of Syrian material help and political backing for Hezbollah and Hamas, curbing their militant tendencies, and diminishing, if not ceasing, Damascus' military–political alliance with Teheran. It can also lead to a more comprehensive Arab–Israeli peace, notably regarding Lebanon and the Palestinians, while helping to settle permanently many Palestinian refugees in Syria. (There are about 350,000 Palestinian refugees in Syria.)

A Syrian–Israeli peace agreement was almost achieved in early 2000, between Syrian President Hafiz al-Assad and Israeli Prime Minister Ehud Barak, with the active mediation of US President Bill Clinton. Unfortunately, that unique opportunity for peace was missed, essentially because of disagreement regarding a strip of land along Lake Tiberias' northeastern bank, 12 km long and a few hundred meters wide.[4]

Following this grave miscarriage, the prospects for Syrian–Israeli peace have significantly diminished, owing to new developments and circumstances. Clinton's successor, George W. Bush, developed intense hostility to Assad's successor, Bashar, because of Syria's continuous involvement in terrorism, its continuous occupation of Lebanon (until April 2005), and particularly its strong opposition to the US occupation of Iraq (March 2003) and its alleged assistance to the Iraqi insurgents.[5] Bush urged Barak's successor, Ariel Sharon, not to resume peace negotiations with Syria unless it capitulated to an American list of demands regarding Iraq, Lebanon terrorism, and democratic reforms. To be sure, Sharon himself, unlike his four predecessors, was highly reluctant to negotiate with Syria, rejecting Bashar's suggestions to renew peace talks with Israel without preconditions.[6] Bashar has indeed periodically made such suggestions, but he also occasionally made crude anti-Jewish, anti-Israeli statements, and has continued to assist Hezbollah and Hamas, thus enraging most Israeli Jews.

Consequently, even if Bashar is willing and capable of delivering peace with Israel – which is somewhat doubtful – Israel's prime minister, Ehud Olmert, and most Israelis, intensely reject the notion of trading the Golan Heights for peace with Syria. Indeed, unlike several cabinet ministers who have advocated negotiating peace-for-Golan with Syria, Olmert stated in late September 2006: "As long as I serve as prime minister, the Golan Heights will remain in our hands because it is an integral part of the State of Israel."[7]

There are several explanations for Olmert's negative attitude toward peace with Syria:

1   He does not trust Bashar's intentions and believes that giving up the

Golan would endanger Israel's strategic interests, including national security and water resources.

2   After his poor performance in the Lebanon war, he cannot afford to further alienate the Israeli public that mostly objects to the return of the Golan. Olmert wishes to regain popularity rather than risk his political future by leading his nation to a painful peace settlement with Syria.

3   Olmert is not in a position to negate Bush's policy toward Bashar, given Israel's vast dependence on Washington, strategically, militarily and diplomatically.

Consequently, although peace with Syria, according to several Israeli politicians and analysts, may serve Israel's regional interests, Olmert's position may further aggravate Israeli–Syrian relations and possibly obstruct Israel's other options, namely: settlements with Lebanon and the Palestinians.

The Lebanese Option

An Israeli–Lebanese political agreement might be possible despite or as a result of the July 2006 war. It could comprise an exchange of prisoners; Israeli withdrawal from the disputed Shabaa Farms (which officially belongs to Syria), and provisions for safeguarding the Israeli–Lebanese border both by the IDF and the Lebanese army. Both Olmert and Fouad Siniora, Lebanon's Prime Minister, wish to reach such agreement: Olmert, in order to demonstrate to the Israeli public that his war aims have been achieved; Siniora, backed by a Sunni–Christian–Druze coalition, seeks to reconstruct Lebanon, please Sunni Arab leaders in the region, as well as the United States, and curtail the influence of Syria and Hezbollah. Alas, it is most unlikely that Siniora could conclude any formal agreement with Israel without the approval of Lebanon's pro-Syrian president, Emile Lahoud, Tehran, Damascus, and particularly of Hezbollah, which seems capable of blocking government actions and perhaps toppling it. Hezbollah is still heavily armed and allied with Damascus and Teheran, and is capable of thwarting such an agreement, for example by firing rockets in Israel. Would or could the Lebanese army and/or the United Nations Interim Force in Lebanon (UNIFIL) prevent such a provocative attack?

The Palestinian Option: The Road Map and Arab League Resolution

Consequently, the remaining option for Israel is to settle the Palestinian problem in a way that is acceptable to most Israelis and to most Palestinians, Arab and Muslim nations and to the international community. The only blueprint for such a solution that so far has been accepted by all these parties is the Road Map of June 2002, designed by the "Quartet" – the United States, the United Nations, the European Union and Russia. It was adopted by the Palestinian and Israeli governments (although Israel accepted it with 14 reservations, which aimed at modifying it, but which were not approved by the Quartet).[8] And even though the Road Map was not implemented, it remains the only internationally endorsed document that outlines the ways and phases to settle this crucial issue (see Appendix).

The gist of the Road Map is a two-state solution, based *inter alia* on UN Security Council (UNSC) resolutions 242 (1967), 338 (1973), 1397 (2002) and the Arab League resolutions (Beirut, 2002). Significantly, the Arab League resolutions, adopted for the first time by 22 Arab nations, called (similar to UNSC resolution 1397) for "the establishment of a Palestinian state on the Palestinian territories occupied since June 4, 1967 in the West Bank and the Gaza Strip with East Jerusalem as its capital"; as well as "a just solution to the problem of Palestinian refugees to be agreed upon in accordance with UN General Assembly Resolution No. 194" (of 1948). If Israel agrees to these terms, "the Arab states will . . . consider the Arab–Israeli conflict over, sign a peace agreement with Israel and achieve peace for all states in the region" (see Appendix).

To be sure, unlike this resolution, the Road Map does not specify the solutions for Jerusalem and the Palestinian refugee problems. It merely indicates that at phase III of the Road Map the parties should negotiate these issues, as well as the issues of borders and Jewish settlements on the basis of UNSC resolutions, plus the Arab League decision.

Still, regarding the most crucial and sensitive problem of the Palestinian refugees, the Arab League resolution (as well the June 2006 Palestinian prisoners' document[9]) mentions UN resolution 194 and not specifically the old Palestinian demand for a "right of return" (*Haqq al-Awda*) – meaning a collective right of return to their pre-1948 homes and lands inside Israel. Resolution 194 does not mention the term *right* but says "that the refugees wishing to return to their homes and live in peace with their neighbors should be permitted to do so at the earliest practical date, and that compensation should be paid for the property of those choosing not to return . . . "[10]

Thus, the Arab League resolution regarding the refugee problem "to be agreed upon . . . in accordance with UN General Assembly Resolution No. 194" pointing out that the refugees "should be permitted" and that "compensation should be paid" etc. – can be interpreted as follows: that Israel has "to agree," and "to permit" . . . through negotiations . . . to admit a certain number of refugees and that it has an option to pay compensation for most refugees who will not return.

Camp David, the *Intifada* and the Gaza Disengagement

As a matter of fact this was the suggestion of President Clinton in his Camp David (July 2000) blueprint. He also advocated that East Jerusalem will be the capital of the Palestinian state and that Israel should render 2% of its land to the Palestinian state in return for the major blocs of Jewish settlements in the West Bank that will be annexed to Israel. Ehud Barak, then Israel's prime minister, accepted Clinton's blueprint, whereas Yasser Arafat, the PLO leader, rejected Clinton's ideas regarding Jerusalem and refugees.

Consequently Israeli–Palestinian peace talks were stalled and, in late September 2000, the Palestinian al-Aqsa *Intifada* erupted against Israel causing great bloodshed and destruction on both sides, as well as aggravating Israeli–Palestinian relations. Ariel Sharon, who was elected Israel's prime minister in early 2001 largely owing to anti-Palestinian feelings among Israeli Jews, refused to renew peace talks with Yasser Arafat, "the terrorist," and "no partner." Arafat, on his part, did not attempt to stop Palestinian violence and incitement against Israel, while both he and Sharon did not implement the provisions of the Road Map of 2002. Sharon, who grudgingly adopted the Road Map with serious reservations, in fact initiated unilateral measures *vis-à-vis* the Palestinians, notably: (a) building a security fence, partly along the 1967 line with the West Bank and partly east of this line on Palestinian territory; and (b) withdrawing Israeli troops and settlements from the Gaza Strip and from the northern West Bank area. Gaining the support of most Israeli Jews (the security fence for example significantly diminished Palestinian terrorist attacks inside Israel), Sharon apparently managed to convince Bush that Arafat was not a partner for negotiations and that Israel's disengagement from Gaza constituted a first step toward the implementation of the Road Map.

Bush, Sharon, Abbas and Hamas

After his reelection as US president on November 2, 2004 and the death of Yasser Arafat on November 11, 2004, Bush has been more motivated to settle the Israeli–Palestinian conflict, through the Road Map and a two-state solution. In November 2004 Bush stated: "I believe we've got a great chance to establish a Palestinian state . . . (and to achieve) a just and peaceful solution of the Arab–Israeli conflict based on two democratic states – Israel and Palestine."[11] Bush has repeatedly stated this notion on various occasions. Secretary of State Condoleezza Rice, for example, was quoted during her meeting with the Palestinian President Mahmud Abbas in early October 2006, as follows: "Ms. Rice said the Bush administration was eager to help Mr. Abbas establish a government that would work with the United States on a two-state solution, a solution in which a democratic Palestine and a democratic Israel can live side by side."[12]

But, as it happened, the Bush administration has been unable or unwilling to induce Mr. Sharon and his successor (since early 2006) Ehud Olmert to engage Abbas in bilateral peace negotiations. Bush also could not or would not prevent Sharon from unilaterally withdrawing from the Gaza Strip in summer of 2005, rather than negotiating and implementing the withdrawal with Abbas' participation. Such moves could probably have bolstered the weak position and low prestige of Abbas, who was anxious to negotiate with Israel and present to his public an important gain. Instead, however, Israeli unilateral action enabled the militant Hamas to claim, and obtain credit, for the armed struggle that allegedly forced Israel to withdraw its settlements from the Gaza Strip.

To be sure, Hamas used this line as well as took advantage of the Palestinian Liberation Organization (PLO) corruption to win the elections in January 2006 – elections that the US had insisted should be implemented democratically. Once in power, Hamas has not changed or abolished its 1988 Charter calling for the elimination of Israel. The Hamas government has also rejected the demands of Israel, the US and most of the international community to recognize Israel and the PLO–Israeli agreements to renounce and stop terrorism. Although it managed to maintain a truce (*hudna*) or cease-fire for several months, the Hamas government would not stop armed attacks against Israel, including launching Qassam rockets on Israeli towns near the Gaza Strip.

The Hezbollah "victory" against Israel apparently encouraged Hamas militants to continue using violence against Israel, thus further reducing the chance for political negotiations with Israel (and for international financial help). Israel continued to employ harsh measures against Palestinians, including targeted killings of terror suspects which occasionally involved killings of civilians. Israeli Jewish civilians affected and enraged by Palestinian violence in southern Israel and, since July 2006, also by Hezbollah's rocket launching into north Israel, have become more "hawkish" toward Palestinians and other Arabs. Many Israelis continued to support the unilateral strategy of Sharon and of his successor, Olmert. But after the Lebanon war, a growing number of Israelis have rejected Olmert's design of "realignment," namely unilateral withdrawal from the West Bank (but not including East Jerusalem, the big blocs of Jewish settlements and "security zones" and perhaps also the Jordan valley).

Following the Lebanon war and under the pressure of public opinion, Olmert has apparently deferred, if not abolished, his new design. He has also frozen the previous government's decision to dismantle "illegal outposts" and allowed the further expansion of Jewish settlements on the West Bank, notably around Jerusalem. At the close of 2006 Fatah and

Hamas were on the verge of civil war. In late December, Prime Minister Abbas called for new Palestinian elections. As a consequence, Fatah and Hamas negotiated the establishment of a unity government, but their agreement did not include a Hamas announcement to recognize the right of the State of Israel to exist nor disavow violence and terrorism as a means to seek its goals – a demand of Israel, the US and the Quartet. As of mid-March 2007 the Palestinian unity government had not been formed; Olmert and Abbas continued meetings in 2007 to seek formulas to renew negotiations with a possibility of a united Fatah and Hamas government and a cease-fire between Israel and Palestine.

Conclusions

Under these circumstances, – i.e., the unwillingness of Fatah and Hamas to reconcile, and of Hamas to recognize Israel and foreswear the use of violence; the growing distrust and antagonism between Israelis and Palestinians; the polarization in the positions of Hamas and the Israeli governments – a larger scale of violence and warfare may develop between Israel and the Palestinians, possibly involving also Hezbollah and Syria.

Several Israeli analysts have suggested that Israel should "manage" the conflict with the Palestinians while maintaining the status quo until more favorable developments will occur. Yet a status quo cannot be managed for long in this volatile region, with its growing religious fanaticism, political instability and economic predicament among many Arabs, as well as deep concerns for their personal and national security among many Jews.

Unfortunately, the leaders of the rival communities are unable or unwilling to combat the mistrust amongst their communities by initiating ideas and adopting measures that would rebuild trust and render hope for peaceful coexistence. The Hamas leaders, notably Khalid Mashal, continue to reject demands and pressures of moderate Palestinians and Arab leaders, not to mention the United States and the international community – to recognize Israel and the previous Israeli–PLO agreements as well as to renounce terrorism. (The Hamas' notion of Israeli withdrawal to the 1967 line in return for *hudna* [truce] is a non-starter for Israel.)

Hamas has undermined continuous attempts by Abbas to form a national unity government with a pragmatic agenda *vis-à-vis* Israel, namely recognizing the Arab League Beirut resolutions (2002), the Road Map (2002) as well as the previous PLO–Israeli agreements since 1993 (Oslo). Senior Arab leaders, Mubarak (Egypt) and Abdallah (Saudi Arabia) have failed to induce Hamas to change its rejectionist position. (Bashar of Syria and Hezbollah obviously support such a position.) The Israeli leaders on their part would not and could not agree to the Hamas government or to any Palestinian government that does not endorse the above-mentioned conditions.

Yet, in order to show good will and render some hope for the future, the Israeli government can stop expanding Jewish settlements, dismantle illegal outposts on the West Bank, and facilitate humanitarian and economic assistance to Palestinians in the Gaza Strip. Other gestures that are likely to improve the tense atmosphere and help somewhat to rebuild trust and strengthen Palestinian pragmatists are, for example, exchange of Palestinian prisoners for Gilad Shalit, the abducted Israeli soldier. Among the released Palestinian prisoners it is worthwhile freeing Marwan Barghuti, a would-be "Palestinian Mandela," charismatic, popular and the initiator of the relatively pragmatic "prisoners' memo." He is likely to play an important role in forging a PLO–Hamas national unity government that possibly would accept the necessary conditions for resuming negotiations with Israel.

Such important steps notwithstanding, the United States must adopt a leading role in rebuilding trust and peace between Israel, the Palestinians and other Arab nations. As we know, President Bush has repeatedly advocated a two-state solution and, unlike his hostile attitude toward Syria, he is able to induce Israel to stop further settlement activities, release Palestinian prisoners and help improve the humanitarian and economic conditions of the Palestinians. Bush must also continue his efforts to encourage pro-American Arab leaders to use their influence on the Hamas to form pragmatic national unity government on the basis of the Arab League resolutions and the Oslo Accords.

Finally, while continuing to work through several diplomatic channels, the United States should convene a new international peace conference on the Israeli–Palestinian issue (if possible also on the Israeli–Syrian–Lebanese problems). This conference should consist also of the Quartet (that issued the Road Map) and the Arab League. It should adopt decisions and measures to renew the Road Map negotiations, shortening its phases in order to move promptly to permanent status negotiations. This may be the only way to avoid further conflict and bloodshed and to promote Israeli–Palestinian trust and peace. This is certainly in the interests of all parties involved, certainly Israel and the Palestinians.

Sunni-Arab regimes could bolster their position and prestige among their public and partly neutralize the so-called Shi'i threat by erasing one of its major objectives. Reviving Israeli–Palestinian mutual trust and negotiations is certainly a vested interest of the United States. It may improve its tarnished image in the Arab and Muslim world, cement a pragmatic pro-American Arab coalition, and perhaps help facilitate a settlement to the critical Iraq problem.

Appendix: The Road Map (June 2006) and Israel's Reservations

Phase I: June 2002 to May 2003

Ending terror and violence, normalizing Palestinian life and building Palestinian institutions:
Palestinian unconditional cessation of violence.

Palestinians prepare for statehood: drafting a constitution, fair and open elections, appointment of interim prime minister or cabinet with an empowered executive authority/decision-making body.

Israel withdraws from Palestinian areas occupied from Sept. 28, 2000.

Israel halts settlement activity and dismantles illegal outposts.

Israel takes measures to improve humanitarian situation, including lifting curfews and easing restrictions on movement of persons and goods.

Quartet monitors actions/progress on both sides.

Arab states end all funding of groups supporting or engaging in violence and terror.

Phase II: Transition – June–December 2003

When Palestinian people have a drafted constitution, statehood will be viable.

First International Conference to be held discussing progress, including goals between Israel and Syria, and Israeli and Lebanon.

Arab states restore pre-*Intifada* links to Israel, such as trade offices.

Creation of independent Palestinian state, with provisional borders.

Enhanced international role in monitoring through the Quartet.

Quartet members promote international recognition of Palestinian state, including possible UN membership.

Phase III: Permanent Status Agreement and End of the Israeli–Palestinian Conflict – 2004–2005

Second International Conference to be convened by the Quartet, in consultation with the parties, at beginning of 2004, to endorse agreement reached on an independent Palestinian state with provisional borders and formally to launch a process with the active, sustained, and operational support of the Quartet, leading to a final, permanent status resolution in 2005.

Parties reach final and comprehensive settlement status agreement that ends the Israeli–Palestinian conflict in 2005, through a settlement negotiated between the parties based on UNSCR 242, 338, and 1397, as well as the Arab League resolution, ending the occupation that began in 1967.

Includes an agreed, just, fair and realistic solution to the refugee issue

A negotiated resolution on the status of Jerusalem that takes into account the political and religious concerns of both sides, and protects the religious interests of Jews, Christians, and Muslims worldwide, and fulfills the vision of two states, Israel and the sovereign, independent, democratic and viable Palestine, living side-by-side in peace and security.

Arab state acceptance of full, normal relations with Israel and security for all the states of the region in the context of a comprehensive Arab–Israeli peace.[13]

In order to bolster the Road Map's legitimacy, the plan was officially endorsed by UN Security Council Resolution 1515 in November 2003. Earlier, as already indicated, the plan had been fully accepted by the Palestinian Authority, under Yasser Arafat's leadership, whereas the Israeli Government, under Ariel Sharon, had acknowledged it with fourteen reservations, and in an indirect mode, as reflected in the following text:

Israeli Government's Decision, 25 May 2003

A. Based on the American administration's note of 23 May, 2003, in which the US committed itself to seriously and fully deal with Israel's remarks concerning the Road(s) Map, while implementing the map, the Prime Minister conveyed Israel's consent to accept the steps defined in the Road(s) Map. The Government approved the Prime Minister's message and decided that all and whole of Israel's remarks to which the administration referred in its note should be implemented, while the Road(s) Map will be materialized. The text of Israel's remarks to the US administration is attached to this decision.

B. The Israeli Government has accepted today the steps defined in the Road(s) Map. It expresses its hope that the political process that will start in accordance with President Bush's address of 24 June 2002, will bring about security, peace and reconciliation between Israel and the Palestinians. The Israeli Government also clarifies that during the political process as well as subsequently, the response to the (Palestinian) refugee issue will not include their admittance and settlement within the boundaries of the State of Israel.[14]

Notes

1   *Al-Majd*, Jordan, October 8, 2001; see also *New York Times*, May 11, 2001.
2   *Los Angeles Times*, August 31, 2006; *Ha'aretz*, August 25, 2006 and October 8, 2006.
3   Cf. Mubarak's remarks, *Ha'aretz,* October 8, 2006.
4   Moshe Ma'oz, *Can Israel and Syria Reach Peace?*, The Baker Institute, Rice University, March 2005; Bill Clinton, *My Life* (New York: Alfred A. Knopf, 2004), pp. 883–86, 903–4.
5   Moshe Ma'oz, *Washington and Damascus: Between Confrontation and Cooperation*, the United States Institute of Peace Special Report, 146, August 2005.
6   Sharon to *Ha'aretz*, September 14, 2004.
7   *New York Times*, September 27, 2006.
8   *Ha'aretz*, May 30, 2003.
9   Text in *Ha'aretz*, June 6, 2006.
10 Dennis C. Howley, *The United Nations and the Palestinians* (New York: Exposition Press, 1975), p. 86.
11 *The Washington Post*, November 13, 2004.
12 *New York Times*, October 5, 2006.
13 "A Performance-Based Roadmap to a Permanent Two-State Solution to the Israeli–Palestinian Conflict," April 30, 2003, US Department of State, <http://w.w.w.state.gov/r/pa/prs/ps/2003/20062.htm>.
14 *Ha'aretz*, May 26, 2003.

CHAPTER 16

The Palestinian Public and What Has Gone Wrong in Israel–Palestine Negotiations

RIAD MALKI

As a Palestinian and an observer of the January 9, 2005 election of Mahmud Abbas (Abu Mazen) to the presidency, I will comment on the Palestinian public's desires as voters went to the polls. I will then address what I believe has gone wrong in Israeli–Palestinian negotiations.

The Palestinian Public

My first point is that on the eve of the Palestinian Authority (PA) presidential elections of January 9, 2005, I was amazed, as a Palestinian observer, to look at the sophisticated level of discussion that was taking place among Palestinians. We were not talking about occupation, we were not talking about the wall or the fence, settlements, etc.; rather, we were talking about matters connected to the elections and future government. For instance, because Hamas had decided to boycott the elections, and others had decided not to vote, a major topic of discussion was about the difference between not participating in the elections and boycotting them, and whether the act of boycotting elections is a democratic decision or an undemocratic one. I had not expected Palestinians would be focusing their discussion on such a topic, and I felt that Palestinians had reached a high level of maturity in politics. For me, this was very important and a lesson about how other people, especially Israelis, should look at Palestinian political development.

The second point is that when most Palestinians were asked very simple questions as they exited the polling stations (such as "what are your priorities, what do you expect from the vote?"), peoples' priorities were very clear. Their greatest concern was with personal security – food, bread, employment, and economic development. This was their first priority – personal security. They then went on to say that their next priority was the rule of law. This related to how many Palestinians perceived history under the PA, and how they want their own society and nation to develop the rule of law and honest government. Their final priority was institutional reform, and when they spoke of reform they were not talking about the three levels of reform that Israel and the international community had been demanding from the PA; i.e., security reform, financial reform, and bureaucratic reform. The Palestinians were talking about comprehensive reform – reform that provides efficient and fair treatment and covers all sectors and layers of government, including judicial reform. They were more demanding than the international community.

The Palestinians' third priority was negotiations with Israel. Negotiations with Israel were not the main priority because they were seeing things from a personal and local level, from the micro to the macro. They began with what most affected their own lives and families, and then looked at the broader picture in which they want an end to conflict and violence.

What Went Wrong?

When we ask the question "what went wrong?" or "what do we need?" I think the answer should be that we have the wrong leaders. The wrong leaders have wasted our time, and have wasted many chances for moving further toward peace during the last decade. Among the many opportunities missed is that all the agreements that were offered to us Palestinians and Israelis did not have a sufficient implementation mechanism verification system, and monitoring system, and they did not have a sufficient enforcement mechanism. We were given agreements and plans that lacked hands and teeth, and the agreements were unintentionally constructed to be disrespected, violated, and ignored because they were fragile and not designed to be enforced.

The second point about what went wrong is that the Oslo Accords – the basis of the whole agreement, the negotiations, and the rapprochement between Palestinians and Israelis – did not address enough of the pending questions. It did not answer the most important questions. It kept the conflict open-ended and allowed leaders to escape their obligations. If we look back into Oslo and how it was implemented and regarded, it was a game that enabled our leaders to escape responsibility and to run away from their obligations. Whether the Mitchell and Tenet Reports, the Zinni Recommendations, or the Road Map, they have not had teeth for implementation and enforcement of their content.

My third point has to do with the role of outside parties. The role of the third parties, if we look back, has been a very shy one. They did not really intervene when it was required of them; they did not really enforce the agreements; they did not push implementation. Their roles were limited to suggestions, and they did not really apply pressure to achieve results. We do hope that in the future active third parties will be able to bring the parties together, to pressure the two sides to reach agreements, and then to fulfill the agreements that are signed.

The fourth point, as suggested by Shaul Gabbay in his chapter in this volume, is that people on both sides, Palestinians and Israelis alike, were not ready for peace. There was no serious effort made by the Israeli government, nor by the PA, nor by the PLO over the years to help people understand the importance of pursuing a negotiated comprehensive peace. Leaders and government officials may have wanted to reach peace, but they did not make the minimum effort needed to create an atmosphere favorable to peace, to convince people of the need to make peace, or explain the dividends that would flow as a result.

On both sides the Palestinians and Israelis were manipulated by their own leaders. Arafat manipulated his people by empty slogans and empty statements, and I believe the same thing happened on the Israeli side. In both countries there was an echo or a mirror image. The Israeli leaders were no better than the late Arafat. Both sets of leaders should be blamed for putting the Palestinian and Israeli populations through such great suffering over the last ten years.

My fifth point is that the continuous disruption of negotiations at each stage, by every crisis, big or small, has delayed for months real and serious negotiations and the prospects for peace. Leaders allowed events to lead them, rather than they leading events. Because of this, we in civil society had to jump in and start to negotiate on the second track, because our leaders were not really interested in evaluating the situations, minimizing the damages, and resolving the crises.

The sixth point is I believe that time has not been an issue or a factor in the thinking and planning of both sides' leaders, the Israelis and the Palestinians. They work as if time is not related to Palestinian and Israeli suffering. There is an urgent need to solve the problems, to reach needed comprises, and bring an end to their peoples' suffering.

My last point is that too few leaders have been ready to take the risks of entering into compromise solutions. Neither the Israelis nor the Palestinians have been ready to do that. I believe that on the Palestinian side Arafat felt that he had only one true partner – Rabin. He did not trust any other partner. The moment Rabin was assassinated, the negotiations stopped, because for the Palestinians there has been no other Israeli leader to replace Rabin. Even when Peres came, he was not Rabin. When Netanyahu took power, he was not Rabin. When Barak ruled, he was not

Rabin. And, obviously, when Sharon came along, he was not Rabin. Until his death, Arafat kept talking about his "partner Rabin," and about the good experience he had enjoyed with him. Even though he negotiated with subsequent Israeli prime ministers, he was not seriously and sincerely negotiating to reach a final compromise and an agreement.

Palestinians observing from a distance and evaluating the negotiations at Camp David felt that the Palestinian delegation team was not sufficiently prepared, and that Arafat was a reluctant participant. We felt he was pushed into the summit. The Palestinians were further weakened by having, in fact, two Palestinian delegations at the negotiations. There was a division in which one group wanted to rush to a compromise, and another that was neither interested in compromise nor an agreement. Moreover, the Palestinian delegation members did not consult seriously with their experts because they thought erroneously they knew all the issues and could resolve them without expert assistance. Failure to get expert advice hurt Palestinians on the several key issues, in particular on Jerusalem.

Finally, the Palestinians as well as the Israelis have to fulfill their own responsibilities regarding the Road Map. Abu Mazen spelled this out very clearly in his inauguration speech. He said he was committed to the implementation of Palestinian responsibilities according to the Road Map regardless of what the Israelis would do. I believe, if given a chance by Hamas, he would do so. But for implementation to take place he will need the cooperation and support of the Israeli government, as well as support from the United States-led Quartet and the Arab League.

CHAPTER 17

An Israeli–Palestinian Agreement: The Security Aspects

REUVEN PEDATZUR

In any future agreement, Israel would need to decide what its minimum military conditions are before agreeing to a territorial compromise. All the conditions are based on the premise that the compromise does not endanger Israel's existence or security. Israel's interests will be served best if a Palestinian state comes into existence as a product of negotiations and mutual consent.[1]

The authors of the Geneva Accord phrased this idea as follows:

> Recognizing that after years of living in mutual fear and insecurity, both peoples [Israel and the PLO] need to enter an era of peace, security and stability, entailing all necessary actions by the parties to guarantee the realization of this era; recognizing each other's right to peaceful and secure existence within secure and recognized boundaries free from threats or acts of force.[2]

General Ya'akov Amidror claims that Israeli strategists, in planning for permanent status negotiations prior to 2000 (the outbreak of the second *Intifada*), sought solutions for two possible types of security threats:

1 A conventional military threat from the eastern front;
2 A terrorist threat from groups that will try to thwart the agreement within the Palestinian territories themselves.

As for the conventional threat, Israel's approach was to ensure that security arrangements should not inhibit Israel from defending itself against a threat from the east. In practice, this meant that:

1 In times of peace and low apparent threat, Israel's military presence in the territories would be minimal, limited to two or three early warning systems;

2   In times of emergency, Israel would be allowed to deploy forces in specified areas in the West Bank that were defined as necessary for Israel's defense.

As for the threat of terrorism, planners believed that a combination of Israeli–Palestinian cooperation and Palestinian self-interest would provide an adequate response. In practice, this meant that:

1   The main responsibility for fighting terrorism within the area of Palestinian control was given to the Palestinian Authority (PA) and delegated to its various security organizations;
2   Agreements to cooperate with PA security apparatuses by providing them with intelligence and assisting their efforts without violating the Palestinians' quasi-sovereignty;
3   Israel would restrict its role at international transit points, such as airports and seaports, to an invisible presence so as not to appear to violate Palestinian quasi-sovereignty;
4   Palestinians themselves would be responsible for protecting their external borders with Jordan and Egypt, with some support and assistance from international forces.[3]

These were the principles that characterized Israel's approach to the negotiations over security arrangements at Camp David in July 2000. Although most of the principles are still valid, they all need to be revisited in light of the war that has been waged against Israel ever since. In addition to these principles, Israel should present several more conditions that will cover other crucial areas of its future security.

Security arrangements are the bedrock of Israel's conditions for Palestinian statehood. As President Clinton stated, "There will be no peace, and no peace agreement, unless the Israeli people have lasting security guarantees. These need not and should not come at the expense of Palestinian sovereignty, or interfere with Palestinian territorial integrity."[4] Without proper security arrangements, Israel will become even more vulnerable than it currently is. This is the reason that Israel should insist on three essential conditions, regarding the Palestinian state. The Palestinian state must be

1   Prohibited from entering into, or participating in, any military pact or alliance with another country, or accepting any foreign military advisers. The Palestinian entity could not annex nor be annexed by any other political entity;
2   Prohibited from permitting the deployment of foreign troops on its territory;
3   Demilitarized.[5]

In order to deal with the security aspects, both sides would have to cover nine major issues:

1   Demilitarization
2   Control over Border Crossings
3   Border Adjustments
4   Agreement on Fighting Terrorism Within the Palestinian Territories
5   Early-warning Stations
6   The Airspace over the West Bank and Gaza
7   The Electromagnetic Sphere
8   The "Safe Passage"
9   The "Jordanian Factor"

Demilitarization

The preliminary condition that would serve as the basis for any agreement would be that Palestine is demilitarized, except for internal security forces possessing light weapons, with a small coast guard and no air force.

Israel agreed in the Oslo Accords that the Palestinians would have police forces, but not an army. "In order to guarantee public order and internal security for the Palestinians of the West Bank and the Gaza Strip, the Council will establish a strong police force."[6]

The Palestinian Authority exceeded the Oslo Accord conditions, but Israel accepted this violation, and agreed to the much bigger force that the Palestinians created. The Israeli–Palestinian Interim Agreement on the West Bank and the Gaza Strip, called "Oslo II" or "Taba," was signed on September 24, 1995, in Taba in Egypt and countersigned four days later in Washington. It is an extensive and complicated document. The agreement permits a Palestinian "police force" of 24,000 personnel to provide security in areas administered by the Palestinian Authority and to combat terrorism. This was a retroactive recognition of forces expanded in violation of the first Oslo Agreement. That police force has now expanded far beyond the limit set by Oslo II and has acquired powerful weapons that are not permitted. Palestinian forces are further bolstered by the armed forces of Hamas and Islamic Jihad that are even more significant since the 2006 electoral victory of Hamas. Palestinian armed forces have not provided security and have not countered terrorism. In fact, they have become a Palestinian Army that served Yasser Arafat until his death and carried out or covertly assisted terrorist actions against Israel. Israel has identified many members of the "police force" who are also members of extremist groups opposed to peace with Israel, and many of them are wanted by Israel for terrorist crimes.

From a military point of view, the real problem is not a strong police force, or even a Palestinian army. The main problem would be the presence of indirect weapons (e.g., rockets and mortars, anti-armor missiles, and anti-aircraft missiles). As the case of the Qassam and Katyusha rockets taught us during the 2006 conflict between Israel and Hezbollah and Hamas, the use of indirect weapons presents a serious challenge to the Israel Defense Force (IDF), and could lead to escalation and even to an Israeli decision to re-occupy territories.

Anti-armor and anti-aircraft missiles create even more complicated dilemmas for the IDF. Because of their size and weight, shoulder-launched missiles can be carried by a single fighter. The weight of the SA-7 launcher and missile is 9.2 kg; its length is 1.44 m., and its effective range is 5.6 km.[7] The weight of the REDEYE launcher and missile is 13.1kg; its length is 1.28 m, and its effective range is 5.5 km.[8]

In the future, the arsenal of the Palestinians will include more modern anti-aircraft missiles, such as the SA-14 and STINGER.[9] The presence of ground-to-air missiles in the West Bank may considerably narrow the capacity to fly not only above the territories but also above Israel proper.

Control over Border Crossings

The issue is the supervision of the Jordan bridges, the border crossings with Egypt, and the airports. Control over border crossings between the Palestinian State and Jordan and Egypt would gradually be shifted from Israel to the Palestinians. Israel and the Palestinian State would establish joint supervisory committees to verify compliance with the security arrangements in their peace treaty.

The Israeli security concerns are how to prevent Palestinian efforts to smuggle weapons and munitions from neighboring countries. According to the Oslo and Geneva accords, the solution would be an invisible Israeli presence, with international forces or Palestinian customs agents, with the ability to check all imports into the Palestinian areas, whether personal or commercial goods.

While preparing for the withdrawal from Gaza, Israel accepted Egypt's offer to beef up its forces on the border between Sinai and the Gaza Strip and to train Palestinian officers. The Egyptians proposed deploying 750 armed troops on the Egyptian side of the Philadelphi route in the Rafah area (on the border between the Gaza Strip and Egypt) to reinforce security and prevent the smuggling of arms into the Gaza Strip. Today, only policemen are deployed there, in keeping with the Israeli–Egyptian peace agreement. Former Israeli PM Ariel Sharon once stated that if Egypt acts to stop the smuggling, the Israel Defense Forces would be able to withdraw from the Philadelphi route.[10]

In the long run, Israel would not be able to control the Palestinian airports. It would be a breach of the Palestinian sovereignty. In order to prevent the Palestinians from using their airports to smuggle arms, US personnel could serve as observers in the airports.

Border Adjustments

In the West Bank, to enhance its margin of security, Israel should seek to expand the coastal plain eastward (*inter alia*, to remove the shoulder-launched missiles far away from Ben-Gurion Airport).

Yet another perceived vulnerability involves the chronic shortage of water. Israel depends in large measure on water sources that are mainly located beyond the pre-1967 frontiers: the aquifer located partly under the West Bank and the water sources of the north located in the Golan Heights and beyond. In 1964–65, the water issue became the focus of a violent confrontation between Israel and Syria, contributing to the escalation that later led to the June 1967 war.[11]

About 60% of Israel's water comes either from aquifers located in the West Bank or from aquifers inside pre-1967 Israel, which are themselves connected to the West Bank. The problematic one, regarding the future agreement, is the Mountain Aquifer, particularly the western portion thereof the Yarkon–Taninim aquifer (named after the two rivers which discharge from it into the Mediterranean Sea). The Mountain Aquifer extends from the eastern approaches of the coastal aquifer under the hills of Judea and Samaria (the "West Bank"). It comprises three portions:

1   The northern potion which discharges into the Jezreel and the Beit Shean valleys;
2   The eastern portion which extends beneath the eastern slopes of the Judean and Samarian hills towards the Jordan Valley; and
3   The western portion – and by far the most important – which constitutes Israel's principal source of high-quality drinking water.[12]

For each of the three sources comprising the Israeli National Water System (Mekorot), hydrologists have set "red lines" that demarcate the levels below which it is considered unsafe to continue extraction. Depleting a source below these levels creates a risk that extensive and irreversible salting or other forms of contamination may begin to occur, *irreparably* endangering the future of the entire source (or major portions of it) as a reservoir of potable water. Accordingly, in any given period, and depending on the prevailing conditions, there is a maximum permissible output or "safe yield", which is the quantity of water that can be extracted from the respective sources without breaching these "red lines."[13] Hence, it is very easy to damage this important reservoir through the unrestricted drilling of wells on the western slopes of the Samarian Mountains.

Another concern of Israel is the issue of the "Eastern Front" (the Arab countries east of the Israeli border – Jordan, Iraq, and Syria). To counter an attack on its eastern front, Israel would like to retain the Jordan Valley, with the Valley's final disposition determined at some future date.

As for Gaza, Israel has no essential security requirements that need to be reflected in border changes. This perception was the basis of Sharon's "Disengagement Plan," in which Israel left the Gaza Strip and dismantled the Jewish settlements there.

Agreement on Fighting Terrorism

To protect against another security fiasco, Israel needs to insist on two new principles in defining security arrangements within the context of a future peace agreement:

1   If the Palestinians do not actively, persistently, and explicitly fight terror, the agreement should allow Israel to take its own counter-terrorism measures in the territory under Palestinian sovereignty.
2   If terrorism is conducted against Israel from Palestinian territories, then the agreement should permit IDF operations in the territory under Palestinian sovereignty.

Israel must insist on retaining the right to operate throughout the territory in perpetuity, not only for a limited number of years, not only in emergency situations, and not only upon the approval of third parties.[14]

Israel also must insist that Palestinians recognize Israel's right to detain, arrest, and interrogate terrorist suspects in the event the Palestinians do not take action against such suspects themselves. Moreover, mechanisms must be created by which the Palestinians share all terrorism-related information with Israel – full transparency is essential.

Early-warning Stations

From an operational viewpoint, there is no great importance to the strategic depth of the West Bank and Golan Heights. While the length of the Sinai peninsular is 200 km, the length of the West Bank and Golan Heights is much smaller. It takes approximately 14 minutes for a fighter jet to cross the Sinai and reach from the Suez Canal to the international border at the speed of 500 knots. These calculations must also include the flight time from the airbase inside Egypt to the Suez Canal and from the international border to the pursued target. This relatively long time, together with the placement of deterrence and reconnaissance stations and a number other early warning mechanisms, allows a sufficient warning period. Because of its size, this warning apparatus will not be suited for the West Bank.

The area of the West Bank is 5,590 square kilometers. The aerial distance from the Abdallah Bridge to Jerusalem is 30 km, and from the Jordan River to Kefar Sava, 59 km. The distance from the Adam Bridge to Petah Tikvah is 60 km. A fighter will pass the distance from Jordan to Jerusalem in 3.5 minutes, and from the Jordan River to Kefar Sava in 7 minutes. Thus, proper deterrence and intelligence stations could provide a suitable alternative to physical occupation of the areas. Because of the short flying distances needed to reach from Jordanian and Syrian territory into Israel, particular importance must be given to early warning systems capable of detecting these aircraft. Israel will maintain at least one early-warning station, Baal Hatzor, near the city of Ramallah.

This and other stations could be manned by joint crews (Israelis and Palestinians). Another option is to have some stations operated by Israelis and others by Jordanian/Palestinian crews, similar to the method implemented at the Camp David accords between Israel and Egypt, or by Americans.

The Airspace over the West Bank and Gaza

The Israeli Air Force would have to be the only military air power that can use this airspace. Israel may agree to a small Palestinian aerial force of unarmed aircraft. This force may include cargo, light reconnaissance, and non-combat helicopters. The activity of the aerial force would be coordinated with the Israeli air force. The West bank must turn into a combat-free air space, from which Syrian and Jordanian planes would be barred. Such an agreement would allow for the formation of a strategic depth, although a rather narrow one.

An agreement to refrain from flying military planes over a country's jurisdiction has precedents. In the agreements signed between Israel and Egypt, the Egyptians agreed to refrain from flying military planes over the Sinai, although being under Egyptian jurisdiction. The agreement states: "Combat planes and reconnaissance flights will only be allowed over areas A and D after concurring with the other side" (area A lies parallel to the Suez canal and gulf on its eastern side and on the western side on Brdawill. Area D is situated in Israel, east of the international border, and parallel to it).[15]

The treaty also outlaws any presence, lifts, and landings of military planes in the entire Sinai: "Only Israeli and Egyptian planes that are noncombative will be allowed to be present in areas A and D after concurring with both sides."[16]

Regarding the other areas of the Sinai (areas B and C), area B is situated at the center of the peninsula, and area C is adjacent to the international border and the coast of Eilat). The treaty specifies:

> Only unarmed Egyptian cargo flights will lift and land in area B. It is possible to maintain eight aircraft. The Egyptian border units will be allowed to have in their arsenal unarmed choppers in area B, and the Egyptian police will have in their armory unarmed choppers exclusively for their use in area C.[17]

Another possibility is to forge an agreement to refrain from military flights west of a particular line east of the Jordan River.

Another agreement that is worth taking a look at is the installation of Israeli anti-aircraft missiles in the West Bank. These missiles would cover the areas under a flight ban for Arab military flights and could be another security mechanism in overlooking the parts of the agreement dealing with the banning of flights in the relinquished territories.

Banning the Construction of New Military Air Fields

The Palestinians would be banned from constructing airfields able to cater to military planes. These fields do not exist today in the West bank; thus, constituting an advantage over the case in the Sinai on the eve of the Camp David Accords. The Egyptian's agreement to refrain from using the air bases left in the Sinai for military use, including the bases constructed by Israel (Etzyon, and Eitam) could be used as an example for this agreement. The Camp David Accords state, "the use of these air bases left by the Israelis near El-Arish, Eitam, and Ofira will be used for non military flights only, including economic use by all nations."[18]

It will be possible to agree on the construction of air bases for civilian use. In the future the Palestinian Authority may be interested in constructing a civilian air base in the West Bank. This also has a precedent. The peace treaty with Egypt states, "It is possible to build in sections A, B, and C [which constitute the 3 sections the Sinai was divided into by the peace treaty] only for civilian air use."[19]

Construction of civilian air bases will be restricted to the use by civilian elements and the Palestinian police force. It will also be possible to offer the Palestinian Authority a joint use of the Atarot airfield in Jerusalem, included within the boundaries of Jerusalem as of June 27, 1967.

Civilian Air Routes

Civilian air routes to Eilat and to South Africa pass through the West Bank. They pass north of Jerusalem into the Jericho area, and from there south

across the western coast of the Dead Sea towards the Arava Valley. There
are two options for the arrangements in this area:

1   The flying routes could be kept the same way, with the agreement of
    both sides.
2   The flying routes could be moved westward, along the international
    border with Egypt.

It is an accepted fact that civilian air routes cross through different borders,
and they do not infringe on the independence of a state. Thus, it looks as
though civilian-flying routes should not present any special problems, and
it will be possible to continue using the present flying routes.

Israeli Air Force Exercises

One of the gravest problems facing the Israeli Air Force after the Sinai
pullout was the lack of exercise area. Losing the right to exercise flights in
the West Bank will pose a hard problem on the air force in this regard.

The air force has grown larger since it had to conduct exercises inside
the Green line prior to 1967. The following statistics illustrate the problem
embodied in the growth in size of the Air Force. On the eve of the Six-Day
War, there were 8,000 soldiers and officers and 200 combat aircraft. In
addition, there were two squadrons of Noratlas, Stratocruiser, DC-3 cargo
planes, and two squadrons of helicopters.

The growth of the Air Force is illustrated with the present data. Today
there are 36,000 soldiers and officers in addition to 55,000 reserve
personnel. The fleet consists of:

1   518 Combat aircraft.
2   58 Transport aircraft.
3   205 Helicopters.[20]

The speed of combat aircraft has also increased substantially since the Six-
Day War, thus demanding larger flying areas for exercise. The different
types of exercises, particularly those using long-distance weapons, require
a large flying zone. The Negev, Jordan Valley and Golan Heights are
already over used by both ground and aerial forces, and the land purchased
for military purpose is increased every year.

In 1984, the overall use of these territories was 50% of the area. In
contrast, the overall land use by the American Ministry of Defense in the
southwest states (California, Nevada, Utah, New-Mexico, and Arizona)
reaches 3%. These states have the highest use for military functions in the
US.[21]

The Golan Heights has hardly any importance for aerial exercises;

therefore, the barring of flights over it will have no substantial effect on the aerial exercises. Because the situation is more complex in the West Bank, Israel must receive assurances allowing its air force to continue exercising over the West Bank. It is also possible to agree on high altitude flying – refraining from low altitude flying, especially over the urban areas. A substantial part of the Air Force's exercises such as dogfight exercises are done anyway at high altitude.

The Electromagnetic Sphere

Israel should insist on two demands:

1   Israel will control this sphere and all the frequencies, both for military and civilian use.
2   Israel will allocate frequencies to the Palestinians.

The regulation of the frequencies is needed because there are military systems that could be jammed by the Palestinians. By using specific frequencies, they can also interfere with civil aviation traffic.[22] This issue was a point of concern for the Israelis from the beginning of negotiations with the Palestinians and was mentioned in the "Agreement on the Gaza Strip and Jericho Area" signed in Cairo on May 4, 1994.[23]

The "Safe Passage"

According to the Oslo Accords, there will be "Arrangements for a safe passage for persons and transportation between the Gaza Strip and Jericho area."[24] Oslo II introduces the concept of "safe passage," granting the right of safe passage to Palestinians wishing to travel between the West Bank and Gaza, necessarily crossing Israeli territory to do so.

But the agreement also includes this text:

> The provisions of this Agreement shall not prejudice Israel's right, for security and safety considerations, to close the crossing points to Israel and to prohibit or limit the entry into Israel of persons and of vehicles from the West Bank and the Gaza Strip.[25]

While it is clear from a reading of the entire document that Israel's security rights take precedence over the right of safe passage, this has been a contentious issue. Until recently, Israel did not implement this part of the agreement. Because the Palestinian State will be composed of two unconnected territories, the "safe passage" should be an essential part of the agreement between Israel and the Palestinians.

Israel may ask for reciprocity by asking for the right for a safe passage on Route 443. The use of this route by Israelis is essential for the future development of Jerusalem. An analysis of Israeli experts emphasizes the importance of this route, and recommends the following:

> The conversion of the Bet Horon route [routes 45/443] into the primary highway between Tel Aviv and Jerusalem. This route, connecting Tel Aviv, Ben-Gurion Airport, Modiin, Bet Horon, and Jerusalem, already serves an ever-increasing fraction of the land traffic to Jerusalem. With improvement, it will become the highway of choice because of both improved travel time and greater safety. Continuing development of plans for rapid rail transport (travel time: 20–30 minutes) along the Bet Horon route. These plans should be executed as soon as they are found to be economically viable with the technology available. The Bet Horon route is the shortest, topographically the smoothest, economically the cheapest of the alternatives. Construction will entail only minimal environmental damage. Rapid transit along this route will create a unified market and employment area comprised of Tel Aviv, Jerusalem, and points between, including the airport. *It is essential that the right of way for road and rail development be protected from interference by the Palestinian Authority.*[26]

The "Jordanian Factor"

It is essential that Jordan be included in any overall peace agreement. Militarily, Jordan is an organic part of the bloc that includes Israel, the West Bank, and the Gaza Strip. The East Bank must be involved in the peace agreement to reduce the military risks that Israel would face. If Jordan were not a party to the peace treaty and military arrangements, Israel would be forced to station permanently a substantial military force on the West Bank.[27] However, if Jordan is brought into the process, the prospect for regional stability will be enhanced immensely.

Jordan can and should be a central player in this process. Israel has a strong interest in ensuring that a Palestinian state be determined with Jordan's consent and participation, and that Palestinian–Jordanian cooperation be enshrined as a structural aspect of Palestinian statehood. Israel has an interest in participating in some elements of Jordanian–Palestinian cooperation, effectively making such cooperation trilateral. Jordan is intrinsically and existentially connected to the Palestinian question in numerous ways.[28]

Notes

1   Ze'ev Schiff, "Israeli Preconditions for Palestinian Statehood," Washington Institute, May 1999. <http://www.washingtoninstitute.org/pubs/pfs/pfs39exe.htm>.

2   "Two Traumatized Societies," *Palestine-Israel Journal*, Vol. 10, No. 4, 2003.
3   Yaakov Amidror, "Israel's Security: The Hard-Learned Lessons," *The Middle East Quarterly*, Vol. XI, No. 1, Winter 2004.
4   The "Clinton Parameter" (January 7, 2001). <http://www.jewishvirtualli-brary.org/jsource/Peace/clintplan.html>.
5   Ze'ev Schiff, "Israeli Preconditions for Palestinian Statehood," ibid.
6   "1993 Declaration of Principles" – Oslo Accords.
7   <http://www.fas.org/man/dod-101/sys/missile/row/sa-7.htm>.
8   <http://www.designation-systems.net/dusrm/m-43.html>.
9   <http://www.fas.org/man/dod-101/sys/land/stinger.htm>.
10 Aluf Benn, "Israel accepts Egyptian offer to increase forces," *Ha'aretz*, December 1, 2004.
11 Shai Feldman, *Israel's National Security; Perceptions and Policy*, wwics.si.edu/subsites/ccpdc/pubs/brgap/chap02.pdf
12 H. Gvirtzman, "Securing the Water Sources in Judea and Samaria," *Nativ*, Vol. 51 (4), 1996 [Hebrew].
13 Martin Sherman, "Water in Israel: The Dry Facts," Herzliya: Interdisciplinary Center, April 2001. (Policy Paper prepared for the 2000 Herzliya Conference, December 2000).
14 Ya'akov Amidror, "Israel's Security: The Hard-Learned Lessons," *The Middle East Quarterly*, Vol. XI, No. 1, Winter 2004.
15 <http://www.jewishvirtuallibrary.org/jsource/Peace/egypt-israel_treaty.html>.
16 Ibid.
17 Ibid.
18 Camp David Accords, September 17, 1978. <http://www.mfa.gov.il/MFA/Peace%20Process/Guide%20to%20the%20Peace%20Process/Camp%20David%20Accords>.
19 Ibid.
20 Jaffee Center for Strategic Studies, *Middle East Military Balance, 2003–2004* <http://www.tau.ac.il/jcss/balance/toc.html>.
21 On the restrictions imposed on the exercises of the US Air Force in Western US, see J. Zane Walley, "Perilous Skies" (<http://www.paragonfoundation.org/perilous_skies.htm>).
22 The issue of Electromagnetic sphere was discussed in the Geneva Accords from October 2003 (article 10) <http://www.ipforum.org/display.cfm?rid=1134>. On the worries of PM Sharon regarding the Electromagnetic sphere, see Aaron Klein, "Sharon's Gaza plan prompts questions," WorldNetDaily.com <http://www.wnd.com/news/article.asp?ARTICLE_ID=41397>.
23 <http://almashriq.hiof.no/general/300/320/327/gaza_and_jericho_00.html>.
24 <http://www.iap.org/oslo.htm>.
25 <http://www.palestinefacts.org/pf_1991to_now_oslo_accords_2.php>.
26 "Professors for a Strong Israel," Statement to the Press – July 30, 1997. <http://www.professors.org.il/releases/30jul97.htm>.
27 Ze'ev Schiff, *Security for Peace, Israel's Minimal Security Requirements* in Negotiations with the Palestinians, The Washington Institute, August 1989. <http://www.washingtoninstitute.org/pubs/pp/pp15exec.htm>.
28 Ze'ev Schiff, ibid.

CHAPTER 18

Did Anything Go Wrong?

MIGUEL A. MURADO

"What went wrong?" In trying to answer this question, one is tempted to respond with a paradox: Did anything, actually, go wrong with the Palestinian–Israeli peace process? In a way, everything has turned out as the most pessimistic had expected. They have been proven right.

One way of seeing the *Intifada* is as a logical consummation of the Oslo Accords. Leaving aside how poorly negotiated those Accords were, they built a ticking bomb that anybody could have heard at the time, but many refused to acknowledge. The peace process did not intend (as any peace process should) to solve the conflict to achieve peace, but to achieve *peace* to solve the *conflict*. Even worse, one side, Israel, was given the right to evaluate and manage the whole process as if it were a neutral power. There were, and still there are, fears that the Palestinians would not be willing to make peace at the crucial point; but then nobody seemed to worry about the question of whether Israel was willing to make peace, too. This was particularly naïve, since it was obvious that while the peace process demanded more from the Palestinians, the final status would depend almost completely on Israel's willingness to make concessions. Naturally, the moment never came.

Or did it? Sometimes I indulge in the fantasy of thinking that the final status talks are taking place: it is the violence of the *Intifada* and its violent repression where both sides negotiate their future. The borders, the shape of a Palestinian state, and even its very existence are being decided in that exchange of cruelty and harm that is war. Needless to say, Israel is winning under these new rules. This form of negotiation is far more violent than the one that took place at Camp David in the year 2000, but certainly no more proactive.

It is worth keeping in mind that, in actuality, Oslo as such, only worked for a few months – from the end of 1993 until the beginning of 1994. Then Baruch Goldstein took his gun and became, ironically enough, the first "suicide terrorist" in the history of the conflict (and I say this ironically because I am aware that this is a tactic the Palestinians have later used far more often). Goldstein's massacre did not, in itself, mark the end of the peace process; but one can argue that Yitzhak Rabin's reaction somehow did. He paralyzed the process, worried by what he interpreted as an upsurge of the anti-Oslo reaction in Israel. He was right. The next year he was assassinated and, let us not forget it, a few months later, a notorious anti-Oslo politician – Binyamin Netanyahu – won the election to replace him.

Under Netanyahu's leadership prospects for an agreement worsened. We are left to wonder of how matters might have progressed (and in what way) had Rabin not been assassinated. However, it was not Netanyahu who put an end to Oslo; he just froze it.

It was during Netanyahu's government when I had the privilege of arriving in Israel and Palestine to work in a very humble capacity in the implementation of Oslo, and I recall that the process was indeed frozen – almost to the point that physicists call "absolute zero". This process was in a coma, but not yet clinically dead. Netanyahu, like Sharon later, understood that it was not in his best interest to terminate the process but to make it last as long as possible. By doing so he could earn precious time and take advantage of the process for his own agenda while killing it by putrefaction.

Oddly enough, it was to be Ehud Barak, who had raised the hopes of so many ill-informed people, that would bury Oslo. Barak's supporters claim that he had his reasons for doing it. That might be partly true, but what cannot be denied is that he made a conscious decision to step away from the Oslo roadmap in the year 2000 and to ignore the Oslo framework. Oslo's core idea was that the final status talks would occur once the Israeli Army had withdrawn from enough territory to allow a reasonably balanced negotiation about the rest. But Barak was not interested in a balanced negotiation; he could not resist the temptation of applying the only peace plan that the Israeli Labour Party has ever had – the Allon Plan in its different denominations. (Beilin's efforts, though undoubtedly generous, can be seen as the newest versions of this plan.) Worst of all, the Oslo process itself allowed Barak to ignore the Oslo prescribed process because it made no provision for a case in which Israel might abandon Oslo. Because Barak's failures to withdraw Israeli troops had the blessings of the White House, President Clinton bears some responsibility in all this, too.

Later in this chapter I will try briefly to consider the Palestinian actions. I am referring mainly to Israel because I think it is wrong to see this conflict as something that involves two sides. Maybe the conflict does, but not its solution. The Palestinians have never been given a status as real negotiators of their future; they do not even have a chair at the gaming table. In English, it is said that you need two to tango. But an Argentinean would find this metaphor rather unfortunate. Tango does indeed require two people, but one of them totally controls the movements of the other.

That was what happened in Camp David 2000. Yasser Arafat was no doubt tricky and indecisive, just two of his numerous defects; but he did not have an offer to consider. There was simply a diktat that the Palestinians could not possibly accept. The common belief that Barak handed them a generous offer goes against logic. No politician ever makes generous offers in a negotiation. Now that we know better what happened that summer at the presidential resort, this common belief goes also against historical understanding.

The failure at Camp David did not unleash the *Intifada*. After Camp David there were talks throughout the months of August and September. And yet I do not think they could have born fruit, just as I do not believe Taba, later in January the following year, might have succeeded. Those two negotiating sessions were again a repeat of the "Oslo process." The violence could have been contained, as it had been many times before, but its outbreak was, in my modest view, inevitable. Both sides saw they could use violence to enhance their positions. Arafat thought he could use the *Intifada* to improve his position in future negotiations, and paid dearly for that mistake. Barak, on the other hand, saw in the violence a chance *not to negotiate* for years.

Once everything was in flames, Arafat used one of his favourite tactics: inaction. He began to travel frantically the world. On the one hand, he wanted to take advantage of the crisis, which he surely saw as something that would not last more than a few days, as had happened with the crisis in May the year before and in October 1998. He believed that the victimized image of the Palestinians could translate into pressure from the international community on Israel. But the terrible lynching of two Israeli reservists in Ramallah quickly followed the pictures of the child Mohammed al-Durah being killed by Israeli soldiers in Gaza. The issue of which side was most responsible for the violence turned simplistically even.

As for Barak, his reaction was typical: siege mentality. Many questions arise when one thinks of Barak's stance toward peace. He had activated the "Field of Thorns" plan during Camp David, a plan to wage all-out war in the Occupied Territories. Its code name was changed to "Magic Melody" and a plan B was added for an even worse-case scenario, named with much optimism, "Distant World." This scenario included the occupation of all of the West Bank and Gaza and the destruction of the Palestinian Authority (PA). These preparations explain the otherwise exceptional readiness of the Israeli Army in the wake of the *Intifada*. Once it all started, Barak activated both "Magic Melody" and the "Lilac Code," which fostered trigger-happiness among the soldiers, and took the *Intifada* from a popular revolt of stone-throwers to a war between states (there really being only one State). In the end, Barak's policies inevitably led to the victory of Sharon in February 2001. It made sense. Barak had convinced the Israelis that harsh treatment was needed and the Israelis chose the harshest doctor. The "Distant World" was not that distant at all.

There is a myth that ought to be debunked; it was not the terror itself but the image of terror that brought Sharon to power. One needs only to check the data to see that there had not been an increase of violence in the weeks before the election. On the contrary, violence had subsided substantially. As for terror attacks, there had been very few until then. In fact, the first of what we could call "catastrophic" attacks happened in June, more than six months after the start of the *Intifada* and several months after Sharon's election. Islamic radicals, who would come to dominate the *Intifada* for long periods of time, had not taken part in the revolt then because Fatah's soldiers had excluded them. Terrorists came on the scene as a result of Arafat's weakness, like Sharon had come as a consequence of Barak's.

I think that everything that could have been done politically was lost in those early months of the *Intifada*. After Sharon's victory, the plot is simple. I would like to stress that I do not demonize Sharon, as many do. I believe that if Sharon ruled Israel it must be because he gave the Israelis what they wanted. I have often encountered young Meretz voters who would emphasize how much they disagree with Sharon and end up expressing views not very different from his. A *Ma'ariv* poll once showed that 40% of Meretz voters actually agreed with Sharon's Palestinian policy. It should not surprise us. Israel is a society based on two principles: ethnicity and fear. Sharon was obsessed with both concepts. It is Israel as a whole that has to question itself about what kind of society it wants to be. It is not just the "Land for Peace" issue. For Israel, the issue is "Land for Democracy" as well.

And what about the Palestinians? The standstill that followed Arafat's death and the subsequent election of Hamas have served to prove, if it needed to be proven, that Arafat might well have been a difficult man, but nowhere near the stumbling block of Israeli political folklore. His successor, Mahmoud Abbas (Abu Mazen), hailed in Israel and the West while he was in the opposition, saw no other path but to follow Arafat's footsteps: the prioritization of unity, a certain degree of ambiguity, reluctance to comply with Israel's security needs, and appealing to the United Nations and the European Union while trying not to anger the United States. It was all that he could do. For Israel he exists only as the symbolic scapegoat of a people that has not yet been authentically recognized as such. And the situation is made even more frustrating and complex after the 2006 election of Hamas.

My contention is not that the *Intifada* is a consequence of the Oslo process. The Israel–Palestine peace process and war process are both one and the same, and not contradictory things. That is why I deem Manichean and useless the idea of the "cooling-off periods," which George Mitchell and then George Tenet proposed. The peace process and the war process are simultaneously with us, whether you call them "Road map" or "Gaza first." If we have learned anything in there past years it is that when there is no violence, delaying action in the peace process just allows time for things to turn violent; and, when there is violence, waiting for it to end without trying for a peace agreement, ensures there will be even more violence.

Sharon was right: This conflict was not about land; it was (and still is) about time. Whoever has time on his side will have the land in his hands. And, to win time there are two options: either losing it in military operations or in negotiating the details of a peace plan. We can rest assured that both strategies have been employed with great success.

CHAPTER 19

A Leaking Reservoir of Trust in Israeli–Palestinian Water Talks

EDWIN G. CORR

The subject of this book is rebuilding and building trust in order to facilitate the Palestinians' and Israelis' negotiation of the cessation of violence and a comprehensive Middle East peace agreement. This chapter examines sharing water and talks about water as they affect the Palestine–Israel search for peace and security. Official and privately sponsored talks and negotiations on water between the Palestinians and Israelis have occupied a special role in citizen-to-citizen diplomacy aimed at rebuilding and building a level of trust needed to advance negotiations. However, whereas meetings and discussions on water have generally contributed to bettering the negotiating atmosphere, the persisting inequities in distribution of water between Israelis and Palestinians and increasing questions about who controls water resources have the potential to exacerbate tensions and conflict rather than ameliorate friction.

The Special Role of Water

Water is the lifeblood of all peoples and civilizations. It is basic for the health and welfare of the individual, the family, and the community. Water has been intimately connected with the rise of civilization in the Middle East.[1] Because water is the source of life, the scarcity of water in the Middle East complicates the political situation and has the potential to make solutions more difficult as the demand for water increases with population growth and economic activity. In different typologies that measure adequacy of water supplies, Israel and Jordan are placed in categories of "absolute scarcity" and the per capita water supply was decreasing until 2005 when the large Ashkelon desalination plant came on line in Israel.[2]

The shared nature of water requires joint management and protection from pollution and there is a strong need for cooperation. Misallocation of water is increasingly regarded as a breach of legal norms because water is considered a humanitarian issue and is often described as a "right."[3] Water is also regarded as a national security issue. Some scholars suggest that whereas wars of the late twentieth century had causes related to energy resources, those of the twenty-first century may be more rooted in contests over water.

Most people believe talks on water have contributed to progress in peace talks. Cooperation and official talks have halted in nearly every area since the start of the second *Intifada* in 2000, but cooperation has continued on water issues. Water agreements are among the few accords reached by Israel and the Palestinian Authority.

Water has been regarded as so important that it should not be politicized. Its negotiation was not a matter of controversy in the 2000 Camp David talks, and, similarly, in the Geneva Accord negotiated by Yossi Beilin and Yasser Abed Rabo, the subject of water was left for later negotiation. This could mean that water issues can be resolved peacefully or it could mean that some aspects of water are so sensitive and potentially confrontational that it is easier to procrastinate than to deal with them. Those aspects are likely to surface eventually. For instance, the question of Israel's positions on Israeli perceived needs for water security as set forth by Rueven Pedatzur in Chapter 17 will sooner or later have to be resolved with the Palestinians who may perceive conflicting needs of their own.

Water Issues Prior to and at the Beginning of the Israeli State

Wells and water have been subjects of controversy in lands of Israel and Palestine since Biblical times, and in modern times especially since the Balfour Declaration of 1917. The British declared that if the water resources of the area could be fully developed, at least four to five million Jewish immigrants could move into TransJordan without displacing Arab occupants. Studies ensued to corroborate or disprove the Balfour allegation. If the studies' or plans' sponsors were pro-Arab, the studies illustrated that the land could not absorb Jewish immigrants of the numbers mentioned by the British in connection the Balfour Resolution. If the sponsors were pro-Zionist, the studies constructed more optimistic projections of water availability.

After Israelis won their independence in 1948–49, they began unilaterally to develop water resources. Two major projects were the draining of the swamps of Lake Huleh in northern Israel and the construction of the National Water Carrier. Both projects enabled Israel to increase exploitation of the Jordan River headwaters, and both provoked conflict with neighboring Arab states, which saw these projects lowering greatly the flow of the Jordan River as encroaching on their water rights, lessening the amounts of water available to them, and contributing to the drying up of the Dead Sea.

In the early 1950s the US Government sent Special Representative Eric Johnston, Head of the International Council of the Authority for Technical Assistance, to the Middle East to create a comprehensive water scheme for the entire region. He did so. All the countries affected generally agreed upon the Johnston Plan. However, when the 1956 Sinai Campaign commenced because of tensions between Israel and Egypt, the Johnston Plan was set aside, and it was never signed. It became, nevertheless, the de facto agreement that Arabs in the region generally attempted to follow, particularly in terms of their water rights versus those of Israel.[4]

The Multilateral Working Group on Water Resources

The Madrid Conference of October 1991 established a bilateral negotiating track between Israelis and Palestinians and a multilateral track among multiple countries to supplement and reinforce the bilateral track. A framework for the multilateral track was created in January 1992 in Moscow to examine technically oriented issues that extend across international boundaries for which resolution thereof is essential for the promotion of long-term regional development and security. Five groups were established plus a steering group to coordinate the work of the five groups. One of these was the Multilateral Working Group on Water Resources (MWGWR).

The vision for and purpose of a working group were to create synergies through awareness of common problems that would encourage the participants in the process to transcend the realm of competing interests and create a situation in which all parties can share benefits. The MWGWR participants' awareness of water scarcity and water quality has aimed at producing cooperation and coordinated efforts to ameliorate water problems.

The MWGWR has made some progress. There have been many meetings, reports issued, and joint efforts in specific areas. The Executive Action Team (EXACT) achievements for enhancement of water data availability has created an impressive structure for the sharing of data among the Israelis, Jordanians, and Palestinians. The most important success in this area is the cordial and continuing communications among professional colleagues of Jordanian, Palestinian, and Israeli agencies that work on water. But whereas important relationships and a spirit of cooperation have been built across natural boundaries among individual experts, the same cannot be said about states' relations on water.

The greatest impediment to greater collaboration and progress has been that the countries of the region consider information about water to be a matter of national security, and national governments often preclude their water agencies from sharing data. When it is shared, there is a general lack of confidence in the reliability of the information provided by other countries. The major disappointment about the MWGWR is that the problems of water scarcity and quality have not yet been addressed in a manner that produces significant solutions and makes water supply and usage notably improved and more equitable.[5]

Aside from the official cooperation of nations collaborating in the MWGWR, three examples of Israeli–Palestinian cooperation on water are sometimes cited: (1) The clean-up of raw sewage from the Palestinian West Bank towns of Nablus and Tulkarm in the Alexander River that Israeli and Palestinian planners began in 1997, and has continued through the worst of the Al Aqsa *Intifada* to the present; (2) an Israeli–Palestinian research project financed by the US Agency for International Development (USAID) to assess damage to the Besor-Khalil watershed in the West Bank and to make recommendations for its restoration; and (3) the Friends of the Earth Middle East Project called the Good Water Neighbors in which seventeen Palestinian, Jordanian and Israeli cross-border communities cooperate to share water conservation best practices.[6]

The Middle East Water Working Groups for Peace Studies Experience

In addition to the Friends of the Earth Middle East Project just mentioned, there have been numerous conferences, workshops, and meetings organized by private institutions to address water issues. For instance, the Israeli–Palestine Center for Research and Information (IPCRI) has held excellent conferences on the subject of water. We now describe another private sector project (in which the author of this paper was a participant), organized by the University of Oklahoma (OU) Center for Peace Studies (CPS), whose secretariat is at OU and whose core institutional members are: the University of Haifa and Netanya Academic College, both in Israel; the University of Bethlehem, Palestine; the Horizon Institute of Jordan, which works with professors of Jordanian universities; and the Cairo Peace Association, and OU.

The Middle East Water Working Groups (MEWWG) grew out of a conference on water held by the CPS at OU in November 2001. Leaders and experts in water in the Jordan Valley attended from the Middle East, the United States, and Europe. A book, *Water in the Jordan Valley: Technical Solutions and Regional Cooperation*, was published on the basis of papers presented at the conference.[7] OU and the Bureau of Education and Cultural Affairs of the US Department of State provided funding for the MEWWG project.

Because of the political situation of the Middle East and sensitivity to restrictions of some governments about their citizens meeting with Israelis, the MEWWG actually was conducted as two projects: the Northern Tier project constituted by water experts from Jordan, Syria, Lebanon, Turkey, and (after the fall of Saddam Hussein) Iraq; and, the Southern Tier project constituted by water experts from Jordan, Israel, and Palestine.

The institutional members of the CPS invited water experts in a private capacity to attend workshops for general discussions on solving water problems. The participants were both technical and economic/social authorities in their fields. Most were professors and many had worked as government officials. Also invited to each meeting were graduate students with the intent of helping to prepare tomorrow's leaders on water. Northern Tier meetings were held in Damascus, Beirut, Ankara, Istanbul, again in Ankara, and Amman. Southern Tier meetings were held in Cyprus, the Dead Sea Spa, Aqaba, and Amman.

The meetings' participants presented no formal papers. Most brought with them vast knowledge accumulated by years of study and practitioner experience. They ostensibly and seriously focused on technical solutions to water problems, and on the premise that solutions emerge within an atmosphere of trust and mutual respect, which working groups can provide. The meetings aimed to increase the knowledge, empathy, and comprehension of the observer students and faculty members involved in the meetings. For the purposes of connecting the experiences of participants in the MEWWG project to the subject of this chapter we will examine two subjects:

1   The growing frustration and disillusionment of the Palestinian participants (and non-participants) in the MEWWG meetings, and
2   The humanization of the "other" (the adversary) in the eyes of the MEWWG participants.

The focus is entirely on the Southern Tier meetings and mostly between the Palestinians and Israelis. Before drawing lessons from the personal interactions, I will set forth the gist of the Palestinian presentations at MEWWG on the water situation in the occupied territories.

The Palestinian Participants' "Facts" and Discouragement about Water in Palestine

In low-key, tempered but firm presentations the Palestinian delegates at each meeting of the MEWWG outlined salient facts about water availability and quality in Palestine. These presentations were made before

Israel's withdrawal from Gaza, but the Israeli water Company, MEKOROT, continues with some arrangements for providing water in Gaza and continues to provide water in the West Bank occupied territories.

Among the facts and statements they made are the following:

1   85% of the Palestinian population is connected to the Israeli-operated water network.
2   Most rural areas have no public sewage systems.
3   12% of Palestinians who reside in 254 communities have no water.
4   The Palestinians therefore have limited access to water and have little control over their water which they must buy from the Israelis.
5   Because Palestinians do not control their water and do not have enough water, they cannot themselves develop a sound water policy.
6   Palestinians have limited access to fresh water, and they use water for multiple purposes, which means perforce that they use water judiciously.
7   Palestinians simply do not have enough water to meet their needs, and they particularly suffer during summers.
8   In some areas Palestinians receive water every two weeks, while neighboring Israeli settlers have water twenty-four hours a day.
9   The lack of law enforcement in the West Bank and frequent violation of Palestinian rights exacerbates the water situation.
10 The springs used for drinking water in many villages are contaminated, but they are the only source of water for drinking.
11 The ratio between Palestinians and Israelis is 1:5; that is, Israelis use five times more water on a per capita basis than do Palestinians.[8]

Comparing the Palestinians' presentations in the MEWWG project with World Bank statistics corroborates generally Palestinians' data. The World Bank sets 1,000 cubic meters of water per capita per annum as the standard in semi-arid countries. Availability of only 500 cubic meters per capita per annum is classified as an "acute" shortage of water and less than 300 cubic meters per capita per annum as a "catastrophic" shortage of water. Many Palestinians have access to no more than 100 cubic meters per capita per annum, and in some seasons communities have no water supply for weeks except for that trucked to the area. [9]

How Private Talks about Water Affect Palestinians and Israelis

The first Southern Tier MEWWG meeting was held in Pano Platres, Cyprus, June 27–29, 2003. The Palestinian delegates had experienced supreme difficulties and delays in traveling through Israeli-occupied Palestine and crossing the international border into Jordan to travel to Amman to spend the night and then fly to Cyprus. The logical short route from Bethlehem would have been from there to the Tel Aviv Airport and on by airplane to Cyprus – a matter of hours rather than two days. On the after-sunset, two-hour bus ride from Cyprus Airport to Pano Platres, it was necessary to keep changing the subject from a Palestinian graduate student's complaints about the bad treatment he had received at the Israeli checkpoints and the border, so as not to poison the discussion atmosphere before the exchanges began. The meeting went extremely well, however, in terms of content and rapport, notwithstanding the Palestinians' description of the lamentable Palestinian water situation in contrast with that of Israeli settlers'.

It was more difficult to persuade Palestinian participants to attend the Dead Sea Spa meeting, December, 2003, and the Aqaba meeting, June 2004, because they did not want the hassle of traveling through Israeli checkpoints and crossing into Jordan. In both meetings the Palestinians again described the lamentable Palestinian water situation in contrast with that of Israeli settlers.

How did the workshops' exchanges and the Palestinian presentation of their disadvantaged water situation affect Israeli participants? They were not surprised by the statistics, but, importantly, it was during the discussion of the inequitable water situation of the Palestinians that Palestinians and Israelis became greatly aware of each other as human beings, not merely as objects they had previously ignored if not despised. One Israeli participant was so impressed that she could not cease talking about how she and most Israelis knew intellectually much about the conditions of life of Palestinians, but they seldom empathize with nor have meaningful interactions with them. Palestinians made similar remarks about views toward Israelis. Once personal exchanges have been experienced, a person must consider the "others'" situation with more understanding instead of in a distant, cold, calculating manner, because the "others" have become fellow human beings.

Palestinian Concerns about Water Control and Distribution

Palestinians may focus more on control of water resources in final peace agreement negotiations. There seem to be more articles and statements asserting Palestinian ownership of aquifers and surface water, and accusing Israel of trying to ensure its control over Palestinian owned water through occupation, location of settlements, and the Israeli's chosen route of the separation barrier. As an example, the August 16, 2004, issue of

Bitterlemons, an internet newsletter that presents Palestinian and Israeli viewpoints on prominent issues of concern, was dedicated to water. Ghassan Khatib, the Palestinian Authority Minister of Labor; Yossi Alpher, a former director of the Jaffee Center for Strategic Studies at Tel Aviv University and a former advisor to Prime Minister Ehud Barak; Abdel Rahman Tamini, the Director of the Palestinian Hydrology Group for Water and Environment Resources Development; and Gidon Bromberg, the Israel Director of Friends of the Earth Middle East, were featured.

Khatib, in "Water and International Law," (and others) asserts that water is one reason behind the Israeli drive to modify borders away from the 1967 lines and that water is also at the core of the settlements issue. Khatib argues that one of the many considerations behind the locating and building of settlements is water, and he says that the Israeli government's practices in the occupied territories have been in violation of international law. In short, he says that Israel is stealing water in that international law prohibits occupiers from using for purposes of its own citizens the water of an occupied power. He also states that Israel is restricting the indigenous population (the Palestinians) from being able to use and enjoy the water that legally belongs to them. He points to Israeli settlers who, in contrast to the Palestinians, have no restrictions on their water usage and on a per capita basis use as much as twenty times the amount of water as do neighboring Palestinians.

Abdel Rahman Tamini, writing about "The Water Wall," says that control over water resources has always been one of the primary objectives of Israeli settlement policy, both within the Jordan River Valley and over coastal aquifers. He alleges that a map of the Israeli security barrier overlaying a map of West Bank aquifers neatly takes in the main basin of the aquifer. Tamini decries the thirty-six ground wells and the 35,000 meters long drip irrigation network that the Israelis encompass with the Wall, and laments the effects on Palestinian agriculture and employment. Tamini warns of the political repercussions of such Israeli actions for final status negotiations over water.

Yossi Alpher in "Things Could Get Worse" points out that Palestinian villages lack running water, that over-pumped wells in the Gaza Strip are producing dangerously poor quality water, and that there are great disparities between settler quality of life with respect to water compared to that of Palestinians. He says that the difference cries out for rectification, while also noting that at the local level cooperation on water has survived the conflict.

Gidon Bromberg, in "A Missed Opportunity to Rebuild Trust," declares that the only two agreements signed by the Palestinians and the Israelis since the beginning of the second *Intifada* have both involved water issues. He believes that lack of greater progress in this area is a lost opportunity. Bromberg says there is no justification for either the Israelis or Palestinians to delay final arrangements on water that he is told are already "99% worked out" between the Israeli government and the Palestinian Authority.[10]

Developing Our Way Out of Water Shortage and Political Friction

The problems of equity and just sharing of water resources among Palestine, Israel and Jordan might not be resolved completely, especially the issue of water resources ownership, but contention over water could be greatly ameliorated by expanding relatively quickly the quantity of water available for the countries of the region. Israel is developing and using new, innovative, scientific and engineering technology for water desalination, which, coupled with cross-border sharing of water, might reverse political tensions surrounding the sensitive issues of water ownership and equitable distribution.[11]

The completion of the Ashkelon desalination plant in 2006 and the completion of two more plants already under contract and construction in Israel scheduled to begin production by the end of 2008 will together increase Israel's potable water by about 20%. Other desalination plants may be built. Should desalination capacity continue to grow, one can envision enough water to provide greater amounts to Palestine to improve equity in distribution. Additional water for Israel might also allow taking less water from the Jordan River so as to restore more water flow downstream in the Jordan to help raise Dead Sea water levels and to provide more water for downstream riparians Jordan and Palestine.

The cost of one F-16 combat plane is more or less the cost of the Ashkelon desalination plant, approximately $250 million. It would take just three similar plants to produce water from the Mediterranean Sea to provide water to meet Jordan's current water deficit. In the long run it would be much cheaper to construct desalination plants and work out the political, technical, and (for Jordan) the security of the pipeline problems of water and transport needed to supply Jordan's water deficit than to continue buying F-16s.[12]

Israel re-uses water at a higher rate than any other country in the world. This rate is likely to continue to rise, and make more water available, in addition to that derived from desalination. Israel also continues to implement water saving conservation measures, and is cutting back on some high water use agricultural crops.

After five years of negotiation, Israel and Turkey signed an agreement in March 2004 for Israel to buy 50 million cubic meters of water a year from Turkey over the next two decades. While the Israel's negotiation of this arrangement may be more for cementing strategic political relations than actually constructing a water pipeline or using tanker ships to bring water to Israel, it is not to be discarded as a way to increase water quantity for Israel, and indirectly, its neighbors.[13]

The long discussed project to save the Dead Sea by pumping, gravity, and channeling water from the Red Sea to the Dead Sea is being studied under the auspices of the World Bank. Some argue that the project would damage ecosystems and it may never come to fruition, but, if so, it could also provide additional water for Jordan, Palestine and Israel. These are a few of the promising projects that might help Israel, Palestine and Jordan develop themselves out of the water challenges now confronting them.

Conclusions

Former Secretary of State Madeline Albright in comments on the Middle East stated that water can be a point of dispute as well as a means to understanding.[14] Talks on and the sharing of water have had a special significance in Israeli–Palestinian–Jordanian relations, and have generally contributed to the overall peace process by assuring continued dialogue even in the worst of times. There is, however, frustration on the part of the Palestinians about lack of more progress, and, especially, over the blatantly obvious inequity between the amount and quality of water available to Israelis compared to the Palestinians, and increasingly over ownership and control of water resources. Attention must be given to this, or water is likely to become a more contentious issue. The best response to this perhaps festering situation would be a comprehensive peace accord. The next best response might be a quick and notable improvement in the Palestinians' water situation, particularly as compared to that of the more affluent Israeli settlers.

Notes

1   Center for Peace Studies/University of Oklahoma, "Proposal for Working Groups to Study Water Resources and Usage in the Middle East," submitted to US Department of State Bureau of Educational and Cultural Affairs, October 4, 2001.

2   Stephen D. Kiser, "Water: The Hydraulic Parameter of Conflict in the Jordan River Basin" in Max G. Manwaring (ed.), *Environmental Security and Global Stability: Problems and Responses* (New York: Lexington Books, 2002), p. 143.

3   Gidon Bromberg, "A Missed Opportunity to Rebuild Trust: An Israeli View" in Palestinian–Israeli Crossfire" <bitterlemonshtml@bitterlemons.org>, August 16, 2004, Edition 30, p. 6.

4   Kiser, "Water," ibid., pp. 135–37.

5   "Regional Water Data Banks Project," published by the Multilateral Working

Group on Water Resources of the Middle East Peace Process, 2002, pp. 1–3, 12.

6 EcoPeace/Friends of the Earth Middle East, "Good Water Neighbors" <http://www.foeme.org/projets.php?ind=32>

7 K. David Hambright, F. Jamil Ragep and Joseph Ginat (eds.), *Water in the Middle East: Cooperation and Technical Solutions* (Norman, OK: University of Oklahoma Press, and Brighton: Sussex-Academic Press, 2006).

8 Melissa Fair, "Working Groups to Study Water Resources and Usage in the Middle East, Southern Tier Meeting 3: Israelis, Jordanians, and Palestinians," A report prepared on the Aqaba, Jordan, June 25–26, 2004 meeting for the University of Oklahoma, International Programs Center, Center for Peace Studies, July 2004, pp. 12–15.

9 Shaul Arlosoroff, a Director of MEKOROT (Israeli National Water Co.) in a lecture at OU College of Public Health, Oct. 7, 2005, as taken from personal notes of William J. Andrews <WilliamJ.Andrews-1@ou.edu>.

10 Bitterlemons HTML version "Palestinian-Israeli Crossfire" <bitterlemonshtml@bitterlemons.org>, August 16, 2004 Edition 30, pp. 2–8. For other articles on ownership and control of water resources see Harald Frederickson, "Return Palestinian Water Rights if not Land: A Proposal," *Middle East Policy*, Vol. XII, No. 1, Spring 2005, pp. 72–78; Ghassan Khatib, "Recognition of Equal Right in the Red-Dead Project," *Middle East Roundtable*, Edition 23, Vol. 3, June 24, 2005. <html-list@bitterlemons-international>; and, again see Kiser, "Water", ibid.

11 Jon Leyne, "Water Factory Aims to Filter Tension" from BBC Online, Sept. 7, 2004 as reported in Common Ground News Service (CG News), Sept. 24, 2004 <cgnews@sfcg.org>.

12 Ibid.

13 Herb Keinon, "Israel–Turkey Water Saga Flows On," *Jerusalem Post*, Oct. 11, 2005.

14 Kiser,"Water", ibid., p. 133.

CHAPTER 20

Rebuilding Israeli–Palestinian Trust by Unilateral Steps

ALON BEN-MEIR

Historically and theologically, the Jews could be, and to a certain extent were being, trusted by Muslims as long as they were subordinate to the Muslims. Since the beginning of Zionism and the establishment of Israel, the Palestinians have been called upon to trust Israelis when they are powerful. Their mistrust is understandable, but the Israeli–Palestinian conflict stands no chance of being solved without overcoming this mistrust, at least at a minimum level. This realization was at the basis of the Oslo talks.[1] However, the trust that was struck at Oslo never extended significantly beyond the walls of the negotiations room. In this chapter, which is primarily addressed to the Israelis, I am suggesting a way to build trust in this conflict.

A Brief Background

I will first make a few points of description:

Trust: The Word and Definition

The English term "trust" shares its root with nouns such as "truth" and "truce", and has to do with predictability, reliability, and risk, indicating the voluntary giving up on conventional control on the other party.[2] Trust may thus be defined, among other definitions, as

1   Nation A trusts nation B in a particular situation when it believes that B will not further its own interests at the expense of A, usually because A believes that B values the prospects of long-run cooperation between the two countries more than it values the short-run gains that would accrue by exploiting its immediate power over A.[3]

2   A bet about the future contingent actions of others.[4]
3   "The generalized expectation that the other will handle his freedom in keeping with . . . the personality which he has presented and made socially visible."[5] "It is strongly associated with risk, both as a problematic situation, and as a means to solve it, by reducing its complexity.[6]

Arabic has several nouns to indicate "trust": *amánah,* the root of which indicates quiet and tranquility. The word itself is associated with compacts or covenants; *wafáq* and *thiqah.* Their opposites are *khiyánah, ghadr,* (Lane: contradiction of wafáq); *makr, nifáq* (which is associated with religious matters; Lane); *and ádam al-thiqah.*[7]

The "trust" addressed in this paper both enables and accompanies substantive moves between Palestinians and Israelis.

History of Mistrust

The most recent phase in the crystallization of mistrust between Israelis and Palestinians was in the aftermath of the negotiations at Oslo 1993, Camp David 2000, Sharm al-Sheikh, and Tabah in late 2000, all of which were followed by the *Intifada.* Both sides failed to live up to their commitments, signifying a sign of mutual untrustworthiness.[8]

Concern of untrustworthiness from the Palestinian side, for example, started with Ehud Barak as Prime Minister of Israel. He started his term as a distrusted prime minister due to the composition of his government and his positions on Jerusalem and the settlements.[9] This mistrust, as well as that on Barak's part, has never been corrected, and contributed greatly towards the eventual collapse of the Oslo peace talks.

This sort of mistrust appears to be rational and founded on relevant evidence on the ground. Other mistrusts, which originated much earlier in history, are more fundamental, and have no less influence on contemporary attitudes. These rest on the Qur'an as well as on formative events, such as the Prophet Muhammad's suspicion of the Jewish Qainuq'a tribe in Medinah that led him to attack them.[10] Generally, the Jews are often depicted in Islamic texts as treacherous, a depiction which is transmitted in Islamic educational systems to date.[11]

For some religious Muslims, negotiating with Israel compels them to make a choice between trusting the Jews/Israelis, and loyalty to the trust that God has put in them.

These two kinds of mistrust are mirrored on the Israeli side both on the political and factual level and on the religio-cultural-historical one: "Esau hates Jacob"; "Ishma'el shall be a wild ass of a man, his hand against everyone and the hand of everyone against him."[12] Drawing on the scriptures in matters of trust, therefore, more often than not, renders building it an act against the word of God, and thus out of the question. God's word is always right on principle, and it may also be easily evidenced by historical events properly interpreted.

Analysis

In putting trust in another party, one starts from a present situation, and fits the other party's interests, and into it the desired and acceptable outcomes. Determining the true interests of the other party is the task of the trusting party, who must also take into consideration that the other party's declarations about interests may not reflect the truth. In order to be able to carry this out, not only "objective" analysis must be exercised but especially acquaintance with the "subjective" approach of the other party.

Some distinctions are in order: the first is between the group and the individual level;[13] the second is between placing and receiving trust; and the third is between the short and the long run.

Trust is easier to build on the personal than on the collective level, and the methods that serve for the former are often inadequate for the latter. Still, the two can hardly be divorced from one another. Both levels share, to a large extent, the quality of being culture-dependent. On the individual level, this dependence is manifested basically in manners of one-on-one conduct, whereas in the collective, basic concepts, history, and education establish the efficacy of confidence-building measures (CBMs).

Secondly, while putting trust in another party is a matter of one's own will, reached by decisions based on interpretation of factual experience, receiving it is entirely dependent on the other party.

Viewing the two as automatically bound together is a common mistake, a mistake made by Barak in a September 5, 1999 speech in the Knesset following the Sharm agreement. In the speech he indicated that among the results of the conference, trust was restored between the sides, but that was not so. Barak had not won Arafat's trust, notwithstanding Arafat expressed the hope that Camp David would be an opportunity to restore the below-zero trust between the two sides. Some Americans had sensed, that was not to be.[14] Even if trust were to have been reached between the two personalities, transmitting it to both publics would have been a different matter all together.

Thirdly, although building trust for the long run rests on having acquired it in the short run, aiming for eternal trust may be detrimental for practical results.

Evaluation

Trust has more to do with a combination of an irrational leap and rationally studied evidence than with an exclusive, rational, interest-based process.[15] Obviously, these aspects of trust are more culture-oriented than "pure" rationality.

This is one of the reasons why rebuilding trust is a difficult operation, and may well be an impossible task. Each party waits for the other to take the initiative; and when one does, it only does so in anticipation of an immediate and favorable response. Failure on the part of the other side to perform as anticipated contributes to increased suspicion towards it. An escalating process is thus promoted, which accompanies and emphasizes the one that reigns due to the conflict itself. Rebuilding trust, on the other hand, may, perhaps, be viewed as an act that aims at creating a positive escalation.[16]

However, experience and analysis show that the chances for trust building by employing conventional attitudes and methods are minuscule. I would, therefore, like to suggest a different approach.

Proposal

Hypotheses

The following proposal rests on a number of hypotheses:

1   Trust, at least on a minimal level, is desirable by both parties although mistrust has its advantages, especially under severe adversarial situations.[17] This is so, if not in the short run, then in the longer run.
2   One of the reasons that the Israelis need trust is that unlike the situation at the end of World War II, Israel is not an absolute victor who can dictate conditions.
3   It is hypothesized in this essay that all the considerations have already been made and a decision was reached to work towards achieving trust with the Palestinians. The following concentrates on the "how?" rather than on "whether to?" It will also avoid the issue of "what to do with trust once it is achieved?"
4   Trust needs to be built in the general public rather than exclusively in the leadership and/or negotiators.
5   Lessons can be drawn from other disciplines, including psychology, where trust plays an important role, particularly in treating phobias, rebuilding trust after spousal infidelity, or recreating trusting relations between parents and their children.

Restructuring Risk-Management

On the basis of these, I make the following suggestion: An attempt to rebuild trust, to the very limited extent that it has ever existed between Palestinians and Israelis, must be undertaken with a long-term approach. It must also be understood that taking the initiative on building trust does not constitute the acceptance of any responsibility, let alone blame, for matters in controversy.

In building trust, risk cannot be avoided. It can, however, be re-framed. Building trust, if it is objective at all, is done through the same channels that are used for issues of substance in a conflict. In such channels, once the initiator has taken the first step, he or she awaits for the other to reciprocate so as to evaluate the risk he has just taken. His or her next step is conditioned on such reciprocation, a process that could be described as vertical. The advantage as well as the disadvantage of such conduct lies in the danger of severing negotiations (both of substance and of building trust) in case of disappointment.

This proposal suggests a horizontally structured risk taking, which offers far greater flexibility. One channel is exclusively allocated for building trust, and it is to be carried on regardless of developments on the ground. On the other hand, other channels which deal with issues of substance must be highly sensitive to such developments, and if need be cut; or else, the process risks further negative escalation.[18]

Thus, the proposed process consists of at least three main stages, which ideally would follow one another in time. However, in the case at hand, the stages have to be run simultaneously:

1   Unilateral steps.[19]
2   Track III.
3   Tracks I and II.

Stages

1 **Unilateral Stage**   The principles for the first and most important stage in rebuilding trust (unlike trust creating) are: (1) Unilaterality,[20] (2) Unconditionality, (3) Graduality, (4) Realism, (5) Calibration to culture, (6) Simultaneity, and (7) Confidentiality.

One of the common-sense conditions for placing trust is mutuality.[21] On the other hand, as the policy of unilateral steps has already gained a foothold in the region's politics, albeit in military and political issues, employing it in the matter of trust ought not be inconceivable. Let Israel (with or without the Palestinians, independently of each other) declare full trustworthiness in a very limited geographical region, on a very limited issue (olive trees or a small neighborhood, for instance), for a very limited period of time (a week, for example). By the end of the above period, the step offer may be continued without waiting for reciprocation on the part of the Palestinians. Further steps could extend beyond one or more of the variables. Unlike the unilateral action taken by Israel to withdraw from Lebanon or Gaza, this proposal calls for a continuous unilateralism.

The unilateral step must not be confined to a timetable because this would constitute a conditioning of sort. The basic fault in confidence-building measures behavior is that it is conditional.[22] In order to overcome this fault, it is proposed that further steps should not be conditioned on direct reciprocity on the part of the Palestinians, thus simplifying and making the need for overt and mutual communication unnecessary.[23]

It is important to emphasize that unconditional altruism is by no means suggested.[24] The proposal does not call on Israel to abandon all other channels of action, but rather to try and break the vicious bond of conditioning in a very restricted domain, time-frame, and locality on a single and restricted channel.

Unlike Barak's approach of setting a timetable and aiming at solving the conflict in one big bang (that includes unprecedented concessions), I am of the opinion that at least, in the domain of forging trust, action cannot be but extremely gradual. In that it shares methods with some psychological means of treating broken trust and phobias. The latter sometimes exercises very gradual desensitization: with every step the patient is led closer to his/her source of fear in order to calm him in preparation for the next step.

Similarly, attempts at persuading one party of the other's complete and eternal trustworthiness are doomed to failure and harming to other more realistic objectives. Therefore, non-utopian expectations should be envisaged, and the trust sought temporal, necessitating constant grooming. One means in such treatment can be, "'benevolent misperception', i.e., a tendency to minimize differences and beliefs, or at least behave as though one believes in the opponent's good intentions."[25]

Traditionally, trustworthiness is of great importance in Islamic culture, as it is strongly connected with faith, and is considered a safeguard against any calamity. Its importance is also indicated by the belief that, along with shame, it will be the first thing that will be removed from the nation of Islam on the road of deterioration should God decide to punish them.[26]

As one of the risks of any CBM, and for that matter, of any step taken between any two or more humans, let alone those who belong to different cultures, is that of misinterpretation or ignoring. It is of essence that intentions be made clear by employing the tools of the other culture.

Unfortunately, the history of the conflict is abundant with such cases, e.g., the release of three prisoners as a gesture towards the Palestinians in preparation for the summit meeting in July 2000. This action was perceived by them as an insult, whose damage outbalanced any benefit that would have been obtained by a more substantial release. Trust was also thwarted by "peripheral" reasons such as personal conduct or leaking the contents of the negotiations. This was the case during the Camp David talks, according to Sher.[27]

Cultural considerations should include precedents, models, literary works, verbal expressions, proverbs, the ability to calibrate explicitness, manners, and knowledge of timing and choice of representatives. This is particularly important as it is the people and not only the leaders or representatives with whom Israel seeks to establish a degree of trust.

In the present case, Islam plays a major role, and must be taken in consideration. Trust (*wafáq*), an institution held by Islam in great esteem, is sometimes defined as "stable and permanent love for the [trusted] until his death, and then for his children and friends."[28]

On the other hand, relating to the future as if it were knowable to and able to be influenced by humans is strongly opposed by Islam. Suffice it to recall the prohibition on making any utterance about the future without adding the *istithná*.[29] If, therefore, as Luhmann puts it, "to show trust is to anticipate the future . . . It is to behave as though the future were certain," then putting trust in anything but God could be questionable on religious grounds.[30] Besides this apprehension regarding the future, Islam also prohibits the believer to take risks,[31] primarily in financial matters (*gharar; salám* contracts), but in other domains as well.[32]

The opposite of trust, i.e., treachery and betrayal, are condemned in the Quran: "Betray not Allah and His messenger, nor knowingly betray your trusts."[33] A person who betrays trust is a hypocrite – a very loaded term in Islam.[34] The loss of trust (*amánah*) is one of the signs of the hour of judgment.[35]

But it is not only on religious grounds that Arabic culture, like all other cultures, cautions against trust, especially when one's enemy presents their better profile to one: "The gentler your enemy's conduct towards you, the more cautious you must be. Security against one's enemy lies in distancing oneself from, and closing-off (*inqib'a*) from him, as it is by befriending and trust that you enable him to fight you."[36]

Two main stumbling blocks must be recognized. First, mistrust is of such magnitude that any action by the other party may be interpreted as corroborating it. Even if this should not be the general reaction, there will be individuals and groups on both sides who will push this interpretation home to people. One of the means to doing so is to accuse those who may agree to attempt collaboration of treason or stupidity.

The newly formed political party Kadima that came to power under Olmert's leadership quickly finds itself on the defensive following the Lebanon débâcle. Although withdrawal from much of the West Bank, unilaterally or through negotiations, is the party's principle tenet, no withdrawal is currently contemplated. Instead, violence between Israel and the Palestinians escalates, especially following the abduction of the Israeli soldier Shalit. Meanwhile, the occupation continues to dehumanize both sides, with no new initiative or prospects for any major breakthrough in the offing to end this consuming conflict.

If withdrawal from the territories seemed a good idea when the Kadima party was created, it is even more so now. Withdrawal must occur under any formula that Israel can work out – as long as its national security is not compromised – with the international community, especially the quartet of the United States, the United Nations, the European Union, and Russia. Meanwhile, Mr. Olmert needs to send clear signals that he remains committed to the idea of ending the occupation and begin to rebuild trust by: (a) making it abundantly clear that he will not tolerate the building of illegal outposts and will dismantle all existing ones, (b) end the expansion of existing settlements with *only minor exceptions*, (c) provide economic incentives and sustainable development projects to Palestinian communities that do not engage in violent activity, (d) remove all road blocks that are not *absolutely critical* to Israel's security, (e) allow Palestinians to legitimately build, plant, and develop their land with no undue restrictions, (f) forsake any form of collective punishment and, finally, (g) release all prisoners who came from Palestinian communities that have not been actively engaged in violence. With or without the support of the Palestinian Authority and regardless of the Authority's political convictions, Israel must build positive inroads into the Palestinian community because, in the final analysis, Israelis and Palestinians must co-exist.

2 Track III Once a reaction, even a minimally positive one, is received from the Palestinians to the unilateral steps, the second stage may be introduced. This would form the third track. The objective of this track is the common creation of a longer-range trust between the peoples rather than only between leaders or negotiators, although the latter is a *sine qua non* for the former.

This can be attempted by establishing the rules of the tracks. The following are some suggestions in this process. The track will continue independently of anything that happens outside of it; there should be no timetable, no sanctions, and no leaks during meetings; and conduct should be according to both cultures. It is assumed that if there is even little trust to start with, the track may work, provided the rules are adhered to.

Among other topics that Track III would tackle are the history, culture, mutual acquaintance, implementation of effective CBMs, and advising leaders of the parties that conduct Tracks II and I. Given the sensitivities, it is recommended that a third party, perhaps Jordan, would take the lead at this stage.

It is of the essence not to aim too high. If indeed mutual mistrust is so basic to the relationship between the parties, and if it has to do with their integrity, perhaps efforts should be made to transform lack of trust into respect for competence.[37]

3 Tracks II and I Negotiators in Tracks II and I should deal with matters of substance and be independent of, and oblivious to, the steps in Track III. This suggested process will stand better chances of success if it is conducted confidentially. It will be up to the leaders to navigate between these tracks and decide the moment when they are to be joined. Thus Track III, the trust-rebuilding track, is intended to precede, enable and then accompany Tracks II and I.

Conclusion

Often behavior creates perception. Since neither side can afford holding the future hostage until full trust is struck, this proposal suggests acting, very cautiously, as though some trust has already been achieved. It suggests that Israel should take unilateral steps in this regard, with the principles of unconditionality, graduality, realism, calibration to culture, and confidentiality, until the other party is ready to reciprocate. Then, a third track should start whose sole objective will be to restore some mutual trust. Simultaneously with Track III, Tracks II and I should continue dealing with substantial matters. In such a way, long-term trust building will not be held hostage to daily events. This gradual process would create a stable and reliable channel between the parties.

Acknowledgments

I would like to thank the following people for their counsel: As'ad Busoul, David Kipper, Neil Weiner and Northwestern University's School of Education and Social Policy for their hospitality.

Notes

1 Yossi Beilin, *Madrikh le-Yonah Petsuah* (Tel Aviv: Yediot Ahronot, 2001), p. 96

2 J. A. Rubin and G. Levinger, "Levels of Analysis in Search of Generalizable Knowledge" in: B. B. Bunker, J. Z. Rubin and Associates (eds.), *Conflict, Cooperation, and Justice* (San Francisco: Jossey-Bass Publishers, 1995), pp. 13–38.

3 Robert Jervis, *Perceptions and Misperceptions in International Relations* (Princeton: Princeton University Press, 1976), p. 44.

4 Piotr Sztompka, *Trust: A Sociological Theory* (Port Chester, NY: Cambridge University Press, 2000), p. 25.

5 Niklas Luhmann, *Trust; and, Power: two Work* (Chichester: Wiley, 1979), p. 39.

6 Niklas Luhmann, "Familiarity, confidence, trust: problems and alternatives" in D. Gambetta (ed.), *Trust: Making and Breaking Cooperative Relations* (Oxford: Basil Blackwell, 1988), p. 95; Luhman, *Trust,* p. 71.

7 Edward William Lane, *An Arabic–English Lexicon* (London and Edinburgh: Williams and Norgate, 1968), p. 1863; Repr. Beirut: Librairie du Liban;

Khiy Ánah is defined by Lane as "to be unfaithful to the confidence or trust that he reposed in him."

8   Robert L. Rothstein, "A Fragile Peace: Could a 'Race to the Bottom' Have Been Avoided?" in: Robert L. Rothstein, Moshe Ma'oz, and Khalil Shikaki (eds), *The Israeli–Palestinian Peace Process: Oslo and the Lessons of Failure; Perspectives, Predicaments, and Prospects* (Brighton & Portland: Sussex Academic Press, 2002), p. 1; Manuel Hassassian, "Why Did Oslo Fail? Lessons for the Future" in Rothstein, Ma'oz, and Shikaki (eds), *The Israeli–Palestinian Peace Process*, p. 120.

9   Robert Malley and Husseun Agha, "The Palestinian–Israeli Camp David Negotiations and Beyond," *Journal of Palestine Studies*, 31:1 (2001), p. 72.

10   *Qu'ran* 2:100; Tabari, *Tafsir* to VII:86, in connection with the verse "If you apprehend treachery from any people (with whom you have a treaty), retaliate by breaking off (relations) with them" (8:58).

11   E.g., Saudi *History of the Muslim State, Grade 5* (2001), pp. 29–30; *Biography of the Prophet and History of the Orthodox Caliphs, Grade 7*, (2000) p. 52; *Dictation, Grade 8*, pt. 1 (2000) p. 24. <http://ajc.org/InTheMedia/PublicationsPrint.asp?did=750>.

12   Rashi's commentary on Gen. 33:4; Gen. 16:12.

13   Luhmann, *Trust*, p. 39 states clearly "Trust is extended first and foremost to another human being." See further distinction in the literature of personal trust, distinction is made between deterrence-based, knowledge-based, and identification-based trust (Fisman and Khanna, 2000, quoting Shapiro, Sheppard, and Cheraskin, 1992).

14   Gilad Sher, *Bemerhak Negi'ah* (*Just Beyond Reach: The Israeli–Palestinian Peace Negotiations 1999–2001*) (Israel: Hemed, 2001), p. 135. The Egyptian ambassador to Tel Aviv is reported to have said that Arafat always complained to President Mubarak about Barak's untrustworthiness.

15   Among others, G. Möllering, "The Nature of Trust: from George Simmel to a Theory of Expectation, Interpretation, and Suspension," *Sociology*, 35:2, (2001), pp. 403–20. On the rational component of CBM ("enlightened self-interest without regard to the hostility between the parties to the conflict"), see Gabriel Ben-Dor, and David B. Dewitt (eds), *Confidence Building Measures in the Middle East* (Boulder, CO: Westview Press, 1994), p. 5. Even more adamant for rationality of CBM's is Adelman on p. 314 in Ben-Dor, and Dewitt, who enumerates the following as assumptions of the institution: "An indifference to values"; "Priority of instrumental rationality"; "A shared basic value attributed to survival"; "A presumption of a shared communication and operational norms, and, in the end, perhaps a Kantian good will . . . "

16   Escalation is sometimes viewed as retaliation for unilateral steps taken by the opponent [N. Alon and H.Omer (in press): *Combatting Demonization: Skills for Furthering Acceptance and Reducing Escalation* (Chapter 4). Lawrence Erlbaum Associates, p. 3], thus it is the main vice, turning it into the positive one might create the positive escalation.

17   Alon and Omer, *in press*, p. 8.

18   Alon and Omer, *in press*, p. 11, quoting Bateson, 1972; Orford, 1986 on "complementary", and "symmetrical" escalation); The mix of resistance with reconciliation has also been shown to reduce escalation. See de Waal, 1993;

Weinblatt, 2004, 2005." (Quoted in Alon and Omer, *in press*, p. 13.).

19 During this phase, an address must be provided by the side that takes the unilateral steps for the other to react, without anticipating, let alone, conditioning on it.

20 The proposal agrees with Ross's definition Marc Howard Ross, *The Culture of Conflict: Interpretations and Interests in Comparative Perspective* (New Haven: Yale University Press,1993), p. 101: "Unilateral action" involves one party taking steps to further what it views as its interests", even if it is not adversarialy motivated.

21 Luhmann, *Trust*, p. 42: "The process demands *mutual commitment* and can only be put to the test by both sides becoming involved in it, in a fixed order, first the truster and then the trusted."

22 See Howard Adelman, "Towards a Confidence Transfornational Dynamic" in Ben-Dor and Dewitt, ibid., pp. 311–32, especially tables on pages 317 and 323, where values, tools, and goals, and the three schools of CBM's are depicted respectively.

23 Luhmann, *Trust*, ibid.,p. 43.

24 For the relative efficacy of conditional and unconditional altruism see Kenneth Clark and Martin Sefton (2001)."The Sequential Prisoner's Dilemma: Evidence on Reciprocation." *Economic Journal*, 111/468, 2001, pp. 51–51.

25 Ross, *The Culture of Conflict,* p. 106, quoting Deutsch, 1973: p. 364.

26 Ibn Abi al-Dunya, Abd Allah ibn Muhammad, pp. 823–94. *Kitáb Mákárim al-Akhláq* (The noble qualities of character), ed. James A. Bellamy. (Wiesbaden: F. Steiner, 1973).

27 Sher, *Just Beyond Reach,* ibid., pp. 25 and 127.

28 Ghazal, *Ábád*, p. 289.

29 *Quran* 18:23–24.

30 Luhmann, *Trust*, p.10

31 Luhmann, *Trust*, p. 42: "[One] must invest in . . . a risky investment. . . . It must be possible for the partner to abuse the trust."

32 Although some argue that "the disapprobation of the practice would appear to relate less to material concerns than to the general Muslim preoccupation with the concept of *Muruwah,"* Susan E. Rayner, *The Theory of Contracts in Islamic Law: a Comparative Analysis with Particular Reference to the Modern Legislation in Kuwait, Bahrain, and the United Arab Emirate* (London; Boston: Graham & Trotman, 1991).

33 *Quran*, 27:8.

34 Ghazal, *Ábád*, p. 337; Ibn Abi al-Dunyá, *Mákárim,* pp.116–17 and 144.

35 Bukhard, *Ñaidi,* 'Ilm, p. 3.

36 E.g., Ibn 'Abd Rabbihi, 'Ilm *ÝIqd* (1940), I, 214ff.

37 For the distinction and its implications in organizations, see Peter Kim, Donald L. Ferrin, Cecily D. Cooper, and Kurt T. Dirks, "Removing the Shadow of Suspicion: The Effects of Apology Versus Denial for Repairing Competence Versus Integrity-Based Trust Violations," *Journal of Applied Psychology*, Vol. 89, No. 1, (2004), pp. 104–18.

PART III

The Mediators

CHAPTER 21

The Changing Face of
the Arab League

CYRUS ALI CONTRACTOR

This chapter discusses the role of the Arab League in the Middle East peace process. There has been a 180-degree turn in the attitude of this organization from complete denial and contempt of Israel to an offer of complete recognition. This indicates important developments unfolding within the Arab League over the past 50 years. This chapter will describe several crucial events affecting the League, and how the League's involvement affected each event. Also explained is the internal wrangling among Arab states that has colored the politics of the region since the formation of the League. I will first discuss the founding of the Arab League based on Arabism, then move to the League's involvement in the 1948 War followed by Sadat's visit to Israel in 1977, and end with a discussion about the 2002 Arab Peace Initiative as proposed by then Crown Prince Abdullah of Saudi Arabia. This involves a normative discussion of what was and was not taboo in the eyes of the Arab world, and how this affected the interactions among the Arab states, and subsequently between these states and Israel.

Founding of the Arab League

Arab leaders were and are "embedded in a structure defined by Arabism and sovereignty that shaped their identities, interests, presentation of self, survival seeking strategies, and strategic interactions."[1] As such, the founding of the Arab League resulted from the discourse involving Arab unity and unification in the late 1930s.

> Arab leaders were beginning to speak of life after colonialism, and the political opposition in many Arab countries began using the theme of Arab unity to embarrass the government and score easy political points. Although

strong divisions existed among Arab leaders, social movements, and intellectuals concerning what unity meant and what practical form it should take, the consensus was emerging that an Arab association of some sort was necessary for an Arab revival and commendable on strategic, political, cultural, and economic grounds. The mix of anticipated independence and Arab nationalism steered the conversation among Arab states and societies toward the future regional order.[2]

However, the meaning of unity was disputed. Was this a discussion about creating a *federation* or just a loose association based on common cultural, economic, and political cooperation? At the heart of the matter is a discussion of sovereignty, and what each state was willing to give up to be a member of this hypothetical organization.

Much of this discord was clarified in 1941 when Britain declared its support for the establishment of some type of regional organization in the Arab world. Much of Britain's concerns and subsequent encouragement for the establishment of such an organization resulted from its war effort, and need for the Arabs to ally with them against the Nazi threat. Even though this support was not initially received with open arms, it sowed the seeds for the formation of what would become known as the League of Arab States.

In the same year, Iraq's prime minister, Nuri al-Said, suggested unification in the Fertile Crescent based on a "Greater Syria" scenario that would include Syria, Transjordan, parts of Lebanon, and Palestine, but which would exclude those states that did not resemble the aforementioned in "their general political and social conditions – that is, unity should include the countries of the Fertile Crescent and exclude Egypt and Saudi Arabia."[3] Political realities, however, caused Said to realize quickly the importance of including Egypt, the most influential and powerful Arab state, in a discussion of Arab unity. Egypt carried the necessary political weight to "make things happen." Consequently, in 1943 Egyptian Prime Minister Mustafa al-Nahhas proposed that Cairo host the first preliminary conference to discuss Arab Unity.[4] Egypt's reason for participating was based less on a deep conviction towards Arab nationalism than that Egypt could emerge as the dominant Arab state, which would further its own interests.[5] This has been the central point in Egyptian foreign policy since the 1920s.

The formation of the Arab League, as well as Arab interactions during the subsequent decades, was colored by three related dynamics.

1   Tensions between statism and nationalism.
2   The fear that an association would encourage interdependence that would threaten states' stability.
3   And the meaning of unity; unification or formal association that does not threaten sovereignty.[6]

Following two weeks of discussion, the Alexandria protocols were formulated which dealt with five basic issues:

> creation of the League of Arab States . . . cooperation in social, economic, cultural, and other matters; consolidation of these ties in the future; a special resolution allowing Lebanon to retain its independence and sovereignty; and a special resolution on Palestine and the need to defend the Palestinian Arabs.[7]

These protocols were signed on October 7, 1944, and resulted in the formation of the Arab League in Cairo on March 22, 1945. Though the League was celebrated as the first post-World War II regional organization, it had little power to bind its member states into an effective organization. The Arab League became a theater for inter-Arab competition, and no real power or unification. It reflected Arab leaders' preoccupation with the "Arab Street." The post-colonial governments for the most part were not representative of the broader populations in their countries (i.e. the Hashemites in Jordan and Iraq) and needed the Arabism mantel to help preserve their own positions.[8]

The League became a tool to establish Arab credentials, and members were peer pressured to abide by the norms of Arabism, thereby becoming a forum of collective legitimation. "The Arab states had already conceded in practice that on certain issues they must proceed multilaterally; the construction of the league formalized this process, and whatever formal or informal decisions that evolved from their discussions would now act as a normative constraint."[9] Therefore, Arab politics became increasingly colored by Arabism, and Arab leaders became increasingly "vulnerable to symbolic sanctioning" if they ignored or disregarded the norms of Arabism. "Increasingly aware of this dynamic, Arab leaders began to use the norms of Arabism to constrain their rivals' foreign policies. This largely symbolic organization had pulled them closer together and increased their mutual vulnerability and susceptibility to symbolic sanctioning."[10]

Arab leaders were forced to worry not only about their respective domestic public opinion, but also the public opinions of other Arab states. This public sphere was incredibly influential in the Arab world. As Lynch argues:

> The assumption that Arab and Islamic societies . . . lack any public sphere within which to publicly debate and discuss political issues seriously misrepresents these societies . . . In contrast to the wider international system, where the networks of non-state actors, global dialogues, and globalized media associated with globalization represent a novel development, the Arab world has decades of experience with political argumentation at the transnational level. Precisely because of the relative closure of domestic public spheres, along with the sense of collective identity born out of the Ottoman and Islamic experience, Arabs have long turned to the transnational level for

political debate . . . What defines the existence of an Arab public sphere is precisely the fact that self-identified Arabs do in fact address and invoke and Arab public.[11]

It was necessary to maintain your Arab credentials. Long story short, the formation of the Arab League based on Arabism was more of a constraint than a benefit. This is especially true in regards to the effect the Arab League had on the possibilities of its individual member states creating normalized relations with Israel. It can be argued that this has prolonged the conflict between Arabs and Israelis. Additionally, the League was probably never intended to actually be effective. Conditions of unanimity and consensus ensured that most proposed actions would never materialize.

Hudson argues that though the League was "successful in organizing a common Arab stand on international issues," it has been abysmal at regulating inter-Arab disputes, and especially the Israeli–Palestinian problem. "The League grew up, as it were, with the Palestinian problem, and for many years it helped organize a solid consensus opposing Israel's establishment and subsequent expansion."[12] Nonetheless, this "unified voice" based on symbolic constraint, which prohibited individual member states from making peace with Israel, helped color the politics of the region for decades. It was not until 2002, and the advent of the Arab Peace Initiative, that the Arab League made a real concerted effort for peace with Israel.

The 1948 Arab–Israeli War and Its Aftermath

The 1948 War between Israel and its Arab neighbors goes a long way to illuminate the weakness and lack of real power that characterized the Arab League. The defeat was humiliating for the Arab states, and the aftermath of that war and the possibility for peace with Israel was doomed due to the symbolic restraints mentioned above. Historical record shows that the events leading up to the war resulted in the defeat of the Arabs.

> Symbolic rather than strategic considerations led the Arab states to resolve on April 16 (1948) to send their armies into Palestine once the mandate ended the following month. Few Arab leaders argued vigorously in private that the Zionists were an implacable military threat, but many readily acknowledged that failure to confront the Zionists would leave them vulnerable at home. In fact, many Arab military officials warned their governments that they might not have the military wherewithal to confront the Zionists; such military dangers, however, paled in comparison to the domestic threats that Arab leaders feared they might face should they fail to go to war.[13]

As the war began in May 1948, the Arab armies of Jordan, Syria, Egypt and Saudi Arabia were not well coordinated. "The result was confusion on the battlefield, bickering between Arab leaders, agreement on coordinated invasion routes that were ignored during the campaign, and a generally disorganized and ineffectual military effort."[14] The result was forever known in the Arab world as *al-nakba* . . . the catastrophe.

The events immediately following the defeat have had a profound effect on the peace process. The Arab states were in complete confusion on how to negotiate the defeat with Israel. Some states found themselves abandoning the League and their "Arabness" by negotiating the end of the war unilaterally, and not collectively as the Arab League. However, public opinion usually brought them back into the Arab fold. "Egypt concluded that any benefits that might be gained from a separate peace were not worth the substantial political costs."[15] Syria found itself in a similar situation, but Jordan actually came the closest to formulating some kind of peace with Israel.

> [King of Jordan] Abdullah's desire for a peace treaty stemmed from his belief that Israel would help Jordan gain political access to the United States . . . his concern that Jerusalem would be internationalized and his belief that a peace treaty with Israel would prevent this . . . and his assumption that the right treaty might elevate his prestige to the Arab world. Abdullah's immediate objective, however, was to complete his annexation of the West Bank.[16]

As this became public knowledge, Abdullah was forced to reconsider. Despite the fact that Egypt itself had contemplated a separate peace with Israel, it used Jordan's maneuvering for Egyptian benefit and Jordan's detriment. This may have had less to do with concern for the Palestinian cause than with fear that an Israeli–Jordanian alliance would threaten Egypt's own power and leadership in the Arab world.[17] Consequently, the Arab League convened in March 1950 and seriously considered expelling Jordan if any peace was made with Israel. To add teeth to the threat of expulsion, the League unanimously adopted a resolution that prohibited any member from negotiation with Israel unilaterally. The Arab League formed the Government of All-Palestine in Gaza to limit Jordan's influence in the Palestinian dilemma. This government was a proxy of Egypt and actually did little more than to serve Egyptian interests in Palestinian lands.

> The decision to form the Government of All-Palestine in Gaza, and the feeble attempt to create armed forces under its control, furnished the members of the Arab League with the means of divesting themselves of direct responsibility for the prosecution of the war and of withdrawing their armies from Palestine with some protection against popular outcry. Whatever the long-term future of the Arab government of Palestine, its immediate purpose, as conceived by its Egyptian sponsors, was to provide a focal point of opposition to Abdullah and serve as an instrument for frustrating his ambition to federate the Arab regions with Transjordan.[18]

Hudson states that the defeat in the war also deepened the animosity among Arab states, and therefore other Arab states hurled "malicious observations . . . about how the [Hashemite family] that won two kingdoms out of the defeat of Arab nationalism in World War I had now joined the new Jewish state in the partition of Palestine."[19] Events that would follow over the subsequent decades were tinted by the taboo of making peace with Israel. Though Abdullah was ultimately restricted from making peace, the Arab public never forgave him for even entertaining the idea, and consequently he was assassinated in 1951 at al-Aqsa Mosque.

So much for Arab unity! If anything, Arab infighting strengthened the Israelis during and after the 1948 War. The costly and ill-advised attack that resulted in the 1948 War proved the disarray of the Arab world and ineffectiveness of the Arab League. Not only were Arab states unable to defeat the lone enemy, the Arab League's collective legitimation resulted in the cold relations between Arab states and Israel. Additionally, the League's position that it could not negotiate with Israel on behalf of the Palestinians effectively divested the member states of any political responsibility while retaining the mantel of the Palestinians' champions. This would be true throughout the conflict with Israel.

Expulsion of Egypt

The decision of Egyptian President Anwar Sadat to address the Knesset in 1977 in a surprise visit to Israel and the subsequent Camp David Accords that followed, resulted in the most serious case of Arab League symbolic sanctioning ever levied upon one of its member states: Egypt's total expulsion from the League. However, Sadat's bold move, though it eventually cost him his life, was the beginning of the paradigm shift from Arabs' complete denial of Israel towards some semblance of normalization between Israel and its Arab neighbors. As Hourani states:

> It was clearly in Sadat's mind to try to put an end to the sequence of wars which, he believed, the Arabs could not win, but there were also wider perspectives: direct negotiations, sponsored by the USA, would eliminate the Soviet Union as a factor in the Middle East; once at peace with Israel, Egypt might follow in the way both of economic support and of a more favourable American attitude towards the claims of the Palestinian Arabs.[20]

Hourani's explanation underlines Sadat's motives as being very interest driven. But, despite the fact that Egypt did gain from its bargaining with Israel, it lost on the normative front, as it was symbolically and materially sanctioned by the Arab League.

That being said, Egypt's eventual loss of legitimacy within the Arab world was not based on one event. Tensions had begun building during much of the 1970s as Egypt, ignoring League policy, unilaterally began to negotiate disengagement from the 1973 Yom Kippur/Ramadan War with Israel. Syria was the first to accuse of Egypt's abandonment of Arabism and the Palestinians, only to later conclude similar disengagement talks with Israel. The Syrian excuse: Theirs was a military negotiation, not a political one as the Egyptians had negotiated with Israel.

Sinai II was the next step that pushed Egypt towards expulsion. Concluded on September 4, 1975, this agreement was a second round of disengagement between Egypt and Israel, and was brokered by the Americans. It resulted in the Sinai being returned to Egyptian hands, and the agreement that further disputes between Israel and Egypt would be settled through diplomatic rather than military means.[21] Again the Syrians were the strongest critics of this move.

> Asad accused Egypt of abandoning the military option, the principle of unanimity among the Arab ranks, the boycott of Israel (because Israel could now use the Suez Canal), and the Palestinians. Later Syria denounced Egypt for dividing the Arab front and transforming the Arab–Israeli conflict into a border conflict.[22]

Sadat was defiant in his defense of his policies, and argued that his motives and actions did not betray the Arab world. He claimed to have found solutions that were conducive to both the collective Arab world/Arabism, but also to Egyptian national interests. The reacquisition of the Sinai was an absolute necessity for Egypt, and was important in regards to greater Arab grievances. He "pleaded for realism and pragmatism, saying he was attempting to deliver peace to the Palestinians through deeds and not words, and he challenged other Arab regimes to follow his lead."[23] In essence, Sadat was arguing that each Arab state had national interests that did not concern the greater Arab nation. As long as those interests did not harm greater Arab interests, the other states should not concern themselves in the internal affairs of others.

The two disengagement negotiations brokered between Israel and Egypt led many of the Arab leaders and observers of the Middle East to predict something more substantial to materialize between the two countries, and as such Sadat's visit to Israel and the Camp David Accords only added fuel to the flame of Arab discontent with Egypt. It is not the point of this chapter to discuss the intricacies or go into the details of Sadat's Knesset visit (Shlomo Gazit's contribution to this volume is an excellent and illuminating view of those events from the Israeli intelligence and military point of view) or the negotiations of Camp David, but instead to glance, albeit briefly, at the response of the Arab League. Former President Jimmy Carter points to the importance of Arabism even in making such an atypical move as going to the Knesset in 1977.

> The Egyptian president laid down in no uncertain terms the strongest Arab
> position, which included Israel's immediate withdrawal from all occupied
> territories and the right of return of all Palestinians to their former homes. I
> found it interesting that Sadat decided not to follow the counsel of his
> advisers that he make the speech in English for the world audience, but to
> deliver it in Arabic for the benefit of his Arab neighbors. The symbolism of
> his presence obscured the harshness of his actual words, so the reaction in the
> Western nations was overwhelmingly favorable and the Israeli public
> responded with excitement and enthusiasm.[24]

Carter also stated that Sadat's main intentions at Camp David were that
"all Israelis leave Egyptian soil in the Sinai and that any bilateral agreement be based on a comprehensive accord involving the occupied
territories, Palestinian rights, and Israel's commitment to resolve peacefully any further disputes with its neighbors."[25] The actions of Sadat were
seen as traitorous by other member states of the Arab League. He had
gained significantly from the Camp David Agreement (formal peace with
Israel, reclaimed all of the Sinai, strengthened relations with the West,
autonomy for occupied Palestinian lands, and future definition of the
status of these lands), but he simultaneously lost much credibility and
popularity in the Arab world.[26] This posed a problem not only for Egypt,
but also for Israel, which in and of itself only further hampered the prospect
for peace.

> Neither the Jordanians nor any Palestinians were willing to participate in the
> subsequent peace talks to help implement the Camp David agreements
> concerning Palestinian rights and the West Bank and Gaza. This rejection
> and the persistent refusal of the Palestinians and most other Arabs to
> acknowledge the legitimacy of Israel's statehood have confirmed the Israeli's
> fears that their existence would again be threatened as soon as their adver-
> saries could accumulate enough strength to mount a military challenge.[27]

Additionally,

> The agreement with Israel . . . was repudiated not only by the Palestinians
> but by most of the Arab states, with greater or lesser degrees of conviction,
> and Egypt was formally expelled from the Arab League, which moved its
> headquarters from Cairo to Tunis. Nevertheless, the advantages to be
> derived from a closer alignment with the United States policy were so great
> and obvious that a number of other Arab states also moved in that direction:
> Morocco, Tunisia, Jordan, and in particular the oil-producing countries of
> the Arabian peninsula . . .[28]

Barnett claims that though Arabism was strong in the epicenter of the
Arab world and less so in the periphery, and that many Arab leaders actually had sympathies for Sadat's position, they were forced to expel him due
to public pressure.[29] Interestingly enough, Carter comments on a brief trip

he took to the Middle East leading up to the events of Camp David in 1978 and found many Arab leaders privately supportive of Sadat's initiative, but because of the constraints of Arab unity under the banner of Arabism, they publicly condemned him as a traitor.[30] Though the taboo of having any dealings with Israel was still ongoing and had a tremendous influence on the behavior of Arab governments, Sadat's pragmatic approach, though initially sanctioned, was beginning to test and break the old paradigm and way of thinking and acting. "Sadat and his critics disagreed publicly about whether his policies were consistent with Arabism, but they largely agreed his policies were narrowing the meaning of Arabism, reducing the range of issues on which they were accountable, and bringing them closer to statism."[31]

At face value it is easy to say that Egypt lost credibility, but a deeper more profound assessment would be that the Arab League was unable to deter Egypt from acting unilaterally. This in and of itself shows the actual ineffectiveness of the League as a sanctioning body. As Hourani argues, the League actually lost much of its already limited authority when Egypt was expelled.[32] If Egypt, the leader of the Arab world and homeland of the most famous Arab nationalist politician, Gamal Abd el-Nasser, was breaking the taboo on negotiations with Israel, then how strong was Arab unity? The League carried much moral weight, but it was unable to affect the behavior of its most prominent member. Egypt's positions in the 1970s were intended to assert Egyptian primacy. Egypt gained US support and knew any Arab sanctions would be temporary and for the most part toothless. Once Egypt broke through the barrier, the Arab world began to move in a different direction.

The 1991 Madrid Peace Talks

As Hudson argues, the Arab League has offered a unified stand and common voice on international issues, most prominently regarding the Palestinian–Israeli conflict. However, the League has been ineffective in regards to material actions. The failure to promote intra-Arab trade and economic development is a clear indicator of the League's ineffectiveness. Additionally, it has failed to organize collective defense against Israel, and it has not been instrumental for most of the peace process.[33] In fact, the Arab League did not participate in the influential Madrid peace talks as a unified organization. This section of the chapter will briefly discuss the Madrid peace talks, and the effect the absence of the Arab League had on the subsequent outcomes.

President George H.W. Bush was instrumental in getting many Arab states and Israel to the negotiating table in Madrid in 1991. Though the Arab League did not participate, many Arab states were willing and ready to rush to Madrid. "According to former Jordanian ambassador Adnan Abu Odeh, many Arabs jumped at the chance to come to Madrid and rid themselves of their pan-Arab commitments."[34] The Madrid talks were a very significant event in the Arab–Israeli peace process because it was the continuation of the changing roles, norms, and behavior of the Arab states in regards to their relations with the Israelis. Some of the reasoning and incentives to participate were simple economic benefits thrown at the feet of many of the Arab states.

> Washington has urged, with considerable success, [Arab states in North Africa and the Gulf] to develop contacts or undertake measures of normalization with Israel even before satisfactory final settlements with the frontline states had been negotiated. It also encouraged these rear-line states to develop economic and other links with Israel to create a network of regional economic interdependence that would underpin a potential Arab–Israeli settlement. The substantial dependence of most Arab states on the United States enticed some to undertake such moves in order to strengthen their ties with Washington.[35]

US advocacy for normalization was a direct response to Arab League ineffectiveness on economic integration. The US model would create an integrated trade and economic network inextricably linked to Israel, a form of backdoor recognition. This again sheds light on the relative weakness of Arabism as a unifying ideology and the Arab League as a body that could effectively "control" its members. It could be argued that the greatest breakthrough of the Madrid talks was its realization. Dennis Ross states, "We were breaking the symbolism of denial – a taboo on direct talks between Arabs and Israelis. We were launching a peace process based on Arab states talking to Israel, with UNSC resolutions 242 and 338 serving as the guiding principles."[36] Though Arabism still played a role in the politics of the region, and not much of a breakthrough was accomplished in Madrid, the idea of these parties sitting at the negotiating table together was incomprehensible a few years earlier. It led to a most important event in 1994, which was the declaration of the Arab League that "although Israel had been the Arab nation's staunchest enemy for fifty years, from now on each country would identify its own enemy."[37] As the perceived threat decreased, the need for Arab unity decreased as well.

Tibi offers that the process that began with the Madrid talks has actually resulted in a new regional formula . . . the "New Middle East." Behind this new terminology is a very important idea that involves the hopes for full regional integration, not just inter-Arab integration. As such, the role of the Arab League would be changed in such an event. "The real issue is the need for regional cooperation that goes beyond the confines of the Arab state system. Middle Eastern peace can only be enduring if combined with the needed economic underpinning to be achieved through regional integration."[38] Tibi also calls for a new definition of the Arab League. He claims that the inclination to regard the Arab League as a way to Arab unity has never gotten farther than plain rhetoric. He offers a rather strong suggestion:

> Arabs need to free themselves from this rhetoric while making efforts at democratization of their societies and the civilianization of their governments in order to strengthen the statehood of existing polities . . . ideological and rhetorical pan-Arabism ought to be buried once and for all, not for the sake of a further fragmentation of Arab politics, but rather, with the aim of establishing a stable Arab integration system based on a democratic, nonethnic, and secular understanding of what it means to be Arab. Without this buildup there can be neither a stable Middle East nor real peace in the region.[39]

The 2002 Arab Peace Initiative – Opportunity Lost

The peace initiative offered by the Arab states in March 2002 was the most comprehensive proposal of peace by the Arab states since the inception of the Arab–Israeli conflict. Put forward by then Crown Prince Abdullah of Saudi Arabia, the Arab Peace Initiative offered full Arab recognition of Israel, as well as peace agreements and normalized relations in return for Israeli withdrawal to the pre-1967 War borders, a just solution to the Palestinian refugee problems, and the recognition of a viable, sovereign, and independent Palestinian state in the West Bank and Gaza with East Jerusalem as the capital. As such the Arab League was in effect arguing for the implementation of United Nations Security Council Resolutions 242 and 338 in regards to the withdrawal from Arab territories, as well as the implementation of United Nations General Assembly Resolution 194 section 11 which dealt with the Palestinian refugee problem. The fundamental guiding principle of the Initiative is the concept of "land for peace." It can also be said that the Arab states finally recognized that a military solution never was and will never be a viable method to settle the conflict. Unfortunately it has not yet been implemented, and as such the conflict still rages on.

A question to ask is whether the Arab Peace Initiative was sincere. Michael Scott Doran suggests that the Saudi plan was not as bold as first interpreted.

> The Saudi plan was not about Palestine-as-place, but rather about balancing the demands of cultural authenticity against the need for an alliance with the United States. In Washington, the Saudis depict it as the work of peacemakers carrying water for American interests. At home, however, Riyadh can point to the plan and depict it as an ultimatum to Washington: "You

Americans roll back the Israelis, or else!" The plan requires no practical action by the Saudis, or, for that matter, by any Arab party until the far-off time when the Americans will have returned the situation in Palestine to its early 1967 status quo, at which stage Riyadh claims it will stand up and be counted. Far from getting themselves dirty with peace-processing, the Saudis cleverly devised a way to avoid touching Palestine for as long as possible, recognizing that in the end it can only burn them. When it comes to managing the conflict the United States is largely on its own, and Washington should plan accordingly.[40]

This possible lack of sincerity may be evident in the dearth of very important substantive issues involving access to water resources, the militarization of the proposed Palestinian state, access to holy sites in Palestine and Jerusalem, access between the West Bank and Gaza, etc. Perhaps these are issues to be discussed during negotiations between the Arab states and Israel, or perhaps the Saudis were only using the Palestinian situation for their own political gains. But the simple fact of the matter is that the Arab League offered peace! Sincere or not, the Bush administration could have used and could still use the offer to persuade Israel to put the Saudis and other Arab states to the test. The failure to do so has been one of the fundamental let downs of the United States as a supposed "equal broker of peace." Instead, advisors to President Bush believed that the road to peace in the Middle East went through Baghdad. As such, the Palestinian issue has been put on the back burner of American concerns, and peace seems further away than ever before.

That being said, what we have witnessed with the Arab League as a regional organization is a complete 180-degree turn. It matured with the Palestinian situation. It was shaped by this conflict and the various Arab leaders have used the Palestinian problem and the greater Arab–Israeli conflict as a tool for both domestic and regional legitimacy. The Arab League itself became a collective legitimizing apparatus, but this collective legitimacy was more of a detriment to peace than a way to peace. Arab state hostility towards Israel was affected as much by symbolic sanctioning and shaming tactics of other Arab leaders and publics as by the existence of Israel and the Palestinian problem. Sadat's bold initiative to separate Arab goals and interests from Egyptian goals and interests, and to have the political savvy to claim that Egyptian interests do not violate the tenets of Arabism, was probably the most significant event in the changing of relations between Israel and the Arab world.

Though Egypt was nevertheless expelled from the Arab League, Sadat was able to shift the way of thinking . . . or perhaps he was the first Arab leader to act on what he really thought was the best course of action, defiant of the conformity of Arabism and the Arab League. He realized that wars with Israel had accomplished nothing. He broke the mold of Arab interaction with Israel to the immediate benefit of Egypt, but not to the detriment of the greater Arab cause. In doing so, Sadat began the normative transformation of the Arab League, Arabism, and the Arab world towards Israel.

As a final note, I intended to offer a brief overview of the Arab League's ineffectiveness at solving the Arab–Israeli conflict, peacefully or through war. The Arab–Israeli conflict is about more than Arab and Israeli interaction, but is influenced heavily by Arab–Arab interaction. The Arab world does not signify a common, unified front. We have witnessed divisions between Iraq and Syria despite their Ba'athist leanings, not to mention both of these countries always having contemptuous relations with Egypt during Sadat's presidency. We see a severe problem involving Lebanon, Syria, Hezbollah, and the non-Arab state of Iran (which also has an ongoing struggle for leadership of the Islamic world with Saudi Arabia). Jordan is overburdened with Palestinian refugees, and is probably the most sincere of all Arab states in wanting to find a solution to the Palestinian problem. This probably explains both former Kings Abdullah and Hussein's pragmatic approaches to Israel. Perhaps Tibi's call for a "New Middle East" based on total integration as a way for peace is worth considering, but the amount of time this would take to implement would be much too long. The hope for peace between Arabs and Israelis cannot wait 15 years for total integration to work its course. Instead, while the initial steps toward economic integration are being worked out and implemented, the United States and European states (despite their own lack of consensus on the issue) should persuade all relevant parties to sit at the negotiating table with the goal of implementing the Arab Peace Initiative. No other state has the ability to "make things happen" as the United States . . . letting this monumental offer by the Arab League slip away will only set things back further.

Acknowledgments

I would like to thank the Center for Peace Studies of the International Program Center at the University of Oklahoma for the opportunity to contribute to this volume. Many thanks to Ambassador Edwin G. Corr for his numerous reviews and edits of this chapter, as well as his guidance and mentoring through the writing process. I am also indebted to Dr. Richard Roberts for his expertise regarding the Arab world and for reviewing my chapter. My discussions with him gave me many insights into the world of Arab politics and helped solidify my thoughts. I would also like to thank Dr. Russell Lucas at Florida International University for always pointing me in the right direction when I need guidance. Lastly I would like to thank Larisa Yun for her editing of this work.

Notes

1   Michael N. Barnett, *Dialogues in Arab Politics: Negotiations in Regional Order* (New York: Columbia University Press, 1998), p. 9. I would like to express my gratitude to Michael N. Barnett as I base much of this chapter on his analysis.

2   Barnett, *Dialogues in Arab Politics*, p. 73.

3   Ibid., p. 76

4   Ibid.

5   Ibid.

6   Ibid., p. 78

7   Ibid., pp. 78–79.

8   For an interesting look at differing perceptions of the "Arab Street" see David Pollack, *The Arab Street: Public Opinion in the Arab World?* (Washington, DC: Washington Institute for Near East Policy, 1992); and Marc Lynch, "Beyond the Arab Street: Iraq and the Arab Public Sphere," *Politics & Society*, Vol. 31, No. 1 (March 2003, pp. 55–91.

9   Barnett, *Dialogues in Arab Politics*, p. 81.

10   Ibid., p. 82

11   Lynch, "Beyond the Arab Street," p. 59.

12   Michael C. Hudson, "Arab Integration: An Overview" in Michael C. Hudson (ed.), *Middle East Dilemma: The Politics and Economics of Arab Integration* (New York: Columbia University Press, 1999), p. 11.

13   Barnett, *Dialogues in Arab Politics*, p. 90.

14   Ibid., p. 91.

15   Ibid., p. 92.

16   Ibid., p. 93.

17   Ibid., p. 94.

18   Avi Shlaim, "Israel and the Arab Coalition" in Eugene Rogan and Avi Shlaim (eds.), *The War for Palestine* (Cambridge: Cambridge University Press, 2001), p. 97.

19   Michael C. Hudson, *Arab Politics: The Search for Legitimacy* (New Haven: Yale University Press, 1977), p. 214. Interestingly, Hudson offers that those loyal to the Hashemite monarchs claim that they were in fact leaders in the Arab world because of their pragmatic approach to the situation. Rather than following some "empty and inflammatory ideological ranting," the Jordanian monarchs strived for realistic goals.

20   Albert Hourani, *A History of the Arab Peoples* (New York: Warner Books, 1991), p. 420.

21   Yoram Meital, *Egypt's Struggle for Peace: Continuity and Change, 1967–1977* (Gainesville: University Press of Florida, 1997), pp. 149–51.

22   Barnett, *Dialogues in Arab Politics*, p. 189.

23   Ibid., p. 190.

24   Jimmy Carter, *Palestine: Peace not Apartheid* (New York: Simon & Schuster, 2006), pp. 42–43.

25   Jimmy Carter, *The Blood of Abraham: Insights into the Middle East* (Boston: Houghton Mifflin, 1985), pp. 43–44.

26   Barnett, *Dialogues in Arab Politics*, p. 188.

27   Carter, *Palestine*, p. 45.

28   Hourani, *A History of the Arab Peoples*, p. 421.

29   Barnett, *Dialogues in Arab Politics*, p. 198.

30   Carter, *The Blood of Abraham*, p. 43.

31   Barnett, *Dialogues in Arab Politics*, p. 199.

32   Hourani, *A History of the Arab People*, p. 423. Also, it should be mentioned

that Egypt was re-admitted to the Arab League in 1989, and subsequently its headquarters returned to Cairo from Tunis.

33   Hudson, *Arab Politics,* p. 11.

34   Barnett, *Dialogues in Arab Politics,* p. 221. This is an interesting premise. Of course, pan-Arabism was a failure and was little more than rhetorical posturing to ensure domestic legitimacy. But beyond that, Arab governments have done little to actually forward the Palestinian cause, which is the issue *par excellence* of Arab unity. However, it seems safe to say that many Arabs are tired of the issue all together. Palestinians are truly a people with no home, and their own "Arab brothers" often do not welcome them. This is especially true after Arafat's support of the Iraqi invasion of Kuwait. Following several discussions with Jordanians of Palestinian descent, it became evident that many Palestinians in Jordan find themselves being treated as second-class citizens. Many Jordanians feel as if they have been overburdened by the Palestinian refugee crisis.

35   Paul Noble, "The Prospects for Arab Cooperation in a Changing Regional and Global System" in Michael C. Hudson (ed.), *Middle East Dilemma: The Politics and Economics of Arab Integration* (New York: Columbia University Press, 1999), p. 64.

36   Dennis Ross, *The Missing Peace: The Inside Story of the Fight for Middle East Peace* (New York: Farrar, Straus and Giroux, 2004), p. 80.

37   Barnett, *Dialogues in Arab Politics,* p. 223.

38   Bassam Tibi, "From Pan-Arabism to the Community of Sovereign Arab States: Redefining the Arab and Arabism in the Aftermath of the Second Gulf War" in Michael C. Hudson (ed.), *Middle East Dilemma: The Politics and Economics of Arab Integration* (New York: Columbia University Press, 1999), pp. 99–100.

39   Tibi, ibid., p. 104.

40   Michael Scott Doran, "Palestine, Iraq, and American Strategy," *Foreign Affairs* (January/February 2003).

CHAPTER 22

The Quartet and US Government Roles in Israeli–Palestinian–Arab Negotiations

EDWIN G. CORR

The "Quartet on the Middle East," sometimes called the "International Quartet," the "Diplomatic Quartet" or simply the "Quartet" is a group of nations and international organizations that came together to deal collectively with the Middle East peace process, especially the Israeli–Palestinian conflict. The Quartet includes the United States (US), Russia, the European Union (EU), and the United Nations (UN). The Quartet was formally established in the fall of 2001 after the Camp David Two, Sharm el-Sheikh and Taba Talks at the end of 2000 and the outbreak of the second *Intifada* in 2001. The purpose of the Quartet is to eliminate or diminish differing and conflicting positions among Quartet members that have plagued past peace efforts. The Quartet also aims at reducing high levels of suspicion and distrust in relations between the EU and Israel, between the UN and Israel, and between the Arabs, EU and Russia on one side and Israel and the US on the other.

The Quartet began by agreeing to provide monitors for efforts to end acts of terrorism and to enforce and verify security agreements proposed by former Senator George Mitchell, retired US Marine Corps General Anthony Zinni and former CIA Director George Tenet in 2001, but these efforts were not successful. Of the Quartet's actions, the most important has been the endorsement of the Middle East "Road Map" that President George W. Bush proposed on June 24, 2002. The Road Map stipulated its implementation in a three-year period, but the three years passed without its implementation.

However, the Quartet has not abandoned the goals of the Road Map. Its representatives meet regularly to coordinate and discuss ways to bring genuine peace and security to the Middle East. The Quartet's efforts are based on the formula of the 1991 Madrid Conference of "land for peace," as set forth in United Nation Security Council resolutions (UNSCRs) 242, 338 and 1397, and now also by the initiative of Saudi Prince Abdallah that Arab nations enter into normal state-to-state relations with Israel in the context of a two-state settlement. The Saudi initiative was approved by the twenty-two nations of the Arab League on March 28, 2002.

The Quartet consults and meets with leaders of states in the region for collaboration on the peace process, especially with Saudi Arabia, Egypt and Jordan. Both Spanish Foreign Minister Miguel Angel Moratinos and Secretary of State Condoleezza Rice have stated in speeches that these three countries might be incorporated into the Quartet.[1]

The members of the Quartet all have played historically important roles in the establishment of Israel and in conflicts as well as the search for peace in the Middle East since Israel's creation. England and France were trustee nations in the region after World War I and the collapse of the Ottoman Empire. Russia historically has attempted to project influence into the Middle East. England's Balfour Resolution led to Israel's founding. The British, French, United Soviet Socialist Republics (USSR) and the United States were all involved in the 1956 Suez Crises. The USSR challenged the United States and European countries for influence in the Middle East throughout the Cold War. At the end of the Cold War, the US and the USSR convened the 1991 Madrid Conference. The following 1993 Oslo Accords by its very name show a European role. After Oslo, there was somewhat of an informal division of work in the Middle East peace process, with the United States in a closer and economic assistance relationship with Israel, Egypt and Jordan while Europeans exercised influence and directed economic aid programs more toward Palestine and selected Arab countries.

The roles of all Quartet members are vital, but many regard the United States' role as being the most critical among the outside mediators because of the United State's very special relationships with Israel. Most of this chapter concentrates on the United States mediation role in the Middle East peace efforts. The focus is on the United States with respect not only to "what went wrong" but also with "what went right." Negotiations have had low and high points since Israel's creation. Some of the most productive negotiating periods have followed times of calamity, violence and war. The years since the beginning of 2001 have been discouraging ones. Hopefully, the situation has reached its "low," and sobered political leaders in the region, and the major powers will return to negotiations in search of a comprehensive peace based on "land for peace" and the "two-state solution."

The Period from 1947 to 1967

The US Government role in the peace process, aside from a key role in the establishment of Israel as an independent state and immediate US diplomatic recognition of Israel by President Harry S. Truman in 1948, was not exceptional from 1949 to 1969 in comparison with US Government attention to other regions. President Truman decided to recognize the State of Israel over the objections of General George C. Marshall, the Secretary of State, whom Truman regarded as the greatest individual of his era. Marshall and the Department of State opposed the creation of a home for the Jews in the Middle East because of concerns related to the incipient Cold War rivalry with the United Socialist Soviet Republic (USSR) that was challenging the West in the Middle East, access to the oil of the Middle East, and recognition that US support for Israel could cause problems in future relations with Arab states.[2]

The Department of State view, based on the commonly held Arab resentment and resistance to Western powers establishing the State of Israel in Palestine, is illustrated in a magazine article by King Abdullah I of Jordan who wrote in 1947:

> Our case is quite simple. For nearly 2,000 years, Palestine has been almost 100 per cent Arab . . . persecution of the Jews was not done by the Arabs; it was done by a Christian nation in the West . . . to ease their consciences, these Christian countries . . . are asking Palestine to accept the entire burden . . . this same America . . . refuses to accept more than a token handful of . . . Jews . . . surely the rest of the wide world . . . [is] generous enough to find [another] place . . . the Zionist settlements in Palestine would have been almost impossible . . . without American money . . . The present catastrophe can be laid almost entirely at your [the United States'] door . . .[3]

Notwithstanding controversy within the Truman administration over establishing the State of Israel within Palestine and little more than normal attention and some modest assistance to Israel during its first twenty years, the US government's and a majority of the American public's support for of the State of Israel has been strong and unwavering. The United States appears to have become slowly but similarly committed to the creation of an independent and viable state of Palestine.[4]

Following the creation of Israel and the Israeli War of Independence against neighboring Arab states that refused to accept its existence, the great American diplomat and UN official Ralph Bunche in 1949 set a pattern for negotiations between Arabs and Israelis. Bunche installed Arab and Israeli representatives in nearby rooms in the same hotel on the Island of Rhodes and, because the Arabs would not meet directly with the Israelis, shuttled between the rooms to extract an armistice agreement from the two sides. This became known within the Department of State as "proximity talks" and evolved into "shuttle diplomacy," as US mediators for years traveled between Israel and neighboring Arab capitals to broker solutions to specific negotiations.

The United States direct role in mediating between Arabs and Israelis was limited until 1969. Three decades passed from the time of Ralph Bunche to when Egyptian President Anwar Sadat and Israeli Prime Minister Menachem Begin joined President Jimmy Carter on the White House lawn in 1979 to sign the first Arab–Israeli Peace agreement. It was another fifteen years before Jordanian King Hussein bin Talal and Israeli Prime Minister Yitzhak Rabin met with President Bill Clinton in Jordan to sign the 1994 Jordan–Israel Peace Accord.[5] The major event involving United States intervention in Arab–Israeli affairs during Israel's first three decades was the Suez Crisis of 1956. The United States and the USSR forced Israel, France and Great Britain to withdraw their forces from Egypt following Egyptian President Gamal Nasser's nationalization of the Suez Canal and those countries' invasion of Egypt.

Between 1946 and 1971, US aid to Israel was about $60 million a year while US aid to the Arab states combined was about three times that amount. US military aid to Israel was minimal. The Department of State took the position that Israel was strong enough to defend itself and was able to obtain needed arms from other suppliers. The US wanted to prevent a United States–USSR arms race in the Middle East in which the United State would be supporting Israel and the Soviets the Arab states.

The US "hands-off" approach began to change in 1962 when President John F. Kennedy's Department of State approved the sale of HAWK anti-aircraft missiles to Israel to off-set the USSR provision to Egypt of long-range bombers. Another major shift occurred in 1968 when President Lyndon Baines Johnson sold Phantom jets to Israel, after which the United States became Israel's principal arms supplier. The US government's goal was to assure Israeli parity if not the superiority of military forces to that of surrounding Arab neighbors in order to assure the security and survival of the State of Israel.[6]

United States Goals and Ideals for the Middle East

President Jimmy Carter set forth US goals for the Middle East in *The Blood of Abraham: Insights Into the Middle East*, enumerating the following:

- Israel and its Arab neighbors to be secure and living in peace.
- Each nation to be autonomous, free of external intervention.
- The Palestinians of the West Bank and Gaza to be given their legitimate rights, including self-determination.

- Israel to withdraw from occupied territories.
- A fully sovereign and independent Lebanon, with all foreign forces withdrawn.
- Economic prosperity and a good life for people of the region.[7]

The list omits three goals Carter that have been overtaken by history and it does not explicitly include the goal of the "two-state solution" that evolved out of the 1991 Madrid Conference and the 1993 Oslo Accords.

President Carter also described American principles and ideals that have guided US negotiators and are recognized as essential to an acceptable Middle East peace:

- The security of Israel must be preserved.
- Differences between adversaries should be resolved by peaceful means, certainly without direct . . . [superpower] military involvement.
- Accommodation must be sought through negotiation with all parties to the dispute, with each having fair representation and the right to participate in free discussions.
- The sovereignty of nations and sanctity of international borders should be honored in order to avoid continuing bloodshed.
- There is no place for terrorism, which tends to subvert peace initiatives and to perpetrate hatred and combat.
- Human rights must be protected, including those generally recognized in the US Constitution and under international law. These would include the right of self-determination, free speech, equal treatment of all persons, freedom from prolonged military domination and imprisonment without trial, the right of families to be reunited, and the right of non-belligerent people to live in peace.[8]

These goals and ideals remain valid, although there was an important shift in semantics. The Carter Administration's language focused on human rights, whereas the Reagan Administration and the current Bush Administration lexicon was and is on democratization and freedom. In practice these ideals are similar. The Carter Administration saw human rights best established through democratic governments, and the Reagan and Bush Administrations regard respect for human rights as an integral part of modern democracy.

The US Government's Role from 1968–2001

Notable involvement of the United States in efforts to achieve peace in the Middle East began when UN envoys were unable to achieve implementation of UN Security Council Resolution 242 after the Six Day War of 1967.

Resolution 242 was adopted in November 1967 with strong US Government backing and has been the basis for peace negotiations from that time to the present. It calls for Israel's withdrawal from occupied territories, the right of all states in the region to live in peace within secure and recognized borders, and a just solution to the refugee problem. Resolution 242 was confirmed by UN Security Council Resolution 338, adopted in October 1973, after Egypt and Syria again attacked Israel (in the Sinai and the Golan Heights) and was again defeated by Israel. Resolution 338 called for a Peace Conference of all parties to the dispute.[9]

The history of negotiation among Israel, Palestinians and neighboring Arab states since 1969 has centered on US-led efforts of great powers and the UN to achieve Israel's withdrawal from territories conquered and occupied in the 1967 and 1973 wars in exchange for Arab states accepting a genuine peace, recognition of Israel's right to exist and be secure, and movement toward normal political and economic relations. There have been failures in the US-led efforts, such as:

- Talks between Israel and Egypt between 1979 and 1981 aimed at autonomy for the West Bank and Gaza in accord with Camp David One.
- United States efforts to broker a peace between Israel and Lebanon after the 1982–1983 Lebanese War, because they were rejected and scuttled by Syria.
- Two major US efforts to mediate a peace between Israel and Syria in 1996 and 2000.
- The Herculean efforts of President Bill Clinton and his team at Camp David Two, Sharm Al-Sheik, and Taba, when negotiators ran out of time with the end of President Clinton's term and the fall of Prime Minister Ehud Barak's government.

There have also been significant successes:

- Secretary of State Henry Kissinger's shuttle diplomacy from 1973 to 1975 under Presidents Nixon and Ford that produced the partial withdrawal agreement of Israel from Egypt and Syria after the 1973 war.
- President Carter and Secretary of State Cyrus Vance brokered Camp David Accords and the Israel–Egypt Peace Treaty during 1978–1979.
- Secretary of State Baker's convening of the groundbreaking Madrid Conference of 1991, leading to the first face-to-face negotiations among Israel, Jordan, Syria and Palestine.
- President Clinton's support of the Oslo Accords of 1993 brokered by the Norwegians by which the Government of Israel and the Palestine Liberation Organization recognized each other as negotiating partners.

- The Jordan–Israel Peace Treaty of 1994, signed in Jordan in the presence of President Clinton, between Israeli Prime Minister Yitzhak Rabin and Jordanian King Hussein bin Talal.[10]

President George W. Bush and Negotiation of an Arab–Palestine-Israel Peace Agreement

George W. Bush campaigned for the US presidency in 2000 to focus more on accomplishing the neo-conservative domestic agenda, and for the United States to decrease and disengage from what he and many of his supporters described as an excessively active and overly engaged foreign policy. He promised to lower the US profile and diplomatic efforts in the Middle East and with North Korea, to refrain from "Quixotic nation building," and to give higher priority to the Western Hemisphere. The new Administration was initially true to its declared intentions, and did, in fact, shelve most diplomatic efforts.

The cooling-off period in foreign relations changed on September 11, 2001 with the Al Qaeda attack on New York City and Washington, D.C. The Administration became absorbed by the US invasion of Afghanistan, war-fighting, and nation-building there; and by alarm about Iraq's Saddam Hussein and supposed weapons of mass destruction. The Bush Administration's attention became monopolized by what President Bush called the "Axis of Evil" (Iraq, Iran and North Korea) and by Afghanistan, all of which were lumped into a "war on terrorism," allegedly aimed at Osama bin Laden and Al Qaeda. Some senior Bush officials began to suggest that the best road to peace in the Middle East and the Islamic world might run through Iraq rather than Israel.

The Clinton presidency draft of a peace agreement for the Middle East that seemed so close to achievement at the end of his term was shelved by President Bush when he took office. After a flurry of unsuccessful US missions to Israel and Palestine in 2001, there was little time to focus on the Israeli–Palestine problem. At the same time, there also is a perception among some critics that his Administration moved so close to Israel that it jeopardized the US role as a "just broker" in Israeli–Palestinian negotiations. Some jokingly said that President Bush had "joined the Likud Party" of Israel. Bush was elected with the backing of the evangelical Christian right, a number of whom support the Likud vision of "Ersatz Israel" (from the Tigris–Euphrates Rivers to Egypt) and have backed Israeli settlements and opposed the "two-state solution." President Bush is allegedly influenced by his roots personally and politically in the evangelical Christian community, which is a key component of the conservative Republican Party base. Moreover, the Israelis were adept in reinforcing the view among many in the US government that Arafat and the PLO, Hamas,

Israeli Jihad and Hezbollah are indistinct from Al-Qaeda terrorists.

There was little progress on Israeli–Palestinian negotiations during the first Bush term, notwithstanding the high-level missions and their recommendations in 2001. The Israeli–Palestinian situation only became more violent and desperate.

Lessons Learned and the Missing Pieces to the Missing Peace

What follows might better be called "lessons indicated" rather than "lessons learned," since the US government currently seems to heed little the advice of earlier participants and students of the Middle East peace process. The experienced US negotiators cited in this section are all committed to the existence of Israel as a Jewish state and to the two-state solution for Palestinians and Israelis.

William B. Quandt, a former US diplomat and Middle East specialist, has written *Peace Process: American Diplomacy and the Arab–Israeli Conflict Since 1967*, which many consider to be the best book on this subject. Quandt suggests certain conditions must be met to produce desirable results. These are:

- "There must be a realistic appraisal of the regional situation . . .
- "The president and his top advisors must be involved and must work in harmony . . .
- "The domestic basis of support for American policy in the region must be constantly developed . . .
- "[S]uccess as a mediator requires a feeling both for the process – the procedures for bringing the parties to negotiations – and for substance . . .
- "There must be a substantial investment in quiet diplomacy in "pre-negotiation" exploration of the terrain, before deals can be cut . . .
- "Pressure sometimes succeeds, but it must be skillfully exerted . . .
- "Timing is crucial for successful negotiations . . . "[11]

Former Secretary of State James A. Baker III said we must remember five historical truisms about this dispute.

> First, there is a catch-22 regarding the issue and it is this: Israel will never enjoy security as long as she occupies the Territories and the Palestinians will never achieve their dream of living in peace in their own state alongside as long as Israel lacks security. It is a tragic version of the old chicken and egg question . . . Second, there is no military solution because neither side will win the conflict by dominating the other . . . Third, a political process and dialogue are essential in the Arab–Israeli dispute. Whenever the political

process breaks down, there will be violence on the ground . . . Fourth, hard-
liners on both sides have been the biggest impediment to the solution,
including Arabs who won't accept Israel's right to exist and Israelis who want
to keep the land . . . And, fifth, only the United States can serve as an effective mediator because of the country's special relationship with Israel.[12]

Aaron David Miller, a US Department of State official for twenty-five
years who worked under six Secretaries of State on Arab–Israeli negotiations, wrote in an article on May 23, 2005:

> For far too long, many American officials involved in Arab–Israeli peace-
> making, myself included, have acted as Israel's attorney, catering and
> coordinating with the Israelis at the expense of successful peace negotiations.
> If the United States wants to be an honest and effective broker on the
> Arab–Israeli issue, then surely it can have only one client: the pursuit of a
> solution that meets the needs and requirements of both sides . . .
> Paradoxically, it is our intimacy with the Israelis that gives America – only
> America – the capacity to be an honest and effective broker.[13]

Miller says that Secretary of State Henry Kissinger, in brokering the
disengagement agreements of the 1970s, Secretary of State James Baker in
fathering the Madrid Conference in 1991, and President Jimmy Carter in
mediating the 1978 Camp David Accords in 1978 and the 1979
Egyptian–Israeli peace treaty, were successful because of a two-client
approach – an attorney for both the Israelis and the Arabs.[14] Miller offers
six "observations that guide him in negotiations on the Middle East:

> First, the Arab–Israeli conflict is not some kind of morality play . . . pitting
> the forces of good on one side against forces of darkness on the other . . .
> we have: a terribly complicated struggle laden with demography, psychol-
> ogy, politics, history and trauma in which each side brings to it legitimate
> needs and requirements that must be resolved . . . Second is end game . . .
> The only rational solution . . . is separation through a process of negotia-
> tion with reciprocity that leads to the creation of two states, Israel and
> Palestine, living in peace and security . . . [Third] . . . Israeli and Palestinian
> lives are inextricably linked. There are only two alternatives: continued and
> protracted violence and confrontation, or alternatively a pathway enlight-
> ened . . . by dialogue in which the parties [Israel and Palestine] take the
> major lead, but the United States takes a major role . . . The United States
> is the only power that has the power to correct that asymmetry . . . [Fourth]
> . . . Wanted, a high level negotiator empowered by the President of the
> United States, with the President's personal authority . . . [Fifth] . . .
> Wanted a serious effort . . . a monitoring force to work with Israelis and
> Palestinians to overcome their suspicions, and to ensure that agreements
> signed are agreements carried out . . . [Sixth] . . . Conventional . . . [or] . . .
> transactional diplomacy must be married to . . . transformational diplo-
> macy, the capacity to change attitudes between people . . . break down the
> walls of suspicion and mistrust . . . [15]

Dennis Ross, the US Government's Middle East negotiator for a decade under three US presidents, identifies in his 800-page book on the peace process some of the missing pieces to the missing peace as:

> The lack of public conditioning for peace, the reluctance to acknowledge the legitimacy of the other side's grievances and needs, the inability to confront comfortable myths, the difficulty of transforming behavior and acknowledging mistakes, the inherent challenge of getting both sides ready to move at the same time, the unwillingness to make choices, and the absence of leadership, especially among Palestinians . . . [16]

Lessons Learned from Other US Mediations

This section will draw lessons from other seemingly intransigent conflicts in which the US government has been instrumental in moving the contending parties toward peace, especially Northern Ireland and El Salvador. Former US Senator George Mitchell played a constructive role in helping Catholics and Protestants of Northern Ireland move toward a peace settlement, and also led a mission to Israel in an to attempt to broker a cease-fire between the Israelis and the Palestinians.

Senator Mitchell set forth four principles for dealing with protracted conflicts:

1   There is no such thing as a conflict that cannot be solved – conflict is created by human beings and can be ended by human beings if the major players are determined to do so.
2   It is important *not* to yield to men of violence who on both sides are determined to wreck the peace process.
3   There must be a willingness among negotiators to genuinely listen to other points of view and to enter into principled compromise – to take risks for peace.
4   Attention must be given to employment and well-being of the people involved.[17]

I will expand on Senator Mitchell's four principles and will draw on my own experiences in dealing with mid-level states conflicts and insurgencies, and especially the peace process in El Salvador from the 1970s into the 1990s. While it is true that all conflicts can be resolved, the time and effort required are related to the length of the conflict, to its intensity, and to the degree of death and destruction. The greater these are, as a general rule, the harder it is to reach resolution. However, it is also true that the intensity and ugliness of a conflict sometimes become so costly that the contenders become convinced of the necessity of reaching an accord in order to halt the death and destruction. Thus, progress is sometimes easier after particularly horrible periods. The possibility for increased success in negotiations may therefore be greater after years of the bloody second *Intifada* and the escalation of armed hostilities between Israel and Hamas and Hezbollah, but the role of the US government as a neutral yet active mediator remains essential to a successful outcome.

Mediators are highly desirable, if not essential, to facilitate negotiations in difficult, long-standing disputes. The mediator must be an entity acceptable to all the contending parties, and to be so, there must be faith in the mediator's fairness and neutrality. For the El Salvador civil war, the Roman Catholic Church was initially welcomed, but belief by the insurgents that the Church was becoming more sympathetic to the Government's position caused a change to the United Nations, which successfully facilitated a peace accord. The overt and behind the scenes roles of the US government throughout the entire peace process were vital to success, even though the US government was not seen as an unbiased mediator. In a number of disputes in recent decades a group of states have served successfully as mediators with titles such as "the Friends of Colombia." The Quartet of the United States, European Union, Russia and the United Nations is playing, or might play, such a role in the Israeli–Palestinian conflict.

The role of mediator has limits. Outside parties rarely, if ever, can impose a lasting solution, unless the solution has some minimal level of acceptance among the contending parties. As a rule, it is easier for an outside great power to prevent things from happening than to cause things to happen. However, an outside power, or mediator, can sometimes tip the balance among the contenders by using its resources and influence to back a specific indigenous or national group that seeks a position or outcome on a matter that is similar to what the outside power or mediator wants. There are limits on what a great a power can do.

There is a rule of thumb that the degree of involvement of the United States as an outside great power in a negotiating situation is determined by the degree of useful dialogue and negotiation occurring among the contending parties. Normally, the less talk and negotiation between them, the more the United States needs to be involved. The greater and more productive the dialogue and negotiations, the less involved the United States need be.

Getting contenders to agree upon an outcome is more difficult when there are strongly competing nationalist sentiments, and when the parties have a strong sense of grievances that they feel should be acknowledged and rectified. As Senator Mitchell and David Aaron Miller argue, helping the contending parties to empathize with the positions of others in the dispute, helps to reach a solution. This is greatly facilitated when the contending parties and the mediators speak each other's languages and understand their protagonists' cultures.

Public diplomacy and non-governmental organizations (NGOs) can be effective in helping to break down barriers, build trust, help the protagonists to see each other as human beings, and in suggesting solutions. However, well meaning NGOs can also damage peace efforts. In the El Salvador negotiation, a well intended mediation effort by a prominent university once derailed promising talks, and it is generally accepted that some NGOs have exacerbated violence in a few instances. Nevertheless, the NGO role in changing attitudes and perceptions in the Middle East situation is essential.

It is also a given that parties to a dispute cannot choose their protagonists' negotiators, nor can outside powers do so. Public statements intended to de-legitimize Arafat by the Governments of Israel and the United States actually strengthened his support among Palestinians and Arabs. In negotiations one needs an interlocutor who can deliver what he negotiates. Roberto D'Aubuisson, the ring leader of "death squads" in El Salvador, was considered malevolent and corrupt by many but in the end his influence with the far right of El Salvador was essential to getting that sector to accept a peace accord.

Outside powers should be careful not to demand actions by one of the parties to a dispute when such actions exceed the party's capacity for their implementation. For instance, demanding that the Palestinian Authority disarm Hamas or Islamic Jihad was beyond the Authority's capacity. This was even more the case after 2000 when the Israelis had greatly damaged many Palestinian police stations and government institutions. Many in the United States demanded that the democratically elected government of President José Napoleon Duarte immediately bring an end to all human rights violations by the Armed Forces or that the US Government cease aid to the country. This was beyond the Salvadoran Government's power, and human rights improvement had to be accomplished incrementally and steadily without losing the war to the insurgents.

Senator Mitchell says that leaders cannot permit extremists to derail peace talks through violence. This may be the most difficult of the challenges confronting peace seekers. Through violence the extremists are able to maintain the cycle in which each contender believes its violent acts to be in response to violent attacks of the foe. In these cases, the cycle must be broken by persuading the contestants not to respond. Outside powers can demand more from the contender whom they support politically and financially, and more can be demanded from a strong legitimately recognized government than from weak government or a non-governmental group.

Much emphasis has been given to influencing and facilitating negotiations among the national contenders, i.e. Israel and Palestine in this case. However, the need for a "roadmap" to peace among the sub-groups within the national contending, negotiating parties may be as important as between them. Both the Israelis and Palestinians need a roadmap for reconciling their internal diversions and disputes, and external powers can also help in this area.

"Truth commissions" and their role in helping prepare the ground for peace negotiations and agreement implementation have become prominent in peace processes. Pundits have urged Israelis and Palestinians to replicate the South Africa truth commission experience. Such advocates should look beyond South Africa to the several truth commission experiences of Latin America, which preceded the South African experience and where lessons can be learned. An important lesson is that there must be a compromise between reaching a peace agreement and the pursuit of absolute justice for all the crimes and violent acts committed. At some point the contenders must determine to forgive but not forget. Agreement should be reached for continued prosecution on a few selected exceptionally repulsive past acts and the remainder should be amnestied. Only in this manner in most cases can a peace be achieved. The contenders must draw a line on the calendar and not seek justice in all cases but only a few, and, of course, for any future criminal acts of violence committed after the peace agreement.

Prospects

More than a decade has passed since the achievement of a major treaty in the Middle East peace process, but as a result of the Oslo Process, the ingredients for a treaty for a final comprehensive agreement seem to be in place. This is because of advances in negotiations during the Clinton years and because of certain important developments under President George W. Bush. What is needed is responsible, accountable leadership on both the Palestinian and Israeli sides in serious and sincere negotiations, with the backing of the Quartet and Arab League, to work out the few remaining tough compromises. The period since 2001 has significant developments, some of which have already been mentioned, in terms of moving toward a peace agreement, including:

- The general acceptance of the "two-state solution," including explicit and public endorsement of it by President George W. Bush, first in November, 2001 and reiterated in such meetings as a summit in Aqaba, Jordan with Prime Minister Sharon, King Abdullah and Prime Minister Mohammed Abbas on June 4, 2003.
- A growing consensus about the components of a final agreement as manifested in such documents as the draft agreement that emerged from the Taba meetings in 2000; and from privately negotiated agreements among private persons (ones who are knowledgeable and have been involved in official talks), such as the Yossi Beilin–Abu Mazen Accord

(1995), the Sari Nuseibeh–Ami Ayalon draft (2002), and the "Geneva Accord" (2003).

- Growing acceptance among Israelis that the demographic trends of higher population growth among Arabs in Israel and the Palestine Authority require a two-state solution lest Israel lose its character as both a Jewish and democratic society. (Maintaining a predominately Jewish democratic state was a major factor in Sharon's decision to withdraw from Gaza – the eventual alternatives being only genocide, mass deportation or apartheid to assure a continuing Jewish majority in Israel.)

- Saudi Arabian Crown Prince Abdullah's initiative that was endorsed by the twenty-two state Arab League on March 28, 2002 for Arab governments to recognize the State of Israel and enter into normal diplomatic and economic relations upon the achievement of a final agreement between Israel and Palestine based on the two-state solution and 1967 boundaries with mutually agreed upon adjustments.

- Cooperation among members of the Quartet (the European Union, Russia, the United Nations and the United States) and their development of a "Roadmap," published on December 20, 2002, to reach a final peace through the two-state solution, even though progress based upon it has stagnated and it is far behind schedule.

- The commitment of Israeli Prime Minister Sharon to end the Israeli occupation of Gaza and to remove Israeli settlements from Gaza and selected sites in the West Bank, and the removal of Israeli troops from Gaza (until the 2006 Israeli war with Hezbollah and Hamas).

- The death of Chairman Arafat and the democratic elections in the Palestine Authority of municipal authorities in December 2004 and of Prime Minister Mohammed Abbas (Abu Mazen) on January 9, 2005, which removed for a period (until the election of Hamas) the excuses of both Israeli Prime Minister Ariel Sharon and President George W. Bush that there was not a legitimate interlocutor in the Palestine Authority with whom to negotiate; and the stroke of Prime Minister Ariel Sharon, which opened space within the Israeli polity for voices favoring negotiations.

- The January 2006 democratic election of Hamas brings the potential of a Palestine government that has the power to control Palestinian terrorism if it can be persuaded by outside powers, including the Arab League it is in Palestinian interests to accept the State of Israel and disavow violence.

During the second George W. Bush campaign for re-election to the Presidency and during his second term, he stressed freedom and democracy as his major goal for the Middle East. However, the combination of disillusionment with the war in Iraq, the surge in oil prices, the

Israel–Hezbollah–Hamas war, United States contention with Iran and Syria, and a general decline worldwide of America's image has brought despair. There is, at the same time, a growing recognition among many Americans that although resolution of the Israel–Palestine situation would not completely cure the problems of the United States in its relations with Arabs and the Islamic world, it would be a very significant step toward restoring moderate Muslims' confidence in the world's pre-eminent super-power.

Americans more and more may be distinguishing to some degree the war in Iraq and especially the Israeli–Palestinian situation from the war on terrorism. Increasingly, Americans are concerned about the United States being able to act as an honest broker between Israel and the Arabs, and not be swayed away from the US's four-decades of commitment to UN Resolution 242 of land for peace for a solution in which Israel's boundaries chiefly follow those of 1967.

This chapter has focused on the vital role of outside mediators, but I want to caution that there are limits to what outsiders can achieve. Palestinian and Israeli leaders will have to make difficult decisions and compromises if there is to be an agreement and peace. Even if the US government, its partners of the Quartet, the Arab League and especially Egypt, Jordan and Saudi Arabia, were to be firm and generous in trying to bring about a resumption of formal negotiations and hold Israel and Palestine accountable for reaching a final agreement, the outside mediators cannot be successful unless both Israel and Palestine are willing to put their own political houses in order, make compromises, and reach prior agreements within their own polities.

Strong radical minorities in both nations wield disproportionate power that block creating effective majorities and obstruct peacemaking. Polls repeatedly show that majorities of Israel and Palestine want and would accept a peace agreement similar to the Clinton proposal and the privately negotiated Geneva Agreement. Unfortunately, the Israelis, in a culture that exalts military power and force over negotiations and compromises, at elections vote for leaders who project toughness and no compromise and who play on the public's security fears. Meanwhile, the Palestinian Authority remains divided between the economically corrupt Fatah and the radically religious Hamas that will not recognize categorically Israel's right to exist. The Palestine government remains institutionally and bureaucratically weak. Only the Israelis and Palestinians can ultimately resolve their internal problems, even with substantial outside assistance.[18]

If the Israelis and Palestinians can manage their own households, because of the huge disparity of power between these two negotiating parties, the United States (in concert with other external mediators) is the essential power at this time that could through firm, fair and balanced proposals and pressures help the two nations to make peace. For the United

States to do this, it too must deal with its own internal opposition to the two-state solution, i.e., the politically powerfully Christian Right and the "neo-conservatives" of the Republican right that have teamed with Israeli governments, the Likud and other right-wing religious parties against the two-state solution. For this to happen, the US president must come to the conclusion that solving the Palestinian–Israeli impasse is of urgent strategic interest to the United States in the war against terrorism, in restoring America's image abroad, and in enhancing internationally US leadership in world affairs.

As stated earlier, the Road Map is in place and ostensibly is still backed by the Quartet. President Bush cannot run for office again and must think about his place in history. Former Secretaries of State Warren Christopher and James Baker, former National Security Advisor Brent Scowcroft, and a host of other respected Americans with international experience have called for President Bush to give the Israeli–Palestinian conflict higher priority. The bi-partisan Iraq Study Group, chaired by James Baker and former Congressman Lee Hamilton, also urged action on Palestine–Israel negotiations.[19] The President and his Secretary of State, Condoleezza Rice, have both announced the US Government's intentions to do so.

It may be that the conditions for another major success in the peace process now exist!

Notes

1   Information on the Quartet was taken from "U.S., U.N., Russia, EU Discuss Road Map to Mideast Peace, December 20, 2002, <http://italy. usembassay.gov/viewer/article.asp?article=/file2002/aliaA2122003.htm>; Gerald M. Steinberg, "The Quartet, The Road Map, and The Future of Iraq: A Realistic Assessment" in "Jerusalem Letter/Viewpoints" No. 489, 10 Tevet 5763/ December 15, 2002 of the Jerusalem Center for Public Affairs, p. 2; "Rice Foresees Need to Expand Middle East Quartet," International Information Programs, Middle East and North Africa, US Department of State, June 21, 2005, p. 1; "International Quartet," <http://vitalperspective. typepad.com/ vital_perspective_clarity/international_quartet/i . . . >; "Quartet on the Middle East," <http://en.wikipedia.org/wiki/ Quartet_on_the_middle_east>.

2   David McCullough, *Truman* (New York: Simon & Schuster, 1992), pp. 600–1, 618–20, 990.

3   His Majesty King Abdullah, "As the Arabs see the Jews," *The American Magazine*, November, 1947

4   The question of what constitutes a viable state is, of course, debatable.

5   Samuel W. Lewis, "The Receding Horizon: The Endless Quest for Arab–Israeli Peace," *Foreign Affairs*, September/October 2004, Volume 83, No. 5, p. 140.

6   Mitchell Bard, "U.S.–Israel Relations: A Special Alliance," from the Jewish Virtual Library. A Division of the American-Israeli Cooperation Enterprise, 2004 <http://www.us-israeli.org/jsource/us-Israel/special.html>.

7   Jimmy Carter, *The Blood of Abraham: Insights Into The Middle East* (Boston: Houghton Mifflin Company, 1985), pp. 18–19.
8   Ibid., p. 203.
9   Ibid., p. xvi.; and Jimmy Carter, *Palestine: Peace not Apartheid* (New York: Simon & Schuster, 2006), pp. 38–39.
10 Lewis, "The Receding Horizon," p. 141.
11 William B. Quandt, *Peace Process: American Diplomacy and the Arab–Israeli Conflict since 1967*, Revised Edition (Washington, D.C.: Brookings Institution Press and Berkeley and Los Angeles: University of California Press, 2001), pp. 383–86.
12 James A. Baker III, "The Future of U.S. Involvement in the Middle East," Remarks of the former Secretary of State at the University of Maryland Anwar Sadat Lecture for Peace, April 14, 2005. (Sent to the University of Oklahoma Center for Peace Studies by Professor Shibley Telhammi of the University of Maryland, April 18, 2005.)
13 Aaron David Miller, "Israel's Lawyer," an article distributed to its membership by the Academy of Diplomacy, May 24, 2005.
14 Ibid.
15 Aaron David Miller, "Arab–Israeli Peace: Is It Still Possible?" Article 2, *Common Ground News Service* (CG News) – November 7, 2003. <http//www.sfcg.org/cgnews/middle-east.cfm>
16 Lewis, "The Receding Horizon," p. 143. This quote is from the Prologue of Dennis Ross, *The Missing Peace: The Inside Story of the Fight for the Middle East* (New York: Farar, Strauss and Giroux, 2004), p. 14.
17 George J. Mitchell, "Negotiating the Settlements to Internal Wars and Terrorism: The Lessons of Northern Ireland" in David L. Boren and Edward J. Perkins (eds.), *Democracy, Morality, and the Search for Peace in America's Foreign Policy* (Norman: University of Oklahoma Press, 2002), pp. 91–92; see also David L. Boren "Preface" to Joseph Ginat, Edward J. Perkins, and Edwin G. Corr (eds.), *The Middle East Peace Process: Vision Versus Reality* (Brighton: Sussex Academic Press and Norman: University of Oklahoma Press, 2002), p. xvi.
18 Phillip C. Wilcox, Jr., "The Holy Land: Can Peace Be Rescued?" *The Foreign Service Journal*, Dec. 2006, Volume 83, No. 12, pp. 21–26. The term "mini-Quartet" I saw first used by Gershon Baskin in "Negotiations, no peace," *The Jerusalem Post*, October 23, 2006.
19 James A. Baker III, "Talking Our Way to Peace," Op-ed contributor, *The New York Times*, Dec. 2, 2004: Warren Christopher, "Diplomacy That Can't Be Delegated," Op-ed contributor, *The New York Times*, Dec. 30, 2004; Brent Scowcroft, "Beyond Lebanon," Op-ed contributor, *The Washington Post*, July 30, 2006; Brent Scowcroft, "Getting the Middle East Back on Our Side," Op-ed contributor, *The New York Times*, January 4, 2007; and *The Iraq Study Group Report: The Way Forward – A New Approach*, James A. Baker, III, and Lee H. Hamilton, Co-Chairs (New York: Vintage Books, 2006), pp. xv, 54–58.

CHAPTER 23

Afterword

JOSEPH GINAT AND SHAUL M. GABBAY

This book summarizes two complementary conferences – the first entitled "What Went Wrong?" and the second "How to Rebuild Trust between Israelis and Palestinians." Understanding the breakdown in trust between Israel and the Palestinians and attempting to rebuild this trust is essential, not only for Israeli–Palestinian relations, but also for the future of the entire Middle East. Peace treaties of the past between Israel, Jordan and Egypt, and agreements between Israel and the Palestinians, have laid a foundation upon which progress towards peace can be built. But further progress towards a regional de-escalation of hostilities, resumption of peace negotiations, and progression of peace between Israel, Jordan, and Egypt are largely dependent on the State of Israeli–Palestinian relations. To overcome decades of socialization and indoctrination it is necessary that monetary incentives and benefits be combined with an all-encompassing regional and international effort to develop trust, and to establish a culture of cooperation in the Middle East. Bitter enemies must be shown that the benefits of co-existence and peace outweigh the perceived necessity of war.

Despite the fact that the conferences took place in 2004 and 2005, as mentioned in Ambassador Edwin Corr's introduction, the contents of the essays in this volume are just as relevant today as they were then, as there has been little progress in the peace process and the contents touch upon cardinal issues which are at the crux of the conflict. The year of 2006 brought additional turmoil and upheavals to the Middle East, including increasingly ruthless terrorism in Iraq and the execution of Saddam Hussein, the election of Hamas to the Palestinian Legislative Council, the outbreak of the Second Lebanon War in July, and Iran's increased pace in developing nuclear capabilities. All of these factors have had a significant impact on the Israeli–Palestinian conflict. To this list, we must add the unilateral disengagement of Israel from the Gaza Strip and the establishment of a number of settlements in the Northern West Bank.

There is no doubt that the year 2007 will be a crucial year with many significant developments in the Middle East. The CPS (Center for Peace Studies) at the University of Oklahoma, the SDC (Strategic Dialogue Center) at Netanya Academic College and ISIME (the Institute for the Study of Israel in the Middle East) – three Centers that work together in tandem, do not only discuss and analyze the developments in the region, but also propose practical solutions for facing the challenges and stabilizing conflict situations. With this in mind, in these concluding remarks we will try to propose practical solutions to the challenges facing the region.

The disengagement from Gaza, initiated by Prime Minister Ariel Sharon, was a highly significant step. However, there were two considerable mistakes in the process:

1   The disengagement should not have been carried out unilaterally, but should have been executed as part of a bilateral process with Palestinian President Mahmoud Abbas, and should have been packaged as a stage in the Road Map peace plan. Nevertheless, the inclusion of Egypt in the disengagement process was a positive development, as was their increased involvement in the post-disengagement period.
2   The second mistake, an internal Israeli matter, was the lack of practical housing, employment and absorption solutions presented to the families evacuated from their homes. Many former residents of the Gaza Strip to this day lack permanent housing.

Following the disengagement, the increase in terrorism originating from the Gaza Strip, specifically in the form of Qassam missiles launched on Israeli civilian targets, and the kidnapping of the Israeli soldier Gilad Shalit, are difficult to explain. Israel left every last inch of the Gaza Strip, evacuated all of the settlements therein, and left the greenhouses intact for Palestinian agricultural use. Israel even left the Philadelphi route at Rafah, which has led to the unimpeded digging of tunnels through which terror organizations smuggle large quantities of explosive materials every month. Despite Israel's full withdrawal from the Gaza Strip, Qassam missiles have constantly targeted Israeli civilians living in towns near Gaza, resulting in Israeli retaliations deep into the Gaza Strip. Recently, a number of Palestinian organizations, led by Hamas, have declared a *tahadiya* (calming), which led to Israel withdrawing its troops from Gaza. However, the Islamic Jihad and other small offshoot organizations have not taken part in the *tahadiya* and continue to launch Qassam missiles daily at Israeli civilian targets. As of December 31, 2006, Israel has refrained from retaliating to these attacks. The current question at hand is how to get out of this quagmire.

The most practical solution for creating the conditions for peace, which was described in Chapter 2, is to reach a comprehensive *hudna* in the Gaza Strip and West Bank. We must move from the stage of *tahadiya*, which according to Islamic law is non-binding, to the stage of *hudna*, which, throughout Islamic history, has never been breached, whether the agreement was signed between Muslims and Muslims or between Muslims and non-Muslims. The signing of a *hudna* does not require as a pre-condition a change in the status quo regarding territorial control or other cardinal issues of disagreements between the parties such as Jerusalem, the Settlements and Refugees. However, during the duration of the *hudna*, negotiations can be conducted on outstanding territorial issues, and territorial changes can be made. During a more peaceful context more fruitful ties could be established which are conducive to the buildup of trust thereby building social capital for the long run.

There are a number of stages in the establishment of a comprehensive *hudna* among all Palestinian organizations and Israel. The first stage would be the signing of a *hudna* among all of the Palestinian organizations in the West Bank and Gaza Strip. The second stage would be the signing of a *hudna* between President Mahmoud Abbas and the various organizations, and the third stage would be the signing of a *hudna* between President Abbas and Israel.

These stages in negotiating the establishing a long-term *hudna* should begin immediately upon the establishment of quiet on the ground. The Egyptian government, which has been very active in the peace process since 2000, and King Abdullah of Jordan, could lend great assistance in constructing the *hudna* agreement. Once the *hudna* is established and Israel and the Palestinians begin negotiating outstanding issues, we would propose that the sides discuss several concepts included in the Saudi proposal, which was adopted by the Arab League and has several articles that can be of assistance during the initial stages of negotiations.

The recent war between Israel and Hezbollah has been named the Second Israel–Lebanon War. We believe that this war should instead be referred to as the first Israel–Iran War. The following analogy accurately illustrates this point – during the war Iran functioned as the water source or "well", Syria functioned as the pipeline, and Hezbollah as the sprinkler. Iran supplied weapons and ammunition to Hezbollah and delivered these arms to Hezbollah via Syria for Hezbollah's use. In addition, Iranian engineers had previously planned and constructed Hezbollah's elaborate bunker system in Southern Lebanon.

Iranian President Ahmadinejad represents the dangerous combination of continually declaring that Israel should be wiped off the map, repeatedly denying the Holocaust, and developing nuclear capabilities. The UN Security Council's decision to apply sanctions to Iran is scoffed at by President Ahmadinejad, as he stated that the day that the United Nations applied sanctions to Iran would be declared an Iranian national holiday.

We do not believe that the free nations of the world have the luxury of permitting Iran to develop a nuclear bomb. Iran has already reached the stage of enriching uranium; the free world must not allow the next step in Iran's nuclear plans to become a reality.

Syria aligned itself with Iran, and lends significant support to Hezbollah's activities. Soon after the Lebanon War ended, Syria resumed its role as the pipeline by which Iranian weapons are being transferred to Hezbollah. Sheikh Nasrallah declared that Hezbollah has re-established its arsenal to levels prior to the outbreak of the war, despite the fact that Israel destroyed much of Hezbollah's missile capabilities during the war.

Syria has declared both directly and indirectly, via senators and third-country visitors to Syria, that it desires to end the conflict with Israel, and has emphasized its desire to reassert its sovereignty over the Golan Heights, the area conquered by Israel in 1967. The Syrians have indicated that if Israel rejects the possibility of negotiations, or if negotiations take place but do not return the Golan Heights to Syrian hands, they will initiate a war with Israel for the purpose of returning the Golan Heights by force. President Assad has indicated such intentions in meetings with United States senators.

In addition, the media reported in 2007 that a close associate of Prime Minister Ehud Olmert, businessman and philanthropist Dan Abraham, met in Washington with Syria's Ambassador to the United States, Ambassador Imad Moustapha. Though it cannot be proven, it is reasonable to assume that, given the close relations between Mr. Abraham and Prime Minister Olmert, Israel's Prime Minister knew of the meeting with the Syrian Ambassador. If this is in fact the case, this meeting can be considered equally as important as the meetings of United States Senators with President Assad. Of equal interest were press reports of a series of secret talks between Israeli and Syrian "non-official" parties in Europe during 2004–6.

We do not believe that it is in Israel's interest to call into question President Bashar Assad's intentions, or to claim that the Syrian President is trying to trick the Western world, before attempting official negotiations. Israel must put President Assad's declarations to the test by engaging in negotiations and checking where they will lead. It is also important that neither side set pre-conditions for negotiations. In addition, it is important that members of the Syrian negotiating team shake hands with their Israeli counterparts when they meet (during negotiations in the 1990s, Hafez El-Assad's directed his negotiating team to refrain from shaking hands with their Israeli counterparts, which had a negative effect on negotiations).

Once official negotiations between the sides are established, it is essential that during the early stages of negotiations President Assad close the headquarters of the Islamic Jihad and Hamas in Damascus, and block the transfer of weapons and ammunitions into Lebanon (the border should be left open for economic trade, but weapon smuggling must be blocked). This must be carried out at an early stage of negotiations, as it would be impossible for the leaders of Israel and Syria to negotiate a peace agreement while nests of terror flourish in Syria's capital city.

Negotiations between Israel and Syria would be obviously scorned by Hezbollah and Iran, as a peaceful settlement between Israel and Syria would create a buffer between Hezbollah and Iran and break the middle link in the Iran–Syria–Hezbollah chain. The creation of such a buffer, severing Syrian cooperation with these extremist elements, is in itself an important reason for Israel to engage in negotiations with Syria.

In Israel, there exist a variety of opinions regarding holding negotiations with Syria. Foreign Minister Tzipi Livni and Defense Minister Amir Peretz both openly support negotiations. However, Israel's Prime Minister Ehud Olmert claims that Syria has yet to prove that it is truly interested in achieving peace. Such a declaration, to our minds, is the result of American pressure. The Prime Minister's hesitancy to engage the Syrians is the result of American opposition to such a scenario, which would enable Syria to return to the "family of nations".

President Bush's anger toward the Syrians is understandable, as the Syrians lied to him during the early stages of the war in Iraq, when they assured the Americans that they had closed their border with Iraq to prevent insurgency. Syria not only allowed insurgency, but assisted insurgents' infiltration into Iraq. While this provokes a desire to retaliate, world leaders should not make decisions based on a desire to punish other leaders for their past behaviors, but on what is best in terms of their own national interests in both the short- and long-term.

The friction that negotiations between Israel and Syria would cause between Syria and Iran and Syria and Hezbollah would be highly beneficial to the United States. In fact, removing Syria from the "Axis of Evil" and welcoming it into the "family of nations" would benefit the United States twofold – not only would the Syrian threat be neutralized but Iran's influence in the region, particularly over Syria and Lebanon, would be weakened.

In addition, the preservation of Lebanon as a unified country under the leadership of the current government is of great importance to the United States. Sheikh Nasrallah has declared his intention to overturn the current Lebanese government and has in 2007 held mass Hezbollah rallies in Beirut to this end. Iran is a great supporter of Nasrallah's goals. However, if Syrian support for Nasrallah's goals is decreased, due to its strategic decision to pursue peace negotiations with Israel, Nasrallah will have great difficulty mustering the required support to carry out such a coup d'état in Lebanon.

We believe that there is nothing to prevent Israel from carrying out peace negotiations on two tracks simultaneously – a *hudna* and negotiations with the Palestinians can be established in parallel while Israeli working groups negotiate a peace agreement with Syria. Once a positive dynamic that creates conditions for peace has been established on a number of fronts – including the possibility of a new national unity Palestinian government, the signing of a *hudna* with the Palestinians, the continuation of quiet on Israel's northern border, and the establishment of negotiations with Syria – it is essential to push this momentum towards parallel solutions both on the Palestinian and Syrian tracks. Such a change in the current difficult status quo in the Middle East would have a positive ripple effect throughout the region, including the reduction of violence and terrorism in Iraq, and stabilization of the precarious situation in that torn country.

Shaul Gabbay, in Chapter 7, argues that building trust is a process that involves interaction on three levels: Governmental, Non-Governmental, and Private/Social. A consolidated effort led by regional actors, supported by the international community, and incorporating real economic incentives must be put to effect in order to establish a culture of interdependence and cooperation in the Middle East. The region has made progress towards peace, but the state of relations between Israel and Jordan and Egypt has not matured into an all-encompassing peace. Normalization remains elusive and interactions largely limited to the governmental level. The cold peace between Israel and its Arab neighbors has been reinforced by a lack of progress and continued escalation of hostilities between Israel and the Palestinians.

In Chapter 2, Joseph Ginat and David Altman write of the importance of understanding the culture of the other in conducting negotiations. The following event underscores the importance of this issue: On Thursday, January 4, 2007, Prime Minister Olmert held a summit meeting with President Hosni Mubarak in Sharm El-Sheikh, which was planned long in advance. A number of hours before the meeting, the Israel Defense Forces entered Ramallah in order to arrest a terrorist. In addition, the air force flew helicopters above Ramallah during the operation. The military operation was not successful, as four civilians were killed and the terrorist was wounded and escaped. During their meeting, President Mubarak could not avoid the issue, and condemned the Israeli military operation both at the beginning and end of the meeting. Naturally, this cast a negative atmosphere upon the meeting.

It is essential to understand the sensitivities of such a meeting between President Mubarak and Prime Minister Olmert, due to opposition forces in Egypt and throughout the Arab world. The Arab world observes such meetings through a magnifying glass. Israel must take into account such sensitivities, and therefore avoid any kind of activities that could harm the atmosphere or enrage the Arab world in the period leading up to such a meeting, and especially on the day of the meeting itself. Needless to say, such a military operation should not have been carried out hours before such an important meeting.

Events within Israel indicate an increased interest in getting talks and negotiations back on track during 2007. On January 8, 2007, the Israeli daily *Ma'ariv* reported disagreement between Israel's Military Intelligence and the Mossad regarding negotiations with Syria. It was reported that Military Intelligence supports engaging in negotiations with President Assad, while the Mossad is convinced that the Syrian President is not really interested in peace but only wants to enter into negotiations with Israel in order to overcome his country's political isolation.

Also on January 8, 2007, Israel's Defense Minister and Chairman of the Labor Party, Amir Peretz, presented a new diplomatic initiative to Labor Cabinet Ministers and Members of Knesset. Minister Peretz spoke of the need to test Syria's seriousness by engaging in negotiations. In addition, he presented a multi-phased plan for achieving a final-status peace accord with the Palestinians, based on the two-state solution, within two and a half years. Peretz's plan involves combining aspects of the Road Map peace plan with the Saudi Initiative adopted by the Arab Summit in 2002.

On January 9, 2007, Israel's Deputy Defense Minister Ephraim Sneh, in an interview on Israel Radio channel 2, spoke of the need to make changes to the Quartet's Road Map peace plan, and update it to the current situation. Ephraim Sneh spoke of two important developments since the Road Map was created, and that the plan needs to take these developments into account:

1   The Hamas government won the Palestinian Authority Legislative Council elections.
2   Moderate Sunni Arab states have unified around certain common interests, many of whom support the Saudi Initiative.

Deputy Minister Sneh argued, and we would agree with his view, that diplomatic plans cannot stand frozen in time, but must adapt to changing circumstances. A perception that may be relevant for a certain time period needs to be adjusted – whether it be adjusted by 20 percent or 80 percent.

Due to a number of factors that we have brought to attention in these final remarks – including internal Palestinian and Israeli processes, Lebanon's instability due to Sheikh Nasrallah's attempts to overthrow the government, the importance of removing Syria from the "Axis of Evil", and Iran's increasingly fast development of nuclear capabilities – we believe that Israel's engagement in negotiations along two tracks, the Palestinian and the Syrian, are essential for the future stability of the Middle East.

This book summarizes two complementary conferences – the first entitled "What Went Wrong?" and the second "How to Rebuild Trust between Israeli and Palestinians". If the relevant governments adopt the propositions that have been expressed in this volume, we believe there will be no need to hold another conference that asks the question of "What went wrong?" In adopting these proposals, governments will take an important step in learning from past mistakes and enabling the involved parties to rebuild trust and negotiate peace.

Contributors

David Altman currently serves as the Senior Vice President for Development and as the Deputy Chair of the S. Daniel Abraham Center for Strategic Dialogue at Netanya Academic College. Prior to his current position, Dr. Altman served as the Director General of the Tel Aviv Foundation, as Director General and Vice President of Bar Ilan University, and as the Academic Assistant to General Moshe Dayan. Dr. Altman has written numerous academic articles and edited a series of six booklets entitled *Moshe Dayan: Background Material on Jordan and the Palestinians*. Dr. Altman has served as a Board Member on a number of important cultural organizations.

Rateb Mohammad Amro is director general and founder of Horizon Center for Studies and Research in Amman. He was director of the Occupied Territories Office of the Ministry of Foreign Affairs and is a retired colonel of the Jordan Army Forces. He is the author of articles and chapters of books, including "A Jordan Perspective" in Joseph Ginat and Edward J. Perkins (eds), *The Palestinian Refugee Problem: Old Problems – New Solutions* and "The Peace Process: A Jordanian Perspective" in Joseph Ginat, Edward J. Perkins, and Edwin G. Corr (eds), *The Middle East Peace Process: Vision Versus Reality*.

Uzi Arad, founding Head of the Institute for Policy and Strategy at the Lauder School of Government, Diplomacy and Strategy of the Interdisciplinary Center Herzliya, established and chairs the annual Herzilya Conference on Israel's National Security. He is an Advisor to the Knesset's Foreign Affairs and Defense Committee. He served in Mossad, rising to Director of Intelligence, and was Advisor to Prime Minister Benyamin Natanyahu. Arad was on the staff of the Hudson Institute and a Research Fellow at Tel Aviv University's Center for Strategic Studies. He earned his PhD at Princeton and has been involved in advanced studies at Harvard. Arad is the author of numerous books and articles.

Gadi Baltiansky is Director General of "Education for Peace Ltd.," an Israeli-based NGO that promotes agreement between Israel and the Palestinians based on the "Geneva Accord" model. He served as Press

Secretary for Israeli Prime Minister Ehud Barak and on Israeli negotiation teams with Syria and the Palestinians. He served as Press Counselor at the Washington Embassy and advisor to the Deputy Foreign Minister. He has published numerous articles, and holds an MA in public administration from the Kennedy School at Harvard and a BA in Political Science and International Relations from the Hebrew University.

Alon Ben-Meir is a noted journalist, author and professor of international relations and Middle Eastern studies at the Center for Global Affairs at New York University. He holds an MA in philosophy and a PhD in international relations from Oxford. Fluent in Arabic and Hebrew, he offers an invaluable perspective on terrorism, ethnic conflict, and international negotiations. He writes a weekly syndicated column for United Press International. His views are sought by television and radio networks. He has authored numerous books, including: *The Middle East: Imperative and Choices,* and *The Last Option.*

David L. Boren is the president of the University of Oklahoma (OU), a former US senator, governor of the State of Oklahoma, and state legislator. He was the longest-serving chairman of the Senate Select Committee on Intelligence. He is widely respected for his lifetime support of education, his distinguished career as a reformer of the American political system, and his innovations as a university president. He graduated in the top one percent of his class at Yale University, was elected to Pi Beta Kappa, was selected as a Rhodes scholar, and earned a Master's Degree from Oxford University. He received a law degree from OU. He served as a member of the Yale University Board of Trustees. He was Chairman of the Department of Political Science and Chairman of the Division of Social Sciences at Oklahoma Baptist University. He is the co-editor, with Edward J. Perkins, of *Preparing America's Foreign Policy for the 21st Century* (1999) and *Democracy, Morality, and the Search for Peace in America's Foreign Policy* (2002) (Norman: University of Okalahoma Press), and is the author of numerous journal articles and chapters in edited works.

Cyrus Ali Contractor is currently completing his Doctorate in Political Science at the University of Oklahoma where he is a Graduate Teaching Associate of American Federal Government as well as a research assistant for the Religious Studies Program, where he focuses on Muslim and Christian interaction. His primary areas of interest in political science are Middle East politics with a special focus on the Islamic Republic of Iran, Shi'a politics and symbolism, and comparative politics in general. He attained both is BA and MA in Political Science from the University of Texas at Arlington.

Edwin G. Corr is a Senior Research Fellow of the International Programs Center (IPC) of the University of Oklahoma (OU). He held the Henry Bellmon Chair as a professor of political science, and was the Director of the Energy Institute of the Americas and the Associate Director of the IPC at OU. He is the author, co-author and co-editor of five books and has published chapters for edited books and journal articles. He served as the United States ambassador to Peru, to Bolivia, to El Salvador, chargé d'affaires in Ecuador and as Deputy Assistant Secretary of State for International Narcotics Matters. He was a Peace Corps director and a US Marine Corps infantry officer.

Shaul M. Gabbay is the Director of the Institute for the Study of Israel in the Middle East (ISIME) at University of Denver. Gabbay holds a PhD from Columbia University and a Post Doctorate from the University of Chicago. His present research topics focus on social networks and social capital in the context of Israel and the Middle East. Gabbay worked and taught at Tel Aviv University, Columbia University, University of Chicago, University of Illinois at Chicago and the Technion, Israel. Gabbay is currently teaching and conducting his research at the Graduate School of International Studies, University of Denver.

Shlomo Gazit is Chairman of the Galili Center for Defense Studies. He was the first Coordinator of Israeli Government operations in the occupied territories (1967–1974), and was Head of Military Intelligence (1974–1979). Gazit has also served as president of Ben-Gurion University (1981–1985), Director General of the Jewish Agency (1985–1988), and as Senior Research Fellow at the Jaffee Center for Strategic Studies. From 1985 to 1986 he headed an Israeli team negotiating with the PLO, and in 1995/6 served as the Israeli prime minister's special delegate to Chairman Yasser Arafat. Among his many publications are *The Carrot and the Stick* and *Trapped Fools*. Gazit holds an MA in history from Tel Aviv University.

Gad G. Gilbar is in the Department of Middle Eastern History at Haifa University, where he previously was Rector. He earned a BA Degree at the Hebrew University and a PhD from the University of London. He was a Senior Research Fellow at the Moshe Dayan Center for Middle Eastern and African Studies at Tel Aviv University. He has been a Visiting Professor at The Hebrew, Harvard, and Lehigh Universities and a Visiting Fellow at RAND. He is the author, editor, and co-editor of six books, of a number of journal articles, and reviews.

Joseph Ginat currently serves as the Vice President of International Relations and Research, and Director of the S. Daniel Abraham Center for Strategic Dialogue at Netanya Academic College. He is also Co-Director of Center for Peace Studies at the University of Oklahoma. He has served as Director of the Israeli Academic Center in Cairo and as Director of the Jewish–Arab Center at Haifa University. Professor Ginat served as an advisor on Arab issues to a number of Prime Ministers and Ministers, and as chairman of several governmental committees that deal with issues related to Israel's Arab population. He has published and edited 14 books and dozens of articles.

His Royal Highness Prince El Hassan bin Talal, son of King Talal bin Abdullah and brother of King Hussein, earned an MA from Oxford University. He was Crown Prince and King Hussein's closest advisor and deputy, and acted as Regent when King Hussein was out of the country. The Prince has initiated, founded and is active in many Jordanian and international institutes and committees. He is the chair and co-chair of prestigious UN commissions and on the boards of many UN and other organizations. His Royal Highness has honored the University of Oklahoma Center for Peace Studies by serving as Chair of its Board of Advisors, and is one of two presidents of the Strategic Dialogue Center of Netanya Academic College. His Royal Highness is the author of five books and many articles.

Menachem Klein is a Senior Lecturer in the Department of Political Science at Bar-Ilan University, Israel. He studied at the Hebrew University, was a Fellow at Oxford University, and a Visiting Professor at MIT. Dr. Klein is a Board Member of *B'etselem*, the Israeli Information Center for Human Rights in the Occupied Territories, an Advisor to the Ministry of Foreign Affairs, and was an Advisory Team Member of Prime Minister Ehud Barak. He is active in many unofficial negotiations with Palestinians, and was a signer of the Geneva Agreement. He is the author of three books and of many journal articles.

Riad Malki is general director and founder of Panorama Center for the Dissemination of Democracy and Community Development in Palestine. He was a professor at Birzeit University, on the steering committee of the Orient House in Jerusalem, active in second-track diplomacy, coordinator of the Arab Program for Democracy, and a steering committee member of the World Movement for Democracy. He received the European Peace Prize in 2000, the Democracy Courage Award in 2004, and the Italian Peace Prize, Lombardi region, in 2005. He is the author of a weekly article in *Al-Ayyam* newspaper in Palestine, and author of many chapters of books.

Moshe Ma'oz is Professor Emeritus of Islamic and Middle Eastern Studies, former Director of the Truman Institute for the Advancement of

Peace at the Hebrew University, and was appointed Dean of Middle Eastern Studies at Netanya Academic College. He is a leading expert on Syria and was assistant advisor on Arab issues to Prime Minister Ben-Gurion, advisor to the Knesset Committee for Foreign Affairs and Defense, advisor on Arab affairs to Defense Minister Ezer Weizman and a member of the Advisory Committees on Arab–Israel Relations to prime ministers Shimon Peres and Yitzhak Rabin. He is an author of five books, including *Asad, The Sphinx of Damascus: A Political Biography* and *Syria and Israel: From War to Peacemaking*.

Dr. Maya Melzer-Geva is lecturer in the Departments of Sociology & Anthropology and of Education at Kinneret Academic College in the Jordan Valley. She is a researcher, program developer and evaluator for The Association for the Advancement of Education in a Multicultural Society. She holds a BA and MA in Sociology and Social Anthropology from Hebrew University in Jerusalem, and a PhD in Education from the University of Haifa. She conducted research on the Georgian Jews who emigrated to Israel since the 1970s, and for the Ministry of Education, Oranim Academic College, the Faculty of Medicine at the Technion – Israel Institute of Technology, and the Center for Humanistic Education at Lochamei Hagetaot.

Mohammad Al-Momani is assistant professor of political science at Yarmouk University. He taught American Government at the University of North Texas (1999–2002) and then joined Rice University where he taught Political Economy and Middle East Politics. He is a Comparative Politics consultant for ETS. He was a policy consultant in the Ministry of Political Development. He is a member of the Institution Council in the Jordanian Institute of Diplomacy and board member in the Jordanian Political Science Association. He has published several articles and is a member of the international professional associations including APSA, ISA, and the Midwest Political Science Association.

Miguel A. Murado is a journalist and a historian. From 1998 to 2000 he worked in the West Bank for the UNDP (United Nations Development Program) as a Media specialist. Then, from 2000 to 2003 he covered the second *Intifada* for the Spanish newspaper *El Mundo*. Currently, he is a diplomatic correspondent for the newspaper *La Voz de Galicia* and author of the book *La Segunda Intifada. Historia de la revuelta palestina (The Second Intifada. A History of the Palestinian Revolt)*, published by Ediciones de Oriente y el Mediterraneo, 2006.

Joseph Nevo is a professor in the Department of Middle East history and a senior research fellow at the Meir and Miriam Ezri Center for Iran and Gulf Studies at the University of Haifa. He has published on the modern political and social history of Jordan, Saudi Arabia, the Palestinian Arab Society before 1948, Palestinian historiography and the Arab–Israeli conflict. His most recent books are *Jordan: In Search of an Identity* and *King Hussein and the Evolution of Jordan's Perception of a Political Settlement with Israel, 1967–1988*. Currently he is a visiting professor at Georgetown University.

Reuven Pedatzur is Academic Director of the S. Daniel Abraham Center for Strategic Dialogue, a senior military affairs analyst with *Ha'aretz*, and Senior Lecturer in Political Science at Netanya Academic College and Tel Aviv University. Dr. Pedatzur is a former combat pilot for the IAF, as well as a commercial pilot. He was a Visiting Scholar (1993–1994) at the Center for Strategic Studies at MIT studying Israel's anti-missile defense system. He has authored many books, chapters and articles including *Rearming Israel: Defense Procurement Through the 1900s* (1991, with Aharon Klieman) and *The Arrow Project and Active Defense: Challenges and Questions* (1993).

Elie Podeh is an Associate Professor, Head of the Department of Islam and Middle East Studies at the Hebrew University of Jerusalem, and editor of *The New East* (Hamizrah Hehadash). He has published several books and articles on inter-Arab relations and the Arab–Israeli conflict, such as: *The Quest for Hegemony in the Arab World: The Struggle Over the Baghdad Pact* (1995); *The Decline of Arab Unity: Rise and Fall of the United Arab Republic* (1999); *The Arab–Israeli Conflict in Israeli History Textbooks, 1948–2000* (2002); *Rethinking Nasserism: Revolution and Historical Memory in Modern Egypt* (edited with Onn Winckler, 2004).

Onn Winckler, PhD, is a Senior Lecturer in the Department of Middle Eastern History at Haifa University, and has served as the Deputy Director of the Jewish–Arab Center there. His major fields of research are the political demography and economy of Arab countries. Recent books include: *Demographic Developments and Population Policies in Ba'thist Syria; Arab Political Demography*; and with Elie Podeh (eds), *Rethinking Nasserism: Revolution and Historical Memory in Modern Egypt*. Dr. Winckler is also the author of chapters of edited books and journal articles.

Index

Stafford Library
Columbia College
1001 Rogers Street
Columbia, Missouri 65216